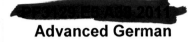

Advanced German

Edited by
Christopher Warnasch and Helga Schier, Ph.D.

❖ LIVING LANGUAGE®

Content in this program has been modified and enhanced from *Starting Out in German* and *Complete Course German: The Basics*, both published in 2008.

Living Language and colophon are registered trademarks of Random House, Inc.

Published in the United States by Living Language, an imprint of Random House, Inc.

www.livinglanguage.com

Editor: Christopher Warnasch
Production Editor: Carolyn Roth
Production Manager: Tom Marshall
Interior Design: Sophie Chin
Illustrations: Sophie Chin

First Edition

Library of Congress Cataloging-in-Publication Data

Advanced German / edited by Christopher Warnasch and Helga Schier.—1st ed.
p.   cm.
ISBN 978-0-307-97161-6
1. German language—Textbooks for foreign speakers—English.   2. German language—Grammar.   3. German language—Spoken German.   4. German language—Self-instruction.   I. Warnasch, Christopher A.   II. Schier, Helga.
PF3129.E5A38 2011
438.2'421—dc23   2011023730

This book is available at special discounts for bulk purchases for sales promotions or premiums. Special editions, including personalized covers, excerpts of existing books, and corporate imprints, can be created in large quantities for special needs. For more information, write to Special Markets/ Premium Sales, 1745 Broadway, MD 3-1, New York, New York 10019 or e-mail specialmarkets@ randomhouse.com.

Acknowledgments

Thanks to the Living Language team: Amanda D'Acierno, Christopher Warnasch, Suzanne McQuade, Laura Riggio, Erin Quirk, Amanda Munoz, Fabrizio LaRocca, Siobhan O'Hare, Sophie Chin, Sue Daulton, Alison Skrabek, Carolyn Roth, Ciara Robinson, and Tom Marshall.

C O U R S E

OUTLINE

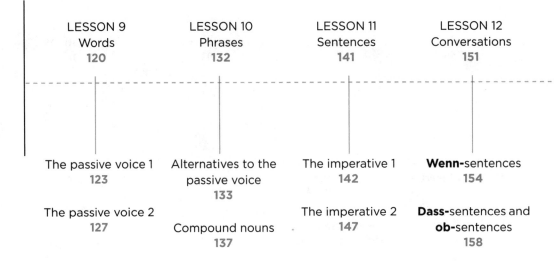
COURSE

UNIT 4: Spare Time Activities 168

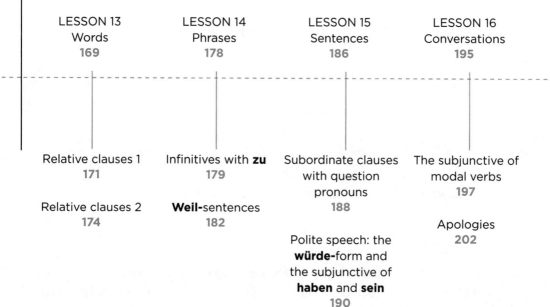
O U T L I N E

How to Use This Course

Willkommen! Welcome to *Living Language Advanced German*!

Before we begin, let's take a quick look at what you'll see in this course.

CONTENT

Advanced German is a continuation of *Intermediate German*.

Now that you've mastered the basics with *Essential* and *Intermediate German*, you'll take your German even further with a comprehensive look at irregular verbs, advanced verb tenses, and complex structures.

UNITS

There are four units in this course. Each unit has four lessons arranged in a "building block" structure: the first lesson will present essential *words*, the second will introduce longer *phrases*, the third will teach *sentences*, and the fourth will show how everything works together in everyday *conversations*.

At the beginning of each unit is an introduction highlighting what you will learn in that unit. At the end of each unit you'll find the Unit Essentials, which review the key information from that unit, and a self-graded Unit Quiz, which tests what you've learned.

LESSONS

There are four lessons per unit for a total of 16 lessons in the course. Each lesson has the following components:

- **Introduction** outlining what you will cover in the lesson.

- **Word Builder 1** (first lesson of the unit) presenting key words and phrases.

- **Phrase Builder 1** (second lesson of the unit) introducing longer phrases and expressions.

- **Sentence Builder 1** (third lesson of the unit) teaching sentences.

- **Conversation 1** (fourth lesson of the unit) for a natural dialogue that brings together important vocabulary and grammar from the unit.

- **Word/Phrase/Sentence/Conversation Practice 1** practicing what you learned in Word Builder 1, Phrase Builder 1, Sentence Builder 1, or Conversation 1.

- **Grammar Builder 1** guiding you through important German grammar that you need to know.

- **Work Out 1** for a comprehensive practice of what you saw in Grammar Builder 1.

- **Word Builder 2/Phrase Builder 2/Sentence Builder 2/Conversation 2** for more key words, phrases, or sentences, or a second dialogue.

- **Word/Phrase/Sentence/Conversation Practice 2** practicing what you learned in Word Builder 2, Phrase Builder 2, Sentence Builder 2, or Conversation 2.

- **Grammar Builder 2** for more information on German grammar.

- **Work Out 2** for a comprehensive practice of what you saw in Grammar Builder 2.

- **Drive It Home** ingraining an important point of German grammar for the long term.

- **Take It Further** sections are scattered throughout the course for expansion on what you've seen so far and for additional vocabulary.

- **Tip** or **Culture Note** for a helpful language tip or useful cultural information related to the lesson or unit.

- **How Did You Do?** outlining what you learned in the lesson.

UNIT ESSENTIALS

You will see the **Unit Essentials** at the end of every unit. This section summarizes and reviews key grammar from the unit, and tests your knowledge of vocabulary by allowing you to fill in your very own "cheat sheet." Once you complete the blanks with the missing vocabulary, the Unit Essentials will serve as your very own reference for the most essential vocabulary and grammar from each unit.

UNIT QUIZ

After each Unit Essentials, you'll see a **Unit Quiz** testing your progress. Your quiz results will allow you to see which sections, if any, you need to review before moving on to the next unit.

PROGRESS BAR

You will see a **Progress Bar** on each page that has course material. It indicates your current position within each unit and lets you know how much progress you're making. Each line in the bar represents a Grammar Builder section.

AUDIO

Look for this symbol ▶ to help guide you through the audio as you're reading the book. It will tell you which track to listen to for each section that has audio. When you see the symbol, select the indicated track and start listening! If you don't see the symbol, then there isn't any audio for that section. You'll also see ⏸, which will tell you where that track ends.

The audio can be used on its own—in other words, without the book—for review and practice when you're on the go. Whether in your car or at the gym, you can listen to the audio to brush up on your pronunciation or review what you've learned in the book.

PRONUNCIATION GUIDE, GRAMMAR SUMMARY, GLOSSARY

At the back of this book you will find a **Pronunciation Guide**, **Grammar Summary**, and **Glossary**. The Pronunciation Guide provides information on German pronunciation and the phonetics system used in this course. The Grammar Summary contains a brief overview of key German grammar from *Essential, Intermediate*, and *Advanced German*. The Glossary (German-English and English-German) includes all of the important words from *Essential, Intermediate*, and *Advanced German*, as well as additional vocabulary.

FREE ONLINE TOOLS

Go to **www.livinglanguage.com/languagelab** to access your free online tools. The tools are organized around the units in this course, with audiovisual flashcards, interactive games, and quizzes for each unit. These tools will help you review and practice the vocabulary and grammar that you've seen in the units, as well as provide some bonus words and phrases related to the unit's topic.

Two-way Prepositions

The Present Perfect
with **haben** (to have)

Expressing Likes and Dislikes

The Present Perfect
with **sein** (to be)

Unit 1:
Shopping

In this first unit you'll learn the vocabulary you'll need if you'd like to update your wardrobe or fill your picnic basket. By the end of this unit, you'll be able to:

☐ Use vocabulary for clothes and food items

☐ Use two-way prepositions and related verb pairs

☐ Express likes and dislikes with verbs such as gefallen (to like) and schmecken (to enjoy)

☐ Speak about the past with the present perfect with haben (to have) and with sein (to be)

☐ Use questions and statements that are helpful when shopping

☐ Use the present perfect of separable verbs and modal verbs

☐ Use the comparative (more, -er) and superlative (most, -est) of adjectives

Look for this symbol ⊙ to help guide you through the audio as you're reading the book. It will tell you which track to listen to for each section that has audio. If you don't see the symbol, then there isn't any audio for that section. You'll also see ⊙ , which will tell you where that track ends.

The Present Perfect
of Separable Verbs

The Comparative of Adjectives

The Present Perfect
of Modal Verbs

The Superlative

Lesson 1: Words

Shopping in a foreign country can be quite a challenge. By the end of this lesson you should be able to:

☐ Use vocabulary for clothes

☐ Use vocabulary for food items

☐ Use two-way prepositions and related verb pairs

☐ Express likes and dislikes with verbs such as gefallen (*to like*) and schmecken (*to enjoy*)

Word Builder 1

▶ 1A Word Builder 1 (CD 7, Track 1)

das Kaufhaus	*department store*
die Boutique	*boutique*
der Kunde/die Kundin	*customer (male/female)*
einkaufen	*to shop*
die Kleider	*clothes*
die Kleidung	*clothing*
das Hemd	*shirt*
die Bluse	*blouse*
der Pullover	*sweater*
die Hose	*pants*
die Jeans	*jeans*
der Rock	*skirt*
das Kleid	*dress*

Two-way Prepositions

The Present Perfect
with **haben** (to have)

Expressing Likes and Dislikes

The Present Perfect
with **sein** (to be)

der Anzug	suit
die Jacke	jacket
der Mantel	coat
die Schuhe	shoes
die Socken	socks
die Krawatte	tie
der Gürtel	belt
der Hut	hat
die Handschuhe	gloves
der Schal	scarf
der Schirm	umbrella
die Uhr	watch
das Regal	shelf
die Umkleidekabine	fitting room
der Spiegel	mirror

✎ Word Practice 1

Time to practice the vocabulary you've just learned. Translate each of the following into German.

1. *the shirt* _____

2. *the pants* _____

3. *the sweater* _____

4. *the shoes* _____

5. *the tie* _____

6. *the jacket* _____

7. *the dress* _____

8. *the suit* _____

9. *the hat* _____

10. *the coat* _____

ANSWER KEY

1. das Hemd; 2. die Hose; 3. der Pullover; 4. die Schuhe; 5. die Krawatte; 6. die Jacke; 7. das Kleid; 8. der Anzug; 9. der Hut; 10. der Mantel

Grammar Builder 1

▶ 1B Grammar Builder 1 (CD 7, Track 2)

TWO-WAY PREPOSITIONS

In *Living Language Intermediate German* you learned that some prepositions are always followed by the dative, and other prepositions are always followed by the accusative. There are also nine prepositions that can be followed by the dative or the accusative. They are called two-way prepositions.

Two-way prepositions introduce the dative case when they indicate a location or position in space. In that case, they answer the question *where?*

Die Kundin kauft <u>in der Boutique</u> **ein.**
The client shops in the boutique.

Two-way prepositions are followed by the accusative case when they indicate a change of location or movement. In that case, they answer the question *to where?*

Two-way Prepositions

The Present Perfect
with **haben** (to have)

Expressing Likes and Dislikes

The Present Perfect
with **sein** (to be)

Die Kundin geht in die Boutique.

The client enters (goes into) the boutique.

PREPOSITION	ACCUSATIVE/DIRECTION	DATIVE/LOCATION
in	Ich packe das Hemd in den Koffer.	Das Hemd ist im Koffer.
in, inside, into	*I'm putting the shirt in the suitcase.*	*The shirt is in the suitcase.*
an	Ich fahre an die Kreuzung heran.	Wir biegen an der nächsten Kreuzung rechts ab.
at, to the side of, to, on	*I'm approaching the intersection.*	*We turn right at the next intersection.*
auf	Ich lege die Handschuhe auf den Tisch.	Die Handschuhe sind auf dem Tisch.
on, on top of, onto	*I'm putting the gloves on the table.*	*The gloves are on the table.*
über	Der Verkäufer hängt den Pullover über das T-shirt.	Ich trage den Pullover über dem T-shirt.
above, over, across	*The salesperson hangs the sweater above the T-shirt.*	*I'm wearing the sweater over the T-shirt.*
unter	Der Verkäufer hängt das T-shirt unter den Pullover.	Ich trage das T-shirt unter dem Pullover.
under, beneath, among	*The salesperson hangs the T-shirt under the sweater.*	*I'm wearing the T-shirt under the sweater.*
vor	Ich stelle mich vor den Spiegel.	Ich stehe vor dem Spiegel.

PREPOSITION	ACCUSATIVE/DIRECTION	DATIVE/LOCATION
in front of, before, ago	*I'm placing myself in front of the mirror.*	*I'm standing (in a standing position) in front of the mirror.*
hinter	**Ich stelle mich hinter dich.**	**Ich stehe hinter dir.**
in back of, behind	*I'm placing myself behind you.*	*I'm standing (in a standing position) behind you.*
neben	**Ich stelle mich neben dich.**	**Ich stehe neben dir.**
beside, next to	*I'm placing myself next to you.*	*I'm standing next to you.*
zwischen	**Ich lege den Pullover zwischen das T-shirt und das Hemd.**	**Der Pullover liegt zwischen dem T-shirt und dem Hemd.**
between	*I'm laying the sweater between the T-shirt and the shirt.*	*The sweater is lying between the T-shirt and the shirt.*

Note that many prepositions, when followed by a definite article in the accusative, form a contraction: **in das** contracts to **ins**, **an das** contracts to **ans**, **auf das** contracts to **aufs**, and so on. As you know, the same is true for many prepositions followed by a definite article in the dative case: **in dem** contracts to **im**, **an dem** contracts to **am**, and **zu dem** contracts to **zum**.

There are a few verb pairs that come up frequently with two-way prepositions. One, the transitive verb in the pair, usually refers to movement/action and needs

an accusative object. The intransitive verb in the pair usually refers to location and does not need an accusative object. If a location is expressed, it's in the dative.

TRANSITIVE (MOVEMENT)		INTRANSITIVE (LOCATION)	
legen	to place, to put (to lay)	liegen	to lie (location)
hängen	to hang	hängen	to hang (to be hanging)
stellen	to place, to put (to stand)	stehen	to stand (to be standing)
setzen	to place, to put (to set)	sitzen	to sit (to be sitting)

✎ Work Out 1

Complete the sentences using the correct case.

1. **Die Kundin steht** _____ . (vor/der Spiegel)

2. **Die Verkäuferin geht** _____ . (in/die Umkleidekabine)

3. **Mein Mann legt die Hose** _____ . (neben/die Schuhe)

4. **Ich kaufe gern** _____ ein. (in/das Kaufhaus)

5. **Warum legst du das Hemd nicht** _____ . (auf/das Regal)

6. **Die Pullover liegen schon** _____ . (auf/das Regal)

ANSWER KEY

1. vor dem Spiegel; 2. in die Umkleidekabine; 3. neben die Schuhe; 4. im Kaufhaus; 5. auf das Regal; 6. auf dem Regal

The Present Perfect
of Separable Verbs

The Comparative of Adjectives

The Present Perfect
of Modal Verbs

The Superlative

Word Builder 2

▶ 1C Word Builder 2 (CD 7, Track 3)

der Supermarkt	*grocery store*
das Brot	*bread*
das Brötchen	*breakfast roll*
das Obst	*fruit*
der Apfel	*apple*
die Orange	*orange*
die Banane	*banana*
das Gemüse	*vegetables*
die Kartoffel	*potato*
die Tomate	*tomato*
die Zwiebel	*onion*
der Mais	*corn*
die Karotte	*carrot*
der Salat	*lettuce*
der Paprika	*pepper (bell, etc.; not the condiment)*
die Gurke	*cucumber*
der Spinat	*spinach*
der Wurstaufschnitt	*cold cuts*
der Schinken	*ham*
die Salami	*salami*
die Lyoner	*bologna*
das Fleisch	*meat*
das Rindfleisch	*beef*
das Kalbfleisch	*veal*
das Schweinefleisch	*pork*

Two-way Prepositions

The Present Perfect
with **haben** (to have)

Expressing Likes and Dislikes

The Present Perfect
with **sein** (to be)

das Lamm	lamb
das Huhn	chicken
die Nudeln	pasta
der Reis	rice
das Gewürz	spice
der Zucker	sugar
das Salz	salt
der Pfeffer	pepper (condiment)
der Paprika	paprika
die Milch	milk
der Joghurt	yogurt
der Käse	cheese
das Getränk	drink
das Wasser	water
das Mineralwasser	mineral water
der Saft	juice
der Orangensaft	orange juice
der Apfelsaft	apple juice
der Wein	wine
das Bier	beer
der Sekt	champagne, sparkling wine

(II)

The Present Perfect
of Separable Verbs

The Comparative of Adjectives

The Present Perfect
of Modal Verbs

The Superlative

✎ Word Practice 1

Choose the most appropriate answer from the three options provided.

1.Lebensmittel gibt es im _____.

a.Kaufhaus

b.Supermarkt

c.Krankenhaus

2.Äpfel und Orangen sind _____.

a.Kleider

b.Gemüse

c.Obst

3.Salz und Pfeffer sind _____.

a.Paprika

b.Fleisch

c.Gewürze

4.Schinken und Lyoner und
Salami sind _____.

a.Wurstaufschnitt

b.Käse

c.Jogurt

5.Bier und Wein und Milch
sind _____.

a.Fleisch

b.Gewürze

c.Getränke

ANSWER KEY

1. b; 2. c; 3. c; 4. a; 5. c

Grammar Builder 2

▷ 1D Grammar Builder 2 (CD 7, Track 4)

EXPRESSING MORE LIKES AND DISLIKES

German features a whole host of verbs to express likes and dislikes.

GEFALLEN AND SCHMECKEN

As you learned in *Living Language Intermediate German,* gefallen and schmecken
always take the dative case: gefallen + dative (*to like someone/something; lit., to be*

Two-way Prepositions

The Present Perfect
with **haben** (to have)

Expressing Likes and Dislikes

The Present Perfect
with **sein** (to be)

pleasing [to someone]); schmecken + dative (*to like [some food]; lit., to taste good [to someone]*).

Gefallen can be used with people and things. Preferences for food are expressed with schmecken.

Obst schmeckt mir.
I like fruit. (lit., Fruit tastes good to me.)

Der Rock gefällt mir.
I like the skirt. (lit., The skirt is pleasing to me.)

Du gefällst mir.
I like you. (lit., You are pleasing to me.)

Note that the subject in the English sentence (*I*) becomes the dative object in the German sentence (mir). The object in the English sentence (*fruit/skirt/you*) is the subject in the German sentence (Obst/Rock/du). Therefore, if the object of liking is in the plural, gefallen and schmecken need to be in the plural as well.

Die Schuhe gefallen mir.
I like the shoes. (lit., The shoes are pleasing to me.)

Bananen schmecken mir nicht.
I don't like bananas. (lit., Bananas are not pleasing to me.)

GERN + VERB (*TO ENJOY, TO LIKE*)

In *Living Language Intermediate German* we also talked about gern + verb. Remember that gern is always used in conjunction with a verb referring to the action enjoyed by the subject.

The Present Perfect
of Separable Verbs

The Comparative of Adjectives

The Present Perfect
of Modal Verbs

The Superlative

Ich kaufe gern ein.
I enjoy shopping.

Ich esse nicht gern Gemüse.
I don't like eating vegetables.

MÖGEN (*TO LIKE*)

Mögen can be used to express likes and dislikes for people, things, and food or drinks.

Ich mag dich.
I like you.

Ich mag Milch.
I like milk.

LIEB HABEN (*TO LIKE*)

Lieb haben is usually used among family members. It can also be used for romantic overtones.

Ich habe dich lieb.
I like you.

LIEBEN (*TO LOVE*)

Lieben is usually reserved for people, expressing romantic love and love within a family. Lieben is rarely used to express enjoyment of a sport, a food, or an activity.

Ich liebe dich.
I love you.

Two-way Prepositions

The Present Perfect
with **haben** (*to have*)

Expressing Likes and Dislikes

The Present Perfect
with **sein** (*to be*)

(II)

✎ Work Out 2

Translate the following sentences using the verb in parentheses.

1. *I like bananas.* (schmecken) _____

   _____

2. *Do you like this T-shirt?* (gefallen) _____

   _____

3. *She doesn't like the shoes.* (gefallen) _____

   _____

4. *My mother loves me.* (lieben) _____

   _____

5. *I like to drink coffee.* (gern + verb) _____

   _____

6. *My father likes wine.* (mögen) _____

   _____

ANSWER KEY
1.Bananen schmecken mir. 2.Gefällt dir das T-Shirt? 3.Die Schuhe gefallen ihr nicht. 4.Meine
Mutter liebt mich. 5.Ich trinke gern Kaffee. 6.Mein Vater mag Wein.

Take It Further 1

German is rather picky with regard to expressing emotions toward people.

1. **Er interessiert mich.** (*I'm interested in him.*) *This usually has romantic overtones.*

The Present Perfect
of Separable Verbs

The Comparative of Adjectives

The Present Perfect
of Modal Verbs

The Superlative

2. **Sie gefällt mir.** *(I like her.) This does not necessarily have any romantic connotations.*

3. **Ich habe ihn gern.** *(I like him.) This might be used in reference to a friend or a distant relative.*

4. **Ich mag dich.** *(I like you.) This usually has romantic overtones or expresses deep devotion to a friend.*

5. **Ich habe dich lieb.** *(I love you.) This usually has romantic connotations or expresses love among family members.*

6. **Ich liebe dich.** *(I love you.) This is reserved for lovers and close family members.*

Ⅱ

✎ Drive It Home

You remember the Drive It Home exercises from *Living Language Essential German* and *Living Language Intermediate German*. They may seem easy, but they are meant to make grammatical structures more automatic by helping you establish grammatical patterns through practice and repetition. Don't skip over these exercises! They'll help you in the long run.

A. Rewrite the sentences below to indicate a change of location, using the verb in parentheses. Follow the example.
   Example: Ich bin im Garten. (gehen) <u>Ich gehe in den Garten.</u>

1. **Wir sind im Kino. (gehen)** _____

   _____

Two-way Prepositions

The Present Perfect
with **haben** (to have)

Expressing Likes and Dislikes

The Present Perfect
with **sein** (to be)

2. **Der Chef ist im Büro. (gehen)** _____

_____

3. **Die Kinder sind in der Schule. (gehen)** _____

_____

4. **Ich sitze auf der Bank. (sich setzen)** _____

_____

5. **Sie steht neben dem Mann. (sich stellen)** _____

_____

B. Rewrite the sentences below to indicate location. Follow the example.
   Example: **Ich hänge die Hose in den Schrank. (hängen)** Die Hose hängt im Schrank.

1. **Ich stelle den Koffer in das Wohnzimmer. (stehen)** _____

_____

2. **Ich lege das Buch auf den Tisch. (liegen)** _____

_____

3. **Ich setze mich auf das Bett. (sitzen)** _____

_____

4. **Wir fahren in die Stadt. (sein)** _____

_____

5. **Ich stelle die Lebensmittel neben die Kasse. (stehen)** _____

_____

ANSWER KEY

A. 1. Wir gehen ins Kino. 2. Der Chef geht ins Büro. 3. Die Kinder gehen in die Schule. 4. Ich setze mich auf die Bank. 5. Sie stellt sich neben den Mann.

B. 1. Der Koffer steht im Wohnzimmer. 2. Das Buch liegt auf dem Tisch. 3. Ich sitze auf dem Bett. 4. Wir sind in der Stadt. 5. Die Lebensmittel stehen neben der Kasse.

How Did You Do?

After this first lesson you should be able to:

☐ Use vocabulary for clothes
(Still unsure? Jump back to page 13.)

☐ Use vocabulary for food items
(Still unsure? Jump back to page 19.)

☐ Use two-way prepositions and related verb pairs
(Still unsure? Jump back to page 15.)

☐ Express likes and dislikes with verbs such as gefallen (*to like*) and schmecken
(*to enjoy*)
(Still unsure? Jump back to page 21.)

✎ Word Recall

Match the English word from column A with the appropriate German translation in column B.

1. *beef*	a. der Apfelsaft
2. *spinach*	b. das Brot
3. *tomato*	c. lieb haben
4. *shirt*	d. das Rindfleisch
5. *supermarket*	e. die Kasse
6. *cashier*	f. der Gürtel
7. *to like*	g. der Spinat
8. *bread*	h. der Supermarkt

Two-way Prepositions

The Present Perfect
with **haben** (*to have*)

Expressing Likes and Dislikes

The Present Perfect
with **sein** (*to be*)

9. *apple juice*

i. **die Tomate**

10. *belt*

j. **das Hemd**

ANSWER KEY
1. d; 2. g; 3. i; 4. j; 5. h; 6. e; 7. c; 8. b; 9. a; 10. f

Lesson 2: Phrases

The phrases in this lesson will help you get your shopping done. By the end of this lesson you should be able to:

☐ Use vocabulary for sizes, weight, and measurements

☐ Speak about the past with the present perfect with haben(*to have*)

☐ Speak about the past with the present perfect with sein(*to be*)

Phrase Builder 1

▶ 2A Phrase Builder 1 (CD 7, Track 5)

Welche Größe … ?	What size … ?
in meiner Größe	in my size
in einer anderen Größe	in a different size
in einer kleineren Größe	in a smaller size
in einer größeren Größe	in a larger size
eine Nummer kleiner	one size smaller
eine Nummer größer	one size larger
in einer anderen Farbe	in a different color
in schwarz	in black
weiß	white

The Present Perfect
of Separable Verbs

The Comparative of Adjectives

The Present Perfect
of Modal Verbs

The Superlative

gelb	yellow
rot	red
blau	blue
grün	green
grau	gray
rosa	pink
violet	purple
kariert	checkered
gestreift	striped
passen	to fit
gut passen zu	to go well with
jemandem gut stehen	to look good on (lit., to suit someone well)
Kann ich ... anprobieren?	Can I try ... on?
Kann ich ... umtauschen?	Can I exchange ... ?
Ich suche ...	I am looking for ...
als Geschenk für ...	as a present for ...

(II)

✎ Phrase Practice 1

Complete the sentences below by following the translations provided.

1. _____ Größe haben Sie? (*What's your size?*)

2. Ich brauche die Hose eine _____ kleiner.

   (*I need the pants one size smaller.*)

3. Haben Sie das Kleid in einer anderen _____ ?

   (*Do you have the dress in a different color?*)

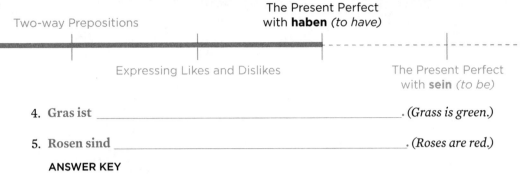

Two-way Prepositions

The Present Perfect
with **haben** *(to have)*

Expressing Likes and Dislikes

The Present Perfect
with **sein** *(to be)*

4. Gras ist _____. *(Grass is green.)*

5. Rosen sind _____. *(Roses are red.)*

ANSWER KEY
1. Welche; 2. Nummer; 3. Farbe; 4. grün; 5. rot

Grammar Builder 1

▶ 2B Grammar Builder 1 (CD 7, Track 6)

THE PRESENT PERFECT WITH HABEN (*TO HAVE*)

To talk about the past, German usually uses the present perfect tense. It's formed
with a helping verb, either **haben** or **sein,** and the past participle of the main
verb, so it looks a lot like the English *I have gone* or *she has spoken.* The major
difference is that the past participle goes to the end of the sentence.

Ich habe ein neues Kleid gekauft.
I bought/have bought/did buy a new dress.

Haben Sie auch die rote Hose gekauft?
Did you also buy the red pants?

Nein, ich habe die rote Hose nicht gekauft.
No, I didn't buy the red pants.

Notice that questions are formed by putting the helping verb first, and in
negatives, **nicht** usually comes before the past participle. You can see from the
examples above, with **gekauft** (*bought*), that the participle is formed with the
prefix **ge-** + stem + the ending **-(e)t.**

INFINITIVE		PAST PARTICIPLE	
kaufen	*to buy*	gekauft	*bought*
sagen	*to say*	gesagt	*said*

The Present Perfect
of Separable Verbs

The Comparative of Adjectives

The Present Perfect
of Modal Verbs

The Superlative

INFINITIVE		PAST PARTICIPLE	
kosten	to cost	gekostet	cost
suchen	to search	gesucht	searched
passen	to fit	gepasst	fit
zeigen	to show	gezeigt	shown
lernen	to learn	gelernt	learned

Regular verbs that end in -d, -t, or a consonant combination add -et to the stem to make pronunciation easier.

arbeiten	to work	gearbeitet	worked

If a verb begins with the prefix be-, ge-, emp-, er-, ver-, or certain others, no ge- is added to form the past participle.

bezahlen	to pay	bezahlt	paid
verstehen	to understand	verstanden	understood

✎ Work Out 1

Rewrite the following sentences in the present perfect. Translate your answers.

1. Ich kaufe eine Hose. _____

_____

2. Mein Freund sucht ein Geschenk für mich. _____

_____

3. Lernen Sie Deutsch? _____

_____

Two-way Prepositions

The Present Perfect
with **haben** (to have)

Expressing Likes and Dislikes

The Present Perfect
with **sein** (to be)

4. **Die Verkäuferin arbeitet in einer Boutique.** _____

_____

5. **Der Anzug passt Ihnen gut.** _____

_____

6. **Wieviel kosten die Schuhe?** _____

_____

ANSWER KEY
1. **Ich habe eine Hose gekauft.** (*I bought a [pair of] pants.*) 2. **Mein Freund hat ein Geschenk für mich gesucht.** (*My friend looked for a gift for me.*) 3. **Haben Sie Deutsch gelernt?** (*Did you learn German?*) 4. **Die Verkäuferin hat in einer Boutique gearbeitet.** (*The saleswoman worked in a boutique.*) 5. **Der Anzug hat Ihnen gut gepasst.** (*The suit fit you well.*) 6. **Wieviel haben die Schuhe gekostet?** (*How much did the shoes cost?*)

Phrase Builder 2
▶ 2C Phrase Builder 2 (CD 7, Track 7)

wiegen	to weigh
auf die Waage legen	to put on the scale
Ich hätte gern …	I'd like …
Ich nehme …	I'll take … , I'll have …
Ich brauche …	I need …
eine Einkaufsliste machen	to make a shopping list
ein Laib Brot	a loaf of bread
ein Liter Milch	a liter of milk
einkaufen gehen	to go (grocery) shopping
bummeln gehen	to go (window-) shopping
an der Kasse	at the cashier, at the cash register

⏸

The Present Perfect
of Separable Verbs

The Comparative of Adjectives

The Present Perfect
of Modal Verbs

The Superlative

✎ Phrase Practice 2

Complete the following sentences.

1. **Bitte legen Sie die Tomaten auf die** _____.

   (Please put the tomatoes on the scale.)

2. **Ich hätte** _____ **zehn Brötchen.** *(I'd like 10 breakfast rolls.)*

3. **Wir** _____ **einen Liter Milch.** *(I need a liter of milk.)*

4. **Möchtest du** _____ **gehen?** *(Do you want to go window-shopping?)*

5. **Bitte bezahlen Sie an der** _____. *(Please pay at the cashier.)*

   ANSWER KEY
   1. **Waage**; 2. **gern**; 3. **brauchen**; 4. **bummeln**; 5. **Kasse**

Grammar Builder 2

▶ 2D Grammar Builder 2 (CD 7, Track 8)

THE PRESENT PERFECT WITH SEIN (*TO BE*)

There are many verbs that use the helping verb sein to form the present perfect tense. Most of them refer to movement or a change of position, such as gehen (*to go on foot*), fahren (*to drive*), or kommen (*to come*), as well as the verbs sein itself and bleiben (*to stay*).

Ich bin in den Supermarkt gegangen.
I went into the supermarket.

Most of these verbs are intransitive, which means they do not take a direct object, and most of them are irregular (strong) verbs. The past participle of irregular verbs is formed with the prefix ge- + stem + the ending -(e)n. Many irregular

Two-way Prepositions

The Present Perfect
with **haben** (to have)

Expressing Likes and Dislikes

The Present Perfect
with **sein** (to be)

(strong) verbs show a stem-vowel change in the past participle. Here are a few common examples.

INFINITIVE		PAST PARTICIPLE	
gehen	to go	gegangen	gone
stehen	to stand	gestanden	stood
finden	to find	gefunden	found

Here are a few examples of strong verbs with no stem-vowel change.

INFINITIVE		PAST PARTICIPLE	
fahren	to drive	gefahren	driven
laufen	to run	gelaufen	run
kommen	to come	gekommen	come

Irregular (strong) verbs are rather unpredictable, so it is best to simply memorize their past participles.

Keep in mind that most verbs that take sein in the present perfect are irregular, but not all irregular verbs take sein in the present perfect. The following are a few common irregular verbs that take haben.

helfen	to help	geholfen	helped
nehmen	to take	genommen	taken
geben	to give	gegeben	given
essen	to eat	gegessen	eaten
trinken	to drink	getrunken	drunk

The Present Perfect
of Separable Verbs

The Comparative of Adjectives

The Present Perfect
of Modal Verbs

The Superlative

✎ Work Out 2

Rewrite these sentences in the present perfect, and then translate.

1. **Ich trinke eine Tasse Kaffee.** _____

_____

2. **Meine Schwester geht einkaufen.** _____

_____

3. **Nehmen Sie ein Taxi?** _____

_____

4. **Die Verkäuferin fährt zur Arbeit.** _____

_____

5. **Die Kundin steht vor dem Spiegel.** _____

_____

6. **Wir geben Ihnen das Geld.** _____

_____

ANSWER KEY

1. **Ich habe eine Tasse Kaffee getrunken.** (*I drank a cup of coffee.*) 2. **Meine Schwester ist einkaufen gegangen.** (*My sister went shopping.*) 3. **Haben Sie ein Taxi genommen?** (*Did you take a taxi?*) 4. **Die Verkäuferin ist zur Arbeit gefahren.** (*The saleswoman drove to work.*) 5. **Die Kundin hat vor dem Spiegel gestanden.** (*The client/customer stood in front of the mirror.*) 6. **Wir haben Ihnen das Geld gegeben.** (*We gave you the money.*)

Two-way Prepositions

The Present Perfect
with **haben** (to have)

Expressing Likes and Dislikes

The Present Perfect
with **sein** (to be)

✎ Drive It Home

A. Let's practice haben as a past tense helping verb. Complete each sentence with
the correct form.

1. Ich _____ Tomaten gekauft.

2. Du _____ endlich Deutsch gelernt.

3. _____ Sie heute gearbeitet?

B. Now let's do the same with sein.

1. Wir _____ in die Stadt gefahren.

2. Ihr _____ gestern angekommen.

3. Sie _____ bummeln gegangen.

C. Now complete the sentence with the correct past participle of the verb in
parentheses.

1. Wir haben an der Kasse _____ . (bezahlen)

2. Ich habe meine Schlüssel _____ . (suchen)

3. Haben Sie meine Schlüssel _____ ? (finden)

4. Seid ihr mit dem Bus _____ ? (fahren)

ANSWER KEY
A. 1. habe; 2. hast; 3. Haben; B. 1. sind; 2. seid; 3. sind; C. 1. bezahlt; 2. gesucht; 3. gefunden; 4. gefahren

The Present Perfect
of Separable Verbs

The Comparative of Adjectives

The Present Perfect
of Modal Verbs

The Superlative

How Did You Do?

Make sure the new material of the lesson feels familiar before you move on. By now, you should be able to:

☐ Use vocabulary for sizes, weight, and measurements
(Still unsure? Jump back to page 28.)

☐ Speak about the past with the present perfect with haben (*to have*)
(Still unsure? Jump back to page 30.)

☐ Speak about the past with the present perfect with sein (*to be*)
(Still unsure? Jump back to page 33.)

 Word Recall

Which of these things are you likely to find in a supermarket? Circle them and then translate.

1. **das Hemd** _____

2. **die Tomaten** _____

3. **die Kasse** _____

4. **die Verkäuferin** _____

5. **die Waage** _____

6. **die Umkleidekabine** _____

7. **das Fahrrad** _____

8. **der Spinat** _____

9. **ein Laib Brot** _____

10. **der Wurstaufschnitt** _____

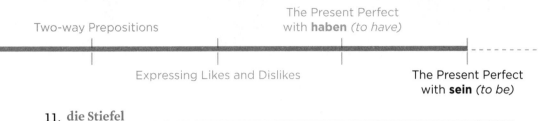

Two-way Prepositions

The Present Perfect
with **haben** (to have)

Expressing Likes and Dislikes

The Present Perfect
with **sein** (to be)

11. **die Stiefel** _____

12. **das Obst** _____

ANSWER KEY
1. *shirt*; 2. *tomatoes*; 3. *cashier*; 4. *female salesperson*; 5. *scale*; 6. *changing room*; 7. *bicycle*; 8. *spinach*;
9. *a loaf of bread*; 10. *cold cuts*; 11. *boots*; 12. *fruit*

Lesson 3: Sentences

Let's move on to some sentences that will help you navigate shopping in a
department store. By the end of this lesson you should be able to:

☐ Use questions and statements that are helpful when shopping

☐ Use the present perfect of separable verbs

☐ Use the present perfect of modal verbs

Sentence Builder 1

▶ 3A Sentence Builder 1 (CD 7, Track 9)

Kann ich Ihnen helfen?	*Can I help you?*
Ich möchte die Hose anprobieren.	*I'd like to try on these pants.*
Kann ich das Kleid anprobieren?	*Can I try on the dress?*
Die Hose steht mir gut.	*The pants look good on me. (lit., The pants suit me well.)*
Kann ich die Krawatte umtauschen?	*Can I exchange the tie?*
Wo ist die Umkleidekabine?	*Where is the fitting room?*
Wo ist die Schuhabteilung?	*Where is the shoe department?*
Haben Sie den Anzug auch in einer anderen Größe/Farbe?	*Do you have this suit in a different size/color?*

The Present Perfect
of Separable Verbs

The Comparative of Adjectives

The Present Perfect
of Modal Verbs

The Superlative

Ich brauche eine kleinere Größe.	*I need a smaller size.*
Ich suche einen blauen Pullover.	*I am looking for a blue sweater.*
Ich brauche ein Geschenk für meinen Mann.	*I need a present for my husband.*
Wo ist die Kasse?	*Where is the cash register?*
Kann ich mit Kreditkarte bezahlen?	*Can I pay with a credit card?*

✎ Sentence Practice 1

Fill in the missing words in the conversation below. The translations are given to help you, but try to identify the missing words without looking at the translations first.

1. Kann ich Ihnen _____? *(Can I help you?)*

2. Ich suche ein _____ für meinen Mann. *(I'm looking for a present for my husband.)*

3. _____ ist die Herrenabteilung? *(Where's the men's department?)*

4. Gleich hier. Wie wär's mit dieser _____? *(Right here. How about a tie?)*

5. Haben Sie die Krawatte auch _____? *(Do you have this tie in a different color?)*

6. Wo ist die _____? *(Where's the cashier?)*

ANSWER KEY
1. helfen; 2. Geschenk; 3. Wo; 4. Kravatte; 5. in einer anderen Farbe; 6. Kasse

Two-way Prepositions

The Present Perfect
with **haben** (to have)

Expressing Likes and Dislikes

The Present Perfect
with **sein** (to be)

Take It Further 1

When looking for your size in the shops, keep in mind that different clothing sizes are used in Europe. Use the following conversion chart for your shopping convenience.

LADIES

Coats, Dresses, Suits							
Europe	36	38	40	42	44	46	
America	8	10	12	14	16	18	
Sweaters, Blouses							
Europe	40	42	44	46	48	50	52
America	32	34	36	38	40	42	44
Stockings							
Europe	35	36	37	38	39	40	41
America	8	8½	9	9½	10	10½	11
Shoes							
Europe	34	35	36	37	38	39	40	41
America	3½	4	4½	5	6	7	8½	9

MEN

Coats, Suits							
Europe	44	46	48	50	52	54	56	58
America	34	36	38	40	42	44	46	48
Shirts							
Europe	37	38	39	40	41	42	43	44
America	14½	15	15½	16	16½	17	17½	18
Shoes							
Europe	39	40	41	42	43	44	45	46
America	6	7	8	9	10	11	12	13

The Present Perfect
of Separable Verbs

The Comparative of Adjectives

The Present Perfect
of Modal Verbs

The Superlative

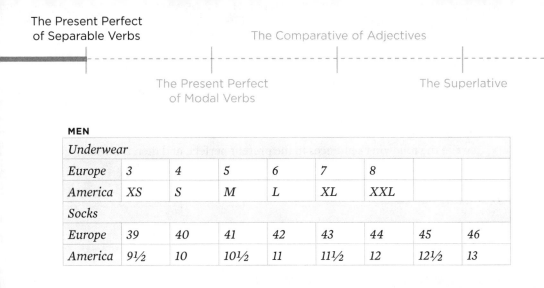

MEN

Underwear								
Europe	3	4	5	6	7	8		
America	XS	S	M	L	XL	XXL		
Socks								
Europe	39	40	41	42	43	44	45	46
America	9½	10	10½	11	11½	12	12½	13

Grammar Builder 1

▶ 3B Grammar Builder 1 (CD 7, Track 10)

THE PRESENT PERFECT OF SEPARABLE VERBS

The present perfect of separable verbs—verbs with a separable prefix—is made
up of the conjugated form of **haben** or **sein** plus the past participle. To form the
past participle, separable verbs place -ge- between the prefix and the stem. There
are regular and irregular separable verbs. Here are a few examples of regular
separable verbs. Their past participle pattern is: prefix + -ge- + stem + -(e)t.

einkaufen	to shop	eingekauft	shopped
absagen	to cancel	abgesagt	cancelled

Here are a few examples of irregular separable verbs. Their past participle pattern
is: prefix + -ge- + stem (with/without stem-vowel change) + -en.

abfahren	to leave	abgefahren	left
mitnehmen	to take along	mitgenommen	taken along
anrufen	to call	angerufen	called

Two-way Prepositions

The Present Perfect
with **haben** (*to have*)

Expressing Likes and Dislikes

The Present Perfect
with **sein** (*to be*)

✎ Work Out 1

Rewrite the following sentences in the present perfect, and then translate.

1. **Der Zug fährt ab.** _____

   _____

2. **Ich rufe dich an.** _____

   _____

3. **Wir kommen gern mit in das Kaufhaus.** _____

   _____

4. **Meine Schwester kauft Gemüse ein.** _____

   _____

5. **Er sagt die Party ab.** _____

   _____

ANSWER KEY

1. Der Zug ist abgefahren. (*The train has left.*) 2. Ich habe dich angerufen. (*I called you.*) 3. Wir
sind gern mit in das Kaufhaus gekommen. (*We liked coming along to the department store./We were
happy to come along to the department store.*) 4. Meine Schwester hat Gemüse eingekauft. (*My sister
shopped for vegetables.*) 5. Er hat die Party abgesagt. (*He cancelled the party.*)

Sentence Builder 2

▶ 3C Sentence Builder 2 (CD 7, Track 11)

Was darf's denn sein?	*What can I get you?*
Ich möchte gern dreihundert Gramm Lyoner.	*I'd like 300 grams of bologna.*
Geschnitten oder am Stück?	*(Would you like this) Sliced or in one piece?*

The Present Perfect
of Separable Verbs

The Comparative of Adjectives

The Present Perfect
of Modal Verbs

The Superlative

Die Salami am Stück, bitte.	The salami in one piece, please.
Darf's sonst noch etwas sein?	Anything else?
Ich nehme zweihundertundfünfzig Gramm Wurstaufschnitt.	I'll have 250 grams of cold cuts.
Darf's etwas mehr/weniger sein?	Can it be a little more/less?
Es darf auch etwas mehr/weniger sein.	It can be a little more/less.
Ich brauche einen Laib Brot.	I need a loaf of bread.
Haben Sie noch Laugenbrötchen?	Do you still have pretzel rolls?
Leider haben wir keine Butter mehr.	Unfortunately we are out of butter.

Ⅱ

✎ Sentence Practice 2

Fill in the missing words in the conversation below. The translations are given to help you, but try to identify the missing words without looking at the translations first.

1. Was _____ denn sein? (*What can I get you?*)

2. Ich _____ gern 300 Gramm Lyoner. (*I'd like 300 grams of bologna.*)

3. _____ haben wir keine Lyoner mehr. (*Unfortunately we are out of bologna.*)

4. Dann nehme ich 300 Gramm _____ . (*Then I'll have 300 grams of cold cuts.*)

5. Darf's auch _____ sein? (*Can it be a little more?*)

6. Ich hätte lieber _____. (*I'd prefer a little less.*)

7. Darf's _____ sein? (*Anything else?*)

8. _____ , das ist alles. (*No thanks, that's all.*)

Two-way Prepositions

The Present Perfect
with **haben** *(to have)*

Expressing Likes and Dislikes

The Present Perfect
with **sein** *(to be)*

ANSWER KEY

1. darf's; 2. hätte; 3. Leider; 4. Wurstaufschnitt; 5. etwas mehr; 6. etwas weniger; 7. sonst noch etwas; 8. Nein danke

Grammar Builder 2

▶ 3D Grammar Builder 2 (CD 7, Track 12)

THE PRESENT PERFECT OF MODAL VERBS

All modal verbs form their present perfect with haben. The past participle is formed by the prefix ge- + stem + -t. If the infinitive has an umlaut, it loses it in the past participle.

Das habe ich nicht gewollt.
I didn't want that.

dürfen	to be allowed to	gedurft	allowed to
können	to be able to	gekonnt	been able to
möchten	to like to	gemocht	liked to
müssen	to have to	gemusst	had to
wollen	to want to	gewollt	wanted to
sollen	to be supposed to	gesollt	been supposed to

The past participles are only used if the modal verb is the main verb, as in **Das habe ich nicht gewollt** (*I didn't want that.*) If there's a second (main) verb, both the modal and the main verb remain in the infinitive and move to the end of the sentence in the present perfect.

Ich habe dir helfen wollen.
I wanted to help you.

Mein Vater hat gut singen können.
My father was able to/could sing well.

The Present Perfect
of Separable Verbs
The Comparative of Adjectives

The Present Perfect
of Modal Verbs
The Superlative

Take It Further 2

Note that verbs ending in **-ieren** do not take the **ge-** prefix in the past participle.

Ich habe telefoniert.
I was on the phone.

Ich habe die Salami probiert.
I tried the salami.

This is also true for separable verbs that end in **-ieren**.

Haben Sie das Kleid anprobiert?
Did you try on the dress?

✎ Work Out 2

Rewrite the sentences using the modals in parentheses, and then translate your answers.

1. **Der Verkäufer hat das Hemd in das Regal gelegt. (müssen)** _____

   _____

2. **Der Kunde hat vor dem Spiegel gestanden. (wollen)** _____

   _____

3. **Die Frau probiert das Kleid an. (dürfen)** _____

   _____

4. Meine Mutter hat ein Geschenk gekauft. (sollen) _____

_____

5. Ich habe Brot geschnitten. (müssen) _____

_____

ANSWER KEY

1. Der Verkäufer hat das Hemd in das Regal legen müssen. (*The salesman must have laid the shirt on the shelf.*) **2.** Der Kunde hat vor dem Spiegel stehen wollen. (*The customer wanted to stand in front of the mirror.*) **3.** Die Frau hat das Kleid anprobieren dürfen. (*The woman was able/allowed to try on the dress.*) **4.** Meine Mutter hat ein Geschenk kaufen sollen. (*My mother should have bought a gift.*) **5.** Ich habe Brot schneiden müssen. (*I had to cut the bread.*)

✎ Drive It Home

Time for driving it all home. Remember, even though these exercises seem very easy, they do help you retain the material you've learned.

A. Complete the sentences with the correct past participle form of the separable verb.

1. Der Zug ist gerade erst_____ . (ankommen)

2. Warum bist du nicht _____? (mitkommen)

3. Ich habe nichts _____ . (einkaufen)

4. Haben Sie die Hose _____? (anprobieren)

5. Wird sind an der falschen Kreuzung _____. (abbiegen)

B. Complete the following sentences with the correct form of the modal verb in parentheses.

1. Ich habe Deutsch lernen _____ . (müssen)

2. Haben Sie das Kleid umtauschen _____? (können)

3. Mein Bruder hat ein Geschenk kaufen _____. (wollen)

The Present Perfect
of Separable Verbs

The Comparative of Adjectives

The Present Perfect
of Modal Verbs

The Superlative

4. **Hast du die Stiefel anprobieren** _____ ? (dürfen)

5. **Der Kellner hat den Wein servieren** _____ . (sollen)

ANSWER KEY

A. 1. angekommen; 2. mitgekommen; 3. eingekauft; 4. anprobiert; 5. abgebogen

B. 1. müssen; 2. können; 3. wollen; 4. dürfen; 5. sollen

How Did You Do?

Before you move on, make sure you know how to:

☐ Use questions and statements that are helpful when shopping
(Still unsure? Jump back to page 38.)

☐ Use present perfect of separable verbs
(Still unsure? Jump back to page 41.)

☐ Use the present perfect of modal verbs
(Still unsure? Jump back to page 44.)

✎ Word Recall

Match the English sentences in column A with the German translations in column B.

1. *What can I get you?*

    a. **Ich möchte ein Pfund Wurstaufschnitt.**

2. *I like you.*

    b. **Die Hose passt gut.**

3. *I'd like a pound of cold cuts.*

    c. **Was darf's denn sein?**

4. *Anything else?*

    d. **Kann ich mit Kreditkarte bezahlen?**

5. *The pants fit well.*

    e. **Darf's sonst noch etwas sein?**

6. *Can I pay by credit card?*

    f. **Ich mag dich.**

ANSWER KEY

1. c; 2. f; 3. a; 4. e; 5. b; 6. d

Two-way Prepositions

The Present Perfect
with **haben** (to have)

Expressing Likes and Dislikes

The Present Perfect
with **sein** (to be)

Lesson 4: Conversations

By the end of this lesson, you should be able to:

☐ Use the comparative of adjectives

☐ Use the superlative of adjectives

Conversation 1

▶ 4A Conversation 1 (CD 7, Track 13 - German; Track 14 - German and English)

Sibylle Wicker's husband has a birthday coming up, and she is out shopping for a present at a clothing boutique.

Verkäufer:	Guten Tag. Kann ich Ihnen helfen?
Sibylle:	Ja, ich suche ein Geschenk für meinen Mann.
Verkäufer:	Eine Krawatte vielleicht?
Sibylle:	Nein, ich habe an einen Pullover gedacht. Hier, der schwarze Pullover ist sehr schön.
Verkäufer:	Das ist ein Damenpullover. Möchten Sie ihn anprobieren?
Sibylle:	Ja, gern. Wo ist denn die Umkleidekabine?
Verkäufer:	Hier. *(Just a few minutes later, Sibylle emerges wearing the sweater.)* Oh, der Pullover steht Ihnen aber gut.
Sibylle:	Danke.
Verkäufer:	Ich habe inzwischen ein Geschenk für Ihren Mann gesucht. Gefällt Ihnen das Hemd?
Sibylle:	Das Hemd? Der Pullover gefällt mir sehr gut. Haben Sie eine passende Hose?
Verkäufer:	Für Sie oder Ihren Mann?
Sibylle:	Für mich.
Verkäufer:	Wie wär's mit der grauen Hose hier?

The Present Perfect
of Separable Verbs

The Comparative of Adjectives

The Present Perfect
of Modal Verbs

The Superlative

Sibylle takes the pants and disappears into the fitting room.

Sibylle:	*(from the fitting room)* **Ich brauche eine kleinere Größe. Und einen Gürtel.**
Verkäufer:	**Hier ist die Hose eine Nummer kleiner, und zwei passende Gürtel. Der schwarze Gürtel ist kürzer.**
Sibylle:	**Der längere Gürtel gefällt mir besser.**

A few minutes later, Sibylle emerges from the fitting room.

Sibylle:	**Ich nehme die Hose, den Pullover, und den längeren Gürtel.**
Verkäufer:	**Gute Wahl. Ich habe inzwischen auch eine Krawatte für das Hemd gefunden.**
Sibylle:	**Hemd? Ich brauche kein Hemd.**
Verkäufer:	**Aber Sie haben doch ein Geschenk für Ihren Mann kaufen wollen.**
Sibylle:	**Oh, das habe ich ganz vergessen. Aber das kann ich auch später machen.**

Salesclerk:	*Hello. Can I help you?*
Sibylle:	*Yes, I'm looking for a present for my husband.*
Salesclerk:	*A tie, perhaps?*
Sibylle:	*No, I was thinking of a sweater. Here, this black sweater is very beautiful.*
Salesclerk:	*That's a woman's sweater. Would you like to try it on?*
Sibylle:	*Yes, please. Where is the fitting room?*
Salesclerk:	*Here. Oh, the sweater looks good on you.*
Sibylle:	*Thanks.*
Salesclerk:	*In the meantime, I've looked for a present for your husband. Do you like the shirt?*
Sibylle:	*The shirt? I like the sweater a lot. Do you have pants that would go with it?*

Two-way Prepositions

The Present Perfect
with **haben** (to have)

Expressing Likes and Dislikes

The Present Perfect
with **sein** (to be)

Salesclerk:	For you or your husband?
Sibylle:	For me.
Salesclerk:	How about these gray pants?
Sibylle:	I need a smaller size. And a belt.
Salesclerk:	Here are the pants one size smaller, and two suitable belts. The black belt is shorter.
Sibylle:	I like the longer belt better.
Sibylle:	I'll take the pants, the sweater, and the longer belt.
Salesclerk:	Good choice. In the meantime, I've also found a tie to go with the shirt.
Sibylle:	Shirt? I don't need a shirt.
Salesclerk:	But you wanted to buy a present for your husband.
Sibylle:	Oh, I forgot all about that. But I might as well do that later.

✎ Conversation Practice 1

Fill in the blanks in the following sentences with the missing words. If you're unsure of the answer, listen to the conversation on your audio one more time.

1. _____ ich Ihnen helfen?

2. Ich suche ein _____ für meinen Mann.

3. Wie wär's mit der _____ Hose hier?

4. _____ Ihnen das Hemd?

5. Ich habe an _____ gedacht.

6. Ich _____ eine kleinere Größe.

7. Der _____ Gürtel gefällt mir besser.

ANSWER KEY

1. Kann; 2. Geschenk; 3. grauen; 4. Gefällt; 5. einen Pullover; 6. brauche; 7. längere

Take It Further 1

The verb denken (*to think*) is a mixed verb, which means that even though it forms the past participle with the prefix ge- plus the ending -t just like regular (weak) verbs, it also has a stem-vowel change, just like irregular verbs.

Ich habe an einen Pullover gedacht.
I was thinking about a sweater.

Other such verbs are bringen (*to bring*), kennen (*to know*), rennen (*to run*), and wissen (*to know*), with the past participles gebracht (*brought*), gekannt (*known*), gerannt (*run*), and gewusst (*known*).

Grammar Builder 1

⏵ 4B Grammar Builder 1 (CD 7, Track 15)

THE COMPARATIVE OF ADJECTIVES

Let's look at the positive, comparative, and superlative forms of groß (*big*).

POSITIVE	COMPARATIVE	SUPERLATIVE
groß	größer	am größten
big	bigger	the biggest

The positive form is simply the basic form you use to describe something, and it's also used in so … wie … (*as … as …*), just like in English.

Das Kleid ist schön.
The dress is beautiful.

Two-way Prepositions

The Present Perfect
with **haben** (to have)

Expressing Likes and Dislikes

The Present Perfect
with **sein** (to be)

Das T-shirt ist so teuer wie der Anzug.
The T-shirt is as expensive as the suit.

The comparative compares persons or things, like the *–er* or *more* forms in English. The connective **als** is used where English uses *than.*

Meine Schuhe sind größer als deine Schuhe.
My shoes are bigger than your shoes.

And also like in English, the German comparative is formed by adding **-er** to the positive.

POSITIVE		COMPARATIVE	
schön	*beautiful*	schöner	*more beautiful*
klein	*small*	kleiner	*smaller*
teuer	*expensive*	teurer	*more expensive*
billig	*cheap*	billiger	*cheaper*
frisch	*fresh*	frischer	*fresher*
grün	*green*	grüner	*greener*
spät	*late*	später	*later*
früh	*early*	früher	*earlier*

Many one-syllable adjectives and adverbs with the stem-vowels **a**, **o**, or **u** add an umlaut in the comparative.

groß	*big*	größer	*bigger*
stark	*strong*	stärker	*stronger*
warm	*warm*	wärmer	*warmer*
kalt	*cold*	kälter	*colder*
jung	*young*	jünger	*younger*
alt	*old*	älter	*older*

Advanced German

The Present Perfect
of Separable Verbs

The Comparative of Adjectives

The Present Perfect
of Modal Verbs

The Superlative

lang	long	länger	longer
kurz	short	kürzer	shorter

Das Hemd ist größer als die anderen.
This shirt is bigger than the others.

If a comparative adjective comes right before the noun, its ending changes depending on the gender, number, and case of the noun.

Wir können uns die teureren Schuhe nicht leisten.
We can't afford the more expensive shoes.

Lass uns doch die grüneren Bananen kaufen.
Let's buy the greener bananas.

Here are some irregular comparatives.

gut	good	besser	better
viel	a lot, much	mehr	more
gern	like	lieber	rather
hoch	high	höher	higher

Das blaue Kleid gefällt mir besser.
I like the blue dress better.

We'll look at the superlative in the next section.

Ⅱ

Two-way Prepositions

The Present Perfect
with **haben** (to have)

Expressing Likes and Dislikes

The Present Perfect
with **sein** (to be)

✎ Work Out 1

Rewrite these sentences with the new subject in parentheses, comparing it to the original sentence. For example, if you see the German equivalent of: *My house is big. (your house)*, you'd write **auf Deutsch**: *Your house is bigger than my house.* Translate your answers.

1. **Meine Schuhe sind teuer. (deine Schuhe)** _____

   _____

2. **Ich bin spät dran. (du)** _____

   _____

3. **Die lange Krawatte ist schön. (kurze Krawatte)** _____

   _____

4. **Das kurze Kleid gefällt mir gut. (das lange Kleid)** _____

   _____

5. **Mein Mantel ist warm. (dein Mantel)** _____

   _____

ANSWER KEY

1. **Deine Schuhe sind teurer als meine Schuhe.** (*Your shoes are more expensive than my shoes.*)
2. **Du bist später dran als ich.** (*You're later than I [am].*) 3. **Die kurze Krawatte ist schöner als die lange Krawatte.** (*The short tie is more beautiful than the long tie.*) 4. **Das lange Kleid gefällt mir besser als das kurze Kleid.** (*I like the long dress more than the short dress.*) 5. **Dein Mantel ist wärmer als mein Mantel.** (*Your coat is warmer than my coat.*)

ⒸⒸ Conversation 2

▶ 4 Conversation 2 (CD 7, Track 16 - German; Track 17 - German and English)

Wilfried is out grocery shopping with his daughter. He is about to realize that perhaps it was not such a good idea to take her along.

Wilfried:	Wir brauchen Orangen, Salat und Tomaten.
Anna:	Ich mag Äpfel lieber als Orangen. Orangen schmecken gut, Äpfel schmecken besser, aber Schokolade schmeckt am besten.
Wilfried:	Mama hat gesagt, wir brauchen Orangen. Sie sind frischer als Äpfel. Und wir brauchen auch Wurstaufschnitt. Wie wär's mit Salami und Schinken?
Anna:	Ich mag Lyoner lieber. Salami schmeckt gut, Lyoner schmeckt besser, aber Schokolade schmeckt am besten.
Wilfried:	Mama hat gesagt, wir brauchen Salami und Schinken. Und wir brauchen noch Brot.
Anna:	Ich mag Brötchen lieber. Brot schmeckt gut, Brötchen schmecken besser, aber Schokolade schmeckt am besten.
Wilfried:	Mama hat gesagt, wir brauchen Brot. Das ist billiger als Brötchen. Und wir brauchen Rindfleisch für das Abendessen.
Anna:	Ich mag Huhn lieber als Rindfleisch. Rindfleisch schmeckt gut, Huhn schmeckt besser, aber Schokolade schmeckt am besten.
Wilfried:	Mama hat gesagt, wir brauchen Rindfleisch. Und wir brauchen auch noch Milch und Wein.
Anna:	Ich mag Apfelsaft lieber als Milch. Und Apfelsaft ist gesünder als Wein. Milch schmeckt gut, Apfelsaft schmeckt besser, aber Schokolade schmeckt am besten.
Wilfried:	Mama hat gesagt, wir brauchen Milch und Wein.

About 20 minutes later, Wilfried and his daughter are at the cashier.

Wilfried:	Haben wir auch alles? Äpfel, Lyoner, Brot, Huhn und Apfelsaft. Ja, wir haben alles.
Anna:	Nein, das wichtigste haben wir ganz vergessen.
Wilfried:	Was denn?
Anna:	Na, die Schokolade.

Two-way Prepositions

The Present Perfect
with **haben** (to have)

Expressing Likes and Dislikes

The Present Perfect
with **sein** (to be)

Wilfried:	*We need oranges, lettuce, and tomatoes.*
Anna:	*I like apples better than oranges. Oranges taste good, apples taste better, but chocolate tastes best.*
Wilfried:	*Mama said we need oranges. They're fresher than apples. And we need cold cuts. What about salami and ham?*
Anna:	*I like bologna better. Salami tastes good, bologna tastes better, but chocolate tastes best.*
Wilfried:	*Mama said we need salami and ham. And we need bread.*
Anna:	*I like breakfast rolls better. Bread tastes good, breakfast rolls taste better, but chocolate tastes best.*
Wilfried:	*Mama said we need bread. That's cheaper than breakfast rolls. And we need beef for dinner.*
Anna:	*I like chicken better than beef. Beef tastes good, chicken tastes better, but chocolate tastes best.*
Wilfried:	*Mama said we need beef. And we need milk and wine.*
Anna:	*I like apple juice better than milk. And apple juice is healthier than wine. Milk tastes good, apple juice tastes better, but chocolate tastes best.*
Wilfried:	*Mama said we need milk and wine.*
Wilfried:	*Do we have everything? Apples, bologna, bread, chicken, and apple juice. Yes, we have everything.*
Anna:	*No, we forgot all about the most important thing.*
Wilfried:	*What's that?*
Anna:	*Well, the chocolate.*

Ⅱ

✎ Conversation Practice 2

Fill in the blanks in the following sentences with the missing words. If you're unsure of the answer, listen to the conversation on your audio one more time.

1. **Orangen _____ gut, Äpfel schmecken besser, aber**

   Schokolade schmeckt am besten.

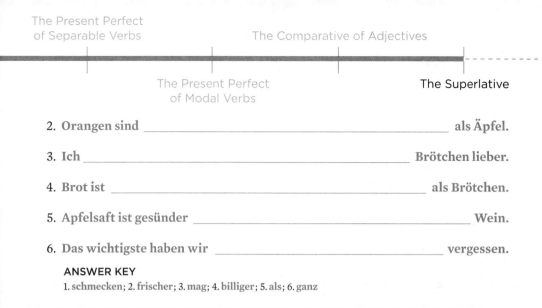

The Present Perfect of Separable Verbs

The Comparative of Adjectives

The Present Perfect of Modal Verbs

The Superlative

2. Orangen sind _____ als Äpfel.

3. Ich _____ Brötchen lieber.

4. Brot ist _____ als Brötchen.

5. Apfelsaft ist gesünder _____ Wein.

6. Das wichtigste haben wir _____ vergessen.

ANSWER KEY
1. schmecken; 2. frischer; 3. mag; 4. billiger; 5. als; 6. ganz

Take It Further 2

The word ganz (*whole, complete*) can be used for emphasis.

Das habe ich ganz vergessen.
I forgot all about that.

Bist du ganz sicher?
Are you absolutely sure?

Du bist schon ganz groß.
You're all grown up. (lit., You're already completely big.)

Grammar Builder 2

4D Grammar Builder 2 (CD 7, Track 18)

THE SUPERLATIVE

The superlative corresponds to English –*est/most*, and is formed by adding -st- plus the appropriate ending for gender, number, and case. For example:

Two-way Prepositions

The Present Perfect
with **haben** (to have)

Expressing Likes and Dislikes

The Present Perfect
with **sein** (to be)

schön → schönst- -er, -e, -es

Das ist die schönste Jacke.
That's the most beautiful jacket.

Das ist mein schönster Pullover.
That is my most beautiful sweater.

The one-syllable adjectives that add an umlaut in the comparative do so in the superlative as well.

warm → wärmst- -er, -e, -es

Das ist die wärmste Hose.
Those are the warmest pants.

If the positive of the adjective ends in -d, -t, -s, -ß, or -z, e- is usually added to the stem to facilitate pronunciation.

alt (*old*) → ältest-

naß (*wet*) → näßest-

Note that the adjective groß is an exception to this rule.

groß (*big*) → größt-

The adjectives with irregular comparatives have irregular superlatives as well.

gut (*good*)	best-
viel (*much*)	meist-
gern (*like, gladly*)	liebst-

The Present Perfect
of Separable Verbs

The Comparative of Adjectives

The Present Perfect
of Modal Verbs

The Superlative

| hoch *(high)* | höchst- |

Das sind die besten Schuhe.

These are the best shoes.

The superlative of adverbs is formed with am and the suffix -en, for example, am besten *(the best)*.

Der Pullover passt am besten zu meiner Hose.

This sweater goes best with my pants.

✎ Work Out 2

Complete the sentences.

1. **Der schwarze Pullover steht mir gut, der blaue Pullover steht mir**

   _____, **und der grüne Pullover steht mir** _____.

   (better, best)

2. **Es ist kalt draußen. Ich ziehe den** _____ **Mantel an.**

   (the warmest)

3. **Welches Kleid ist** _____, **das blaue oder das gelbe?**

   (more beautiful)

4. **Die weißen Schuhe sind teuer, die schwarzen Schuhe sind** _____,

   und die braunen Schuhe sind _____.

   (more expensive, most expensive)

5. **Der blaue Rock ist kurz, der gelbe Rock ist** _____,

   und der rosa Rock ist _____. *(shorter, shortest)*

Two-way Prepositions

The Present Perfect
with **haben** (to have)

Expressing Likes and Dislikes

The Present Perfect
with **sein** (to be)

ANSWER KEY
1. besser, am besten; 2. wärmsten; 3. schöner; 4. teurer, am teuersten; 5. kürzer, am kürzesten

✎ Drive It Home

Complete the sentences with the correct comparative in A and the correct
superlative in B.

1. **Meine Hose ist eng.**

a. **Deine Hose ist** _____.

b. **Peters Hose ist** _____.

2. **Unser Haus ist groß.**

a. **Euer Haus ist** _____.

b. **Das Hause meiner Eltern ist**

_____.

3. **Der grüne Pullover ist teuer.**

a. **Der rote Pullover**

ist _____.

b. **Der schwarze Pullover**

ist _____.

4. **Ich bin noch jung.**

a. **Meine Schwester ist** _____.

b. **Mein Bruder ist** _____.

5. **Die Bananen sind frisch.**

a. **Die Orangen sind** _____

_____.

b. **Die Trauben sind** _____

_____.

ANSWER KEY
1. a. enger; b. am engsten; 2. a. größer; b. am größten; 3. a. teurer; b. am teuersten; 4. a. jünger; b. am
jüngsten; 5. a. frischer; b. am frischesten

How Did You Do?

Before you move on to the next lesson, make sure you can:

☐ Use the comparative of adjectives
(Still unsure? Jump back to page 51.)

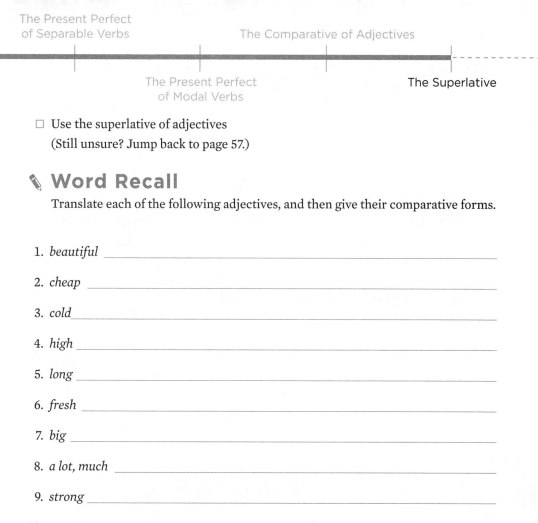

The Present Perfect
of Separable Verbs

The Comparative of Adjectives

The Present Perfect
of Modal Verbs

The Superlative

☐ Use the superlative of adjectives
(Still unsure? Jump back to page 57.)

✎ Word Recall

Translate each of the following adjectives, and then give their comparative forms.

1. *beautiful* _____

2. *cheap* _____

3. *cold* _____

4. *high* _____

5. *long* _____

6. *fresh* _____

7. *big* _____

8. *a lot, much* _____

9. *strong* _____

10. *young* _____

ANSWER KEY
1. **schön, schöner**; 2. **billig, billiger**; 3. **kalt, kälter**; 4. **hoch, höher**; 5. **lang, länger**; 6. **frisch, frischer**;
7. **groß, größer**; 8. **viel, mehr**; 9. **stark, stärker**; 10. **jung, jünger**

Don't forget to practice and reinforce what you've learned by visiting **www.livinglanguage.com/languagelab** for flashcards, games, and quizzes for Unit 1!

Unit 1 Lesson 4: Conversations

Unit 1 Essentials

Vocabulary Essentials

Test your knowledge of the key material in this unit by filling in the blanks in the following charts. Once you've completed these pages, you'll have tested your retention, and you'll have your own reference for the most essential vocabulary.

SHOPPING FOR CLOTHES

	department store
	boutique
	customer (male/female)
	to shop
	clothes
	clothing
	to like
	Can I help you?
	I'd like to try on ...
	Can I try on ... ?
	... look(s) good on me. (lit., ... suit[s] me well.)
	Can I exchange ... ?
	Where is the fitting room?
	Where is the shoe department?
	Do you have ... in a different size/color?
	I am looking for ...
	Where is the cashier?
	Can I pay with a credit card?

GROCERY SHOPPING

	grocery store
	bread
	breakfast roll
	fruit
	vegetables
	cold cuts
	to taste, to like
	What can I get you?
	I'd like …
	(Would you like this) sliced or in one piece?
	In one piece, please.
	Anything else?

If you're having a hard time remembering these words and phrases, don't forget to check out the supplemental flashcards for this unit online. Go to **www. livinglanguage.com/languagelab** for a great way to help you practice vocabulary.

Grammar Essentials

Here is a reference of the key grammar that was covered in Unit 1. Make sure you understand the summary and can use all of the grammar it covers.

TWO-WAY PREPOSITIONS

PREPOSITION	ACCUSATIVE/DIRECTION	DATIVE/LOCATION
in	Ich packe das Hemd in den Koffer.	Das Hemd ist im Koffer.
in, inside, into	*I am putting the shirt in the suitcase.*	*The shirt is in the suitcase.*
an	Ich fahre an die Kreuzung heran.	Wir biegen an der nächsten Kreuzung rechts ab.
at, to the side of, to, on	*I am approaching the intersection.*	*We turn right at the next intersection.*
auf	Ich lege die Handschuhe auf den Tisch.	Die Handschuhe sind auf dem Tisch.
on, on top of, onto	*I am putting the gloves onto the table.*	*The gloves are on the table.*
über	Der Verkäufer hängt den Pullover über das T-shirt.	Ich trage den Pullover über dem T-shirt.
above, over, across	*The salesperson hangs the sweater above the T-shirt.*	*I am wearing the sweater over the T-shirt.*
unter	Der Verkäufer hängt das T-shirt unter den Pullover.	Ich trage das T-shirt unter dem Pullover.
under, beneath, among	*The salesperson hangs the T-shirt under the sweater.*	*I am wearing the T-shirt under the sweater.*

PREPOSITION	ACCUSATIVE/DIRECTION	DATIVE/LOCATION
vor	Ich stelle mich vor den Spiegel.	Ich stehe vor dem Spiegel.
in front of, before, ago	I am placing myself in front of the mirror.	I am standing in front of the mirror.
hinter	Ich stelle mich hinter dich.	Ich stehe hinter dir.
in back of, behind	I am placing myself behind you.	I am standing behind you.
neben	Ich stelle mich neben dich.	Ich stehe neben dir.
beside, next to	I am placing myself next to you.	I am standing next to you.
zwischen	Ich lege den Pullover zwischen das T-shirt und das Hemd.	Der Pullover liegt zwischen dem T-shirt und dem Hemd.
between	I am laying the sweater between the T-shirt and the shirt.	The sweater is lying between the T-shirt and the shirt.

TRANSITIVE AND INTRANSITIVE VERB PAIRS

TRANSITIVE (MOVEMENT)		INTRANSITIVE (LOCATION)	
legen	to place, to put, to lay	liegen	to lie (location)
hängen	to hang	hängen	to hang
stellen	to place, to put	stehen	to stand
setzen	to place, to put	sitzen	to sit

THE PRESENT PERFECT

Auxiliary **haben** or **sein** + past participle of the main verb:

Ich <u>habe</u> **ein neues Kleid** <u>gekauft</u>.

I bought/have bought/did buy a new dress.

Ich <u>bin</u> **in den Supermarkt** <u>gegangen</u>.

I went into the supermarket.

REGULAR PAST PARTICIPLES

INFINITIVE		PAST PARTICIPLE	
kaufen	*to buy*	gekauft	*bought*
sagen	*to say*	gesagt	*said*
kosten	*to cost*	gekostet	*cost*

IRREGULAR PAST PARTICIPLES

INFINITIVE		PAST PARTICIPLE	
gehen	*to go*	gegangen	*gone*
finden	*to find*	gefunden	*found*
nehmen	*to take*	genommen	*taken*

SEPARABLE VERB PAST PARTICIPLE

einkaufen	*to shop*	eingekauft	*shopped*
absagen	*to cancel*	abgesagt	*cancelled*
abfahren	*to leave*	abgefahren	*left*
mitnehmen	*to take along*	mitgenommen	*taken along*

MODAL PAST PARTICIPLES

dürfen	*to be allowed to*	gedurft	*allowed to*
können	*to be able to*	gekonnt	*been able to*
möchten	*to like to*	gemocht	*liked to*
müssen	*to have to*	gemusst	*had to*
wollen	*to want to*	gewollt	*wanted to*
sollen	*to be supposed to*	gesollt	*been supposed to*

THE COMPARATIVE AND SUPERLATIVE OF ADJECTIVES

POSITIVE	COMPARATIVE	SUPERLATIVE
klein (*small*)	kleiner	am kleinsten
groß (*big*)	größer	am größten
gut (*good*)	besser	am besten

Unit 1 Quiz

Let's put the most essential German words and grammar points you've learned so far to practice in a few exercises. It's important to be sure that you've mastered this material before you move on. Score yourself at the end of the review and see if you need to go back for more practice, or if you're ready to move on to Unit 2.

A. Complete the sentences using the phrases in parentheses.

1. Ich habe das Kleid _____ Kaufhaus gekauft. (in the)

2. Wir fahren _____ Stadt. (into the)

3. Bitte legen Sie das Hemd _____ Tisch. (onto the)

4. Die Kundin steht _____ Kasse. (next to the)

5. _____ nächsten Kreuzung müssen Sie links abbiegen. (at the)

B. Rewrite the sentences in the present perfect.

1. Ich gehe einkaufen. _____

_____

2. Du vergisst die Schokolade. _____

_____

3. Die Kundin probiert die Hose an. _____

_____

4. **Der Kuchen schmeckt mir gut.** _____

   _____

5. **Wir fahren mit dem Auto.** _____

   _____

6. **Sie müssen an der Kasse bezahlen.** _____

   _____

7. **Ich suche mir einen Pullover aus.** _____

   _____

8. **Wir können die Orangen selbst wiegen.** _____

   _____

9. **Warum lauft ihr so schnell?** _____

   _____

10. **Ich hänge das Bild auf.** _____

    _____

C. Complete the sentences with the comparative and superlative of the adjective in parentheses.

1. Ich bin reich. Du bist _____. Mein Bruder ist
_____. (reich)

2. Meine Mutter ist 35 Jahre alt. Mein Vater ist _____.
Mein Großvater ist _____. (alt)

3. Das Haus in der Bergallee gefällt mir _____ als
das Haus in der Bahnhofstrasse, aber das Haus in der Landhausstrasse gefällt
mir _____. (gut)

4. Wir fahren _____ mit der Strassenbahn als mit
dem Auto, aber _____ fahren wir mit dem Bus. (gern)

5. Der Sportler joggt schnell. Ich jogge _____, aber
mein Sohn Gabriel joggt _____. (schnell)

How Did You Do?

Give yourself a point for every correct answer, then use the following key to tell whether you're ready to move on:

0-7 points: It's probably a good idea to go back through the lesson again. You may be moving too quickly, or there may be too much "down time" between your contact with German. Remember that it's better to spend 30 minutes with German three or four times a week than it is to spend two or three hours just once a week. Find a pace that's comfortable for you, and spread your contact hours out as much as you can.

8-12 points: You would benefit from a review before moving on. Go back and spend a little more time on the specific points that gave you trouble. Reread the Grammar Builder sections that were difficult, and do the Work Outs one more time. Don't forget about the online supplemental practice material, either. Go to **www.livinglanguage.com/languagelab** for games and quizzes that will reinforce the material from this unit.

13-17 points: Good job! There are just a few points that you could consider reviewing before moving on. If you haven't worked with the games and quizzes on **www.livinglanguage.com/languagelab**, please give them a try.

18-20 points: Great! You're ready to move on to the next unit.

| | | points

ANSWER KEY

A. 1. im; 2. in die; 3. auf den; 4. neben der; 5. An der

B. 1. Ich bin einkaufen gegangen. 2. Du hast die Schokolade vergessen. 3. Die Kundin hat die Hose anprobiert. 4. Der Kuchen hat mir gut geschmeckt. 5. Wir sind mit dem Auto gefahren.
6. Sie haben an der Kasse bezahlen müssen. 7. Ich habe mir einen Pullover ausgesucht. 8. Wir haben die Orangen selbst wiegen können. 9. Warum seid ihr so schnell gelaufen? 10. Ich habe das Bild aufgehängt.

C. 1. reicher/am reichsten; 2. älter/am ältesten; 3. besser/am besten; 4. lieber/am liebsten;
5. schneller/am schnellsten

Unit 2:

At a Restaurant

Congratulations on completing Unit 1, and welcome to Unit 2! In this unit you'll learn the vocabulary and grammar for eating out and trying the culinary specialties while traveling through different countries and regions. By the end of this unit you'll be able to:

☐ Read the menu at a restaurant

☐ Order at a restaurant

☐ Use the simple past of **haben**, **sein**, and **werden**

☐ Use past time expressions

☐ Speak about the past with the simple past of regular (weak) verbs

☐ Speak about the past with the simple past of irregular (strong) verbs

☐ Use the simple past of modal verbs

☐ Use the simple past of mixed verbs

☐ Express possession with the genitive case

☐ Use prepositions with the genitive case

The Simple Past
of Modal Verbs

Expressing Possession: the Genitive

The Simple Past
of Mixed Verbs

Prepositions with
the Genitive

Lesson 5: Words

By the end of this lesson you'll be able to:

☐ Read the menu at a restaurant

☐ Use the simple past of **haben, sein,** and **werden**

☐ Use past time expressions

Word Builder 1

▶ 5A Word Builder 1 (CD 8, Track 1)

das Restaurant	*restaurant*
die Kneipe	*neighborhood bar*
der Kellner	*waiter*
die Kellnerin	*waitress*
der Ober	*waiter*
die Bedienung	*waitress*
das Essen	*meal*
das Mittagessen	*lunch*
das Abendessen	*dinner*
die Vorspeise	*appetizer*
die Hauptspeise	*main course*
die Nachspeise	*dessert*
der Nachtisch	*dessert*
das Getränk	*beverage*
die Suppe	*soup*
die Süßspeise	*sweets, dessert*

die Spezialität	specialty, special
die Rechnung	check
das Trinkgeld	tip
bestellen	to order
empfehlen	to recommend

✎ Word Practice 1

Answer the multiple choice questions below.

1. The person serving you food in a restaurant is _____.
a. ein Kellner
b. ein Verkäufer
c. eine Kneipe

2. Schokolade, Kuchen, and Eis are _____.
a. Getränke
b. Suppen
c. Süßspeisen

3. Food unique to a certain region is _____.
a. der Nachtisch
b. die Suppe
c. die Spezialität

4. Once you've eaten you've got to pay _____.
a. die Rechnung
b. die Bedienung
c. die Kneipe

5. You first eat die Vorspeise, then die Hauptspeise, and finally _____.
a. das Abendessen
b. die Nachspeise
c. die Kellnerin

ANSWER KEY
1. a; 2. c; 3. c; 4. a; 5.b

The Simple Past
of Modal Verbs

Expressing Possession: the Genitive

The Simple Past
of Mixed Verbs

Prepositions with
the Genitive

Grammar Builder 1

▶ 5B Grammar Builder 1 (CD 8, Track 2)

SIMPLE PAST OF SEIN, HABEN, AND WERDEN

Even though the present perfect is the most commonly used past tense, the verbs **haben** and **sein** often use the simple past tense to refer to events in the past. Here are the forms.

HABEN (*TO HAVE*)			
ich hatte	*I had*	wir hatten	*we had*
du hattest	*you had*	ihr hattet	*you had*
er/sie/es hatte	*he/she/it had*	sie/Sie hatten	*they/you had*

SEIN (*TO BE*)			
ich war	*I was*	wir waren	*we were*
du warst	*you were*	ihr wart	*you were*
er/sie/es war	*he/she/it was*	sie/Sie waren	*they/you were*

Ich war gestern schon in diesem Restaurant.
I was in this restaurant yesterday.

Ich hatte Eis zum Nachtisch.
I had ice cream for dessert.

Werden (*to become*) is another verb commonly used in the simple past. Here are its forms.

WERDEN (*TO BECOME*)			
ich wurde	*I became*	wir wurden	*we became*
du wurdest	*you became*	ihr wurdet	*you became*
er/sie/es wurde	*he/she/it became*	sie/Sie wurden	*they/you became*

Gestern war mein Geburtstag. Ich wurde vierzig Jahre alt.
Yesterday was my birthday. I turned forty [years old].

✎ Work Out 1

Rewrite these sentences in the simple past, and then translate your answers.

1. **Das Essen ist heute aber gut.** _____

   _____

2. **Wir haben keinen Nachtisch.** _____

   _____

3. **Unser bester Kellner ist krank.** _____

   _____

4. **Er wird heute zwanzig Jahre alt.** _____

   _____

5. **Dieses Restaurant ist das teuerste in der ganzen Stadt.** _____

   _____

The Simple Past
of Modal Verbs

Expressing Possession: the Genitive

The Simple Past
of Mixed Verbs

Prepositions with
the Genitive

6. **Die Kneipe hat keinen Tisch mehr frei.** _____

ANSWER KEY

1. Das Essen war heute aber gut. (*The food today was really good.*) 2. Wir hatten keinen Nachtisch. (*We had no dessert.*) 3. Unser bester Kellner war krank. (*Our best waiter was sick.*) 4. Er wurde heute zwanzig Jahre alt. (*He turned twenty today.*) 5. Dieses Restaurant war das teuerste in der ganzen Stadt. (*This restaurant was the most expensive in the whole city.*) 6. Die Kneipe hatte keinen Tisch mehr frei. (*The neighborhood bar had no more free tables.*)

Word Builder 2

▶ 5C Word Builder 2 (CD 8, Track 3)

die Speisekarte	menu
die Weinkarte	wine list
der Tisch	table
das Glas	glass
die Tasse	cup
der Teller	plate, bowl
der Löffel	spoon
das Messer	knife
die Gabel	fork
das Besteck	silverware
die Serviette	napkin
der Geburtstag	birthday
feiern	to celebrate

(II)

✎ Word Practice 2

Translate each of the following.

1. *to celebrate* _____

2. *table* _____

3. *fork* _____

4. *knife* _____

5. *cup* _____

6. *napkin* _____

7. *plate, bowl* _____

8. *birthday* _____

ANSWER KEY
1. feiern; 2. der Tisch; 3. die Gabel; 4. das Messer; 5. die Tasse; 6. die Serviette; 7. der Teller; 8. der Geburtstag

Grammar Builder 2

▶ 5D Grammar Builder 2 (CD 8, Track 4)

TIME EXPRESSIONS FOR THE PAST

There are a few important common time expressions used when talking about past events.

gestern	yesterday
vorgestern	the day before yesterday
letzt-	last
vorletzt-	the ... before last
(vor)letzte Woche	last week/the week before last

(vor)letzten Monat	last month/the month before last
(vor)letztes Jahr	last year/the year before last
früher	earlier
vor einer Stunde	an hour ago
vor vielen Jahren	many years ago

Note that letzt- works like an adjective and adjusts in number, gender, and case to the noun it describes.

Ich war letzte Woche in Tübingen.
I was in Tübingen last week.

In den letzten Tagen war ich oft im Restaurant essen.
In the last few days, I went out to dinner a lot. (lit., In the last few days, I was often eating in a restaurant.)

Vor vielen Jahren war hier eine Kneipe.
Many years ago, there was a neighborhood bar here.

(II)

✎ Work Out 2

Rephrase the sentence in the simple past using the time expressions in parentheses.

1. **Ich bin in Dresden.** *(yesterday)* _____

_____

2. **Haben Sie heute Geburtstag?** *(last week)* _____

_____

3. Wo bist du? *(the day before yesterday)* _____

_____

4. Er wird morgen fünfzig Jahre alt. *(last year)* _____

_____

5. Hat dein Vater in einer Stunde Zeit? *(an hour ago)* _____

_____

ANSWER KEY

1. Ich war gestern in Dresden. 2. Hatten Sie letzte Woche Geburtstag? 3. Wo warst du vorgestern?
4. Er wurde letztes Jahr fünfzig Jahre alt. 5. Hatte dein Vater vor einer Stunde Zeit?

✎ Drive It Home

A. Complete the sentences using the correct form of the simple past of sein.

1. Wir _____ gestern in der Stadt.

2. Ich _____ noch nie in Afrika.

3. _____ ihr heute schon in der Schule?

B. Now complete the sentences using the correct form of the simple past of haben.

1. Gestern _____ Sie den Nachtisch.

2. Das Restaurant _____ keine Weinkarte.

3. _____ ihr denn gestern wirklich keine Zeit?

C. Now complete the sentences using the correct form of the simple past of werden.

1. Mein Vater _____ letzten Montag fünfundachtzig Jahre alt.

2. Als ich dreißig Jahre alt war, _____ ich Lehrerin.

3. Gestern _____ Sie endlich Vater.

ANSWER KEY
A. 1. waren ; 2. war ; 3. Wart ; B. 1. hatten ; 2. hatte ; 3. Hattet ; C. 1. wurde ; 2. wurde ; 3. wurden

☀ Tip!

Ask **Wo ist die Toilette?** if you have to use the bathroom. **Das Badezimmer** is where you take your bath or a shower and brush your teeth. Public restrooms are referred to as **Toiletten** or **W.C.** Look for **Herren** for the men's restrooms, and **Damen** for the women's restrooms.

How Did You Do?

Before you move on to the next lesson, make sure you know how to:

☐ Read the menu at a restaurant
(Still unsure? Jump back to page 73.)

☐ Use the simple past of **haben**, **sein**, and **werden**
(Still unsure? Jump back to page 75.)

☐ Use past time expressions
(Still unsure? Jump back to page 78.)

✎ Word Recall

Match the English words in column A with the German translations in column B.

1. *menu*	a. das Essen
2. *neighborhood bar*	b. der Teller
3. *lunch*	c. gestern
4. *meal*	d. das Mittagessen
5. *to order*	e. das Frühstück
6. *yesterday*	f. die Kneipe

7. *breakfast*

8. *plate*

g. die Speisekarte

h. bestellen

ANSWER KEY
1. g; 2. f; 3. d; 4. a; 5. h; 6. c; 7. e; 8. b

Lesson 6: Phrases

By the end of this lesson you should be able to:

☐ Speak about the past with the simple past of regular (weak) verbs

☐ Speak about the past with the simple past of irregular (strong) verbs

Phrase Builder 1

6A Phrase Builder 1 (CD 8, Track 5)

einen Tisch bestellen	*to reserve a table, to make reservations*
einen Tisch reservieren	*to reserve a table, to make reservations*
Auf welchen Namen?	*Under which name?*
ein Tisch für vier	*a table for four*
ein Tisch für 20 Uhr	*a table for 8:00 p.m.*
ein Tisch am Fenster	*a table at the window*
ein Tisch im Nebenzimmer	*a table in a separate room*
ein Tisch auf der Terrasse	*a table on the terrace*
Wie wär's mit … ?	*How about … ?*
Darf ich … empfehlen?	*May I recommend …*
Ich empfehle …	*I recommend …*
als Vorspeise	*as an appetizer*

The Simple Past
of Modal Verbs

Expressing Possession: the Genitive

The Simple Past
of Mixed Verbs

Prepositions with
the Genitive

als Hauptspeise	as a main course
als Nachspeise	for dessert
Was darf's sein?	What can I get you?
Noch etwas?	Anything else?

Phrase Practice 1

Translate the following phrases from English to German.

1. *What can I get you?* _____

2. *to reserve a table* _____

3. *Under which name?* _____

4. *a table at the window* _____

5. *How about … ?* _____

6. *I recommend* _____

ANSWER KEY
1. Was darf's sein? 2. einen Tisch reservieren; 3. Unter welchem Namen? 4. ein Tisch am Fenster;
5. Wie wär's mit … ? 6. Ich empfehle …

Grammar Builder 1

6B Grammar Builder 1 (CD 8, Track 6)

THE SIMPLE PAST OF REGULAR (WEAK) VERBS

The simple past is mostly used in writing, in speeches that refer to the past, in stories or fairy tales, and, as discussed above, with the verbs **haben**, **sein**, and **werden**. Regular, or weak, verbs form their past tense by adding the past tense

marker, -t-, similar to -ed in English, and the personal endings, -e, -est, -e, -en, -et, and -en, to the stem of the verb.

ich	stem + t + e	ich hörte (I heard)
du	stem + t + est	du hörtest
er/sie/es	stem + t + e	er/sie/es hörte
wir	stem + t + en	wir hörten
ihr	stem + t + et	ihr hörtet
sie	stem + t + en	sie hörten
Sie	stem + t + en	Sie hörten

If the verb stem ends in -d or -t, insert -e- between the stem and the past tense ending—for example, antworten er antwort_e_te.

Er bestellte den Schweinebraten.
He ordered the pork roast.

Ich hörte viel Gutes über dieses Restaurant.
I heard many good things about this restaurant.

Der Koch eröffnete ein neues Restaurant.
The cook opened a new restaurant.

⏸

✎ Work Out 1

Rewrite the sentences in the simple past.

1. **Wer bestellt die Käsespätzle?** _____

   _____

2. **Ich arbeite in einer Kneipe.** _____

   _____

3. **Wir suchen lange nach dem Restaurant.** _____

   _____

4. **Der Kellner redet zu viel.** _____

   _____

5. **Der Nachtisch schmeckt mir gut.** _____

   _____

ANSWER KEY
1. Wer bestellte die Käsespätzle? 2. Ich arbeitete in einer Kneipe. 3. Wir suchten lange nach dem Restaurant. 4. Der Kellner redete zu viel. 5. Der Nachtisch schmeckte mir gut.

Phrase Builder 2

⊙ 6C Phrase Builder 2 (CD 8, Track 7)

Eine Speisekarte, bitte.	*A menu, please.*
Ich nehme …	*I'll have …*
Ich möchte gern …	*I'd like …*
ein Teller Suppe	*a bowl of soup*
ein Glas Wein	*a glass of wine*
eine Flasche Wein	*a bottle of wine*

| Simple Past of **sein**, **haben**, and **werden** | | The Simple Past of Regular (Weak) Verbs | |
| Time Expressions for the Past | | | The Simple Past of Irregular (Strong) Verbs |

eine Tasse Kaffee	a cup of coffee
ein Kännchen Kaffee	a portion (lit., a small pot) of coffee
mit Zucker	with sugar
ohne Zucker	without sugar
mit Milch	with milk
ohne Milch	without milk
Die Rechnung, bitte.	The check, please.
Alles zusammen?	One check? (lit., All together?)
ein Trinkgeld geben	to leave a tip, to tip
aufrunden	to round up (the amount)
Stimmt so.	Keep the change. (lit., This is correct.)

(II)

✎ Phrase Practice 2

Complete the German phrases to match the English in parentheses.

1. Ich _____ gern (I'd like)

2. eine _____ Kaffee (a cup of coffee)

3. _____ Zucker (with sugar)

4. _____ zusammen? (One check?)

5. ein _____ geben (to leave a tip)

6. _____ so. (Keep the change.)

ANSWER KEY
1. möchte; 2. Tasse; 3. mit; 4. Alles; 5. Trinkgeld; 6. Stimmt

The Simple Past
of Modal Verbs

Expressing Possession: the Genitive

The Simple Past
of Mixed Verbs

Prepositions with
the Genitive

Grammar Builder 2

▶ 6D Grammar Builder 2 (CD 8, Track 8)

THE SIMPLE PAST OF IRREGULAR (STRONG) VERBS

All strong verbs show a stem-vowel change in the past tense—for example, bitten
ich bat. In addition, strong verbs add the following endings.

ich	stem-vowel change + -	ich bat *(I asked for)*
du	stem-vowel change + st	du batst
er/sie/es	stem-vowel change + -	er/sie/es bat
wir	stem-vowel change + en	wir baten
ihr	stem-vowel change + t	ihr batet
sie/Sie	stem-vowel change + en	sie/Sie baten

Note that the first person singular and third person singular do not have an ending.

If the verb stem ends in -d or -t, insert -e- between the stem with stem-vowel
change and the ending in the second person singular and plural—for example:
finden du fandest.

As it is hard to know which verbs are strong verbs, it is best to simply memorize
the past tense forms along with the infinitives. You can refer to the Grammar
Summary for a list of common strong verbs. Here are a few.

INFINITIVE	SIMPLE PAST	
lesen	las	*to read*
finden	fand	*to find*
sprechen	sprach	*to speak*
rufen	rief	*to call, to yell*
trinken	trank	*to drink*
essen	aß	*to eat*

Time Expressions for the Past

The Simple Past of Irregular (Strong) Verbs

INFINITIVE	SIMPLE PAST	
nehmen	nahm	to take
empfehlen	empfahl	to recommend
gefallen	gefiel	to like (lit., to be to one's liking)
gehen	ging	to go
kommen	kam	to come
sitzen	saß	to sit

Nach langem Suchen fanden wir das Restaurant endlich.
After searching for a long time, we finally found the restaurant.

Der Kellner empfahl den Rinderbraten.
The waiter recommended the beef roast.

Dieses Restaurant gefiel mir schon immer.
I always liked this restaurant.

Ⅱ

✎ Work Out 2
Rewrite the sentences in the simple past.

1. **Der Koch empfiehlt den Sauerbraten.** _____

_____

2. **Wir finden das Restaurant nicht.** _____

_____

3. Lesen Sie die Speisekarte? _____

   _____

4. Ich sitze am Fenster. _____

   _____

5. Der Kellner gefällt mir. _____

   _____

ANSWER KEY
1. Der Koch empfahl den Sauerbraten. 2. Wir fanden das Restaurant nicht. 3. Lasen Sie die
Speisekarte? 4. Ich saß am Fenster. 5. Der Kellner gefiel mir.

✎ Drive It Home

Rewrite the following sentences using the correct form of the simple past.

1. Ihr lest die Speisekarte. _____

2. Was trinkst du? _____

3. Meine Freundin isst das Sauerkraut. _____

   _____

4. Ich nehme den Sauerbraten. _____

5. Wir rufen den Kellner. _____

6. Der Kellner hört uns nicht. _____

   _____

7. Ich öffne meine Tasche. _____

8. Wir zahlen mit Kreditkarte. _____

   _____

Simple Past of **sein**,
haben, and **werden**

The Simple Past of Regular
(Weak) Verbs

Time Expressions for the Past

The Simple Past of Irregular
(Strong) Verbs

ANSWER KEY

1. Ihr last die Speisekarte. 2. Was trankst du? 3. Meine Freundin aß das Sauerkraut. 4. Ich nahm den Sauerbraten. 5. Wir riefen den Kellner. 6. Der Kellner hörte uns nicht. 7. Ich öffnete meine Tasche. 8. Wir zahlten mit Kreditkarte.

⚡ Tip!

Table manners are different in German-speaking countries from those in the U.S. During a meal, always show both of your hands rather than keeping one hand under the table. It is not customary to cut your food, then put the knife down and change the hand holding the fork to eat. Instead, always hold your fork in the left hand and your knife in the right hand.

How Did You Do?

By now you should be able to:

☐ Speak about the past with the simple past of regular (weak) verbs (Still unsure? Jump back to page 83.)

☐ Speak about the past with the simple past of irregular (strong) verbs (Still unsure? Jump back to page 87.)

✎ Word Recall

To review the vocabulary you learned in the last two lessons, fill in the German equivalents for the following English phrases:

1. *A menu, please.* _____

2. *I'll have …* _____

3. *a small pot of coffee with sugar* _____

4. *The check, please.* _____

5. *to round up (the amount)* _____

6. *to make reservations* _____

7. *May I recommend …* _____

8. *I recommend …* _____

9. *as a main course* _____

10. *Anything else?* _____

ANSWER KEY
1. **Eine Speisekarte bitte;** 2. **Ich nehme … ;** 3. **ein Kännchen Kaffee mit Zucker;** 4. **Die Rechnung, bitte;** 5. **aufrunden;** 6. **bestellen, reservieren;** 7. **Darf ich … empfehlen;** 8. **Ich empfehle … ;** 9. **als Hauptspeise;** 10. **Sonst noch etwas?**

Lesson 7: Sentences

By the end of this lesson you should be able to:

☐ Order at a restaurant

☐ Use the simple past of modal verbs

☐ Use the simple past of mixed verbs

Sentence Builder 1

▶ 7A Sentence Builder 1 (CD 8, Track 9)

Ich möchte einen Tisch für zwei Personen reservieren/bestellen.	*I'd like to reserve a table for two people.*
Um welche Uhrzeit?	*For what time?*
Um 19 Uhr.	*For 7:00 p.m.*
Auf welchen Namen, bitte?	*What's the name, please?*
(Auf) Schneider.	*(In the name of) Schneider.*

Können wir einen Tisch im Garten haben?	Could we have a table in the garden?
Im Garten ist leider nichts mehr frei.	Unfortunately, there is no more room in the garden.
Ich habe eine Reservierung für Schneider.	I have a reservation for Schneider.

✎ Sentence Practice 1

Complete the sentences below. The translations in parentheses will guide you to the correct word.

1. Ich möchte einen Tisch _____. (*I'd like to reserve a table.*)

2. Um _____ Uhrzeit? (*For what time?*)

3. Auf welchen _____? (*What's the name?*)

4. Kann ich einen Tisch _____ haben? (*Can I have a table at the window?*)

5. Am Fenster ist _____ mehr frei. (*There's no more room at the window.*)

ANSWER KEY

1. bestellen; 2. welche; 3. Namen; 4. am Fenster; 5. nichts

The Simple Past
of Modal Verbs

Expressing Possession: the Genitive

The Simple Past
of Mixed Verbs

Prepositions with
the Genitive

Grammar Builder 1

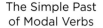 7B Grammar Builder 1 (CD 8, Track 10)

THE SIMPLE PAST OF MODAL VERBS

Modal verbs form the past tense by adding the past tense marker, -t-, and a
personal ending: -e, -est, -e, -en, -et, or -en.

DÜRFEN *(TO BE ALLOWED TO)*	
ich durfte	wir durften
du durftest	ihr durftet
er/sie/es durfte	sie/Sie durften

KÖNNEN *(TO BE ABLE TO)*	
ich konnte	wir konnten
du konntest	ihr konntet
er/sie/es konnte	sie/Sie konnten

MÖCHTEN *(TO LIKE TO)*	
ich mochte	wir mochten
du mochtest	ihr mochtet
er/sie/es mochte	sie/Sie mochten

MÜSSEN *(TO HAVE TO)*	
ich musste	wir mussten
du musstest	ihr musstet
er/sie/es musste	sie/Sie mussten

WOLLEN *(TO WANT TO)*	
ich wollte	wir wollten
du wolltest	ihr wolltet
er/sie/es wollte	sie/Sie wollten

The simple past is commonly used with modal verbs.

Ich wollte heute im Restaurant essen.
I wanted to eat in the restaurant today.

Meine Mutter konnte leider nicht mitkommen.
Unfortunately, my mother couldn't come along.

Wir mussten zu Hause bleiben.
We had to stay home.

Ⅱ

✎ Work Out 1

Rephrase the sentences in the simple past.

1. Willst du heute im Restaurant essen? _____

   _____

2. Möchten Sie ein Glas Wein trinken? _____

   _____

3. Sie kann nicht mitkommen. _____

   _____

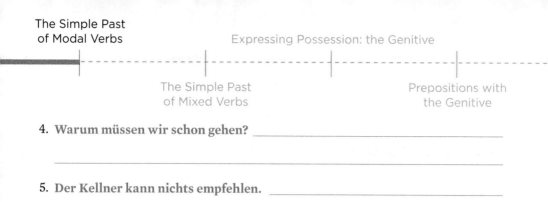

The Simple Past
of Modal Verbs

Expressing Possession: the Genitive

The Simple Past
of Mixed Verbs

Prepositions with
the Genitive

4. Warum müssen wir schon gehen? _____

_____

5. Der Kellner kann nichts empfehlen. _____

_____

ANSWER KEY

1. Wolltest du heute im Restaurant essen? 2. Mochten Sie ein Glas Wein trinken? 3. Sie konnte nicht mitkommen. 4. Warum mussten wir schon gehen? 5. Der Kellner konnte nichts empfehlen.

Sentence Builder 2

▶ 7C Sentence Builder 2 (CD 8, Track 11)

Können wir bitte eine Speisekarte haben?	Could we have a menu, please?
Was darf's denn sein?	What can I get you?
Was empfehlen Sie?	What do you recommend?
Das klingt aber gut.	That sounds good.
Ich nehme den Rostbraten.	I'll have the roast.
Wir brauchen noch ein Messer.	We need a knife.
An unserem Tisch fehlt eine Gabel.	We are missing a fork at our table.
Guten Appetit!	Enjoy your meal!
Bitte bringen Sie mir noch ein Glas Rotwein.	Please bring me another glass of red wine.
Die Rechnung, bitte.	The check, please.
Ist das Trinkgeld inklusive?	Is the tip included?
Stimmt so.	That's correct.
Vielen Dank.	Thank you.

✎ Sentence Practice 2

Complete the dialogue below.

Kellner: Was (1) _____ denn sein?

Gast: Was (2) _____ Sie?

Kellner: Der (3) _____ ist sehr gut.

Gast: Dann (4) _____ ich den Rostbraten.

Kellner: Und zu trinken?

Gast: Ein (5) _____ Rotwein, bitte.

Kellner: Kommt sofort.

ANSWER KEY

1. darf's 2. empfehlen 3. Rostbraten 4. nehme 5. Glas

Grammar Builder 2

⊙ 7D Grammar Builder 2 (CD 8, Track 12)

THE SIMPLE PAST OF MIXED VERBS

Like weak verbs, mixed verbs in the simple past add the past tense marker, -t-, and the past tense endings -e, -est, -e, -en, -et, -en But like strong verbs, they also undergo a stem-vowel change.

BRINGEN*(TO BRING)*	
ich brachte	wir brachten
du brachtest	ihr brachtet
er/sie/es brachte	sie/Sie brachten

DENKEN*(TO THINK)*	
ich dachte	wir dachten
du dachtest	ihr dachtet
er/sie/es dachte	sie/Sie dachten

The Simple Past
of Modal Verbs

Expressing Possession: the Genitive

The Simple Past
of Mixed Verbs

Prepositions with
the Genitive

KENNEN *(TO KNOW)*	
ich kannte	wir kannten
du kanntest	ihr kanntet
er/sie/es kannte	sie/Sie kannten

RENNEN *(TO RUN)*	
ich rannte	wir rannten
du ranntest	ihr ranntet
er/sie/es rannte	sie/Sie rannten

WISSEN *(TO KNOW)*	
ich wusste	wir wussten
du wusstest	ihr wusstet
er/sie/es wusste	sie/Sie wussten

(II)

✎ Work Out 2

Rewrite the sentences in the simple past.

1. Kennen Sie das Restaurant schon? _____

_____

2. Ich denke an den Salat als Vorspeise. _____

_____

3. Der Kellner bringt die Rechnung. _____

_____

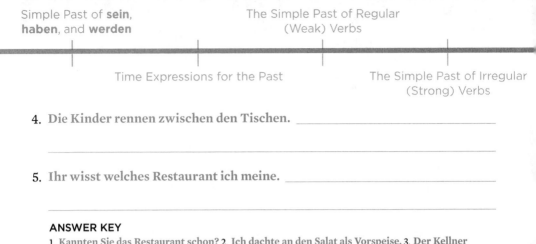
4. Die Kinder rennen zwischen den Tischen. _____

_____

5. Ihr wisst welches Restaurant ich meine. _____

_____

ANSWER KEY
1. Kannten Sie das Restaurant schon? 2. Ich dachte an den Salat als Vorspeise. 3. Der Kellner brachte die Rechnung. 4. Die Kinder rannten zwischen den Tischen. 5. Ihr wusstet, welches Restaurant ich meinte.

✎ Drive It Home

A. Fill in the blanks with the simple past of the modal verbs in parentheses.

1. Wir _____ im Restaurant essen. (wollen)

2. Ich _____ einen Tisch bestellen. (sollen)

3. Der Kellner _____ die Speisekarte nicht finden. (können)

4. Die Kinder _____ nicht im Restaurant spielen. (dürfen)

5. Ich _____ mit Kreditkarte bezahlen. (müssen)

B. Fill in the blanks with the simple past of the mixed verbs in parentheses.

1. _____ Sie ich habe schon bezahlt? (denken)

2. Der Gast _____ den Kellner persönlich. (kennen)

3. Du _____ nicht wo die Toilette ist. (wissen)

4. Wir _____ genug Geld mit. (bringen)

5. Der Kellner _____ zwischen den Tischen herum. (rennen)

ANSWER KEY
A. 1. wollten; 2. sollte; 3. konnte; 4. durften; 5. musste
B. 1. Dachten; 2. kannte; 3. wusstest; 4. brachten; 5. rannte

⊕ Culture Note

Das Mittagessen (*lunch*) is the main meal of the day for most people in
Germany, Austria, and Switzerland. That's when people eat their **Käsespätzle**
or their **Schnitzel**. Many companies offer employees a hot midday meal at the
company's cafeteria, and companies without a cafeteria offer meal tickets for
local restaurants. School-age children who cannot go home for lunch eat a hot
meal in the school cafeteria, which is usually staffed by volunteering parents.
Das Abendessen (*dinner*) is usually just a light meal consisting of **belegte Brote**
(*open-faced sandwiches*) sampling the wide variety of **Wurst** (*cold cuts*) and **Käse**
(*cheese*) to be found particularly in the south of Germany and Switzerland. **Das
Frühstück** (*breakfast*) consists of **Brötchen** (*fresh baked breakfast rolls*) with
Marmelade (*marmalade*), **Gelee** (*jam*), or **Wurst** (*cold cuts*) and **Käse** (*cheese*),
or the famous **Müesli** (*granola and dried fruit mixed with either milk or yogurt*),
which originated in Switzerland. Between lunch and dinner, people enjoy **Kaffee
und Kuchen** (*coffee and cake*), particularly on the weekends.

How Did You Do?

You probably know by now how to:

☐ Order at a restaurant
(Still unsure? Jump back to page 91.)

☐ Use the simple past of modal verbs
(Still unsure? Jump back to page 93.)

☐ Use the simple past of mixed verbs
(Still unsure? Jump back to page 96.)

✎ Word Recall

Fill in the chart with either the English or German translation of the word or phrase.

der Kellner	1.
die Speisekarte	2.
3.	*to recommend*
4.	*Anything else?*
Stimmt so.	5.
6.	*The bill please.*
7.	*I'd like the soup, please.*
Noch ein Glas Wein bitte.	8.
9.	*Enjoy your meal!*
wissen	10.

ANSWER KEY

1. *waiter*; 2. *menu*; 3. **empfehlen** ; 4. **Sonst noch etwas?** 5. *That's correct. (No change.)* 6. **Die Rechnung, bitte.** 7. **Ich hätte gern die Suppe.** 8. *Another glass of wine, please.* 9. **Guten Appetit!** 10. *to know (facts)*

Lesson 8: Conversations

By the end of this lesson you should be able to:

☐ Express possession with the genitive case

☐ Use prepositions with the genitive case

ⓐ Conversation 1

▶ 8A Conversation 1 (CD 8, Track 13 - German; Track 14; German and English)

Rainer wants to take his girlfriend out to dinner for her birthday.

The Simple Past
of Modal Verbs

Expressing Possession: the Genitive

The Simple Past
of Mixed Verbs

Prepositions with
the Genitive

Rainer: (*on the phone*) Ich möchte für heute Abend um 20 Uhr einen Tisch für zwei Personen reservieren. Auf Schäfer.

At the restaurant

Rainer: Zur Feier des Tages trinken wir eine Flasche Champagner. Du hast schließlich nicht jeden Tag Geburtstag.

The waiter returns with the champagne.

Rainer: Auf dein Wohl, Caroline.

Caroline: Zum Wohl!

Rainer: (*handing her a present*) Alles Gute zum Geburtstag!

Caroline: Oh. Warst du schon einmal in diesem Restaurant?

Rainer: Nein, aber ich wollte schon immer mal hier essen. Es gehört dem Bruder eines Kollegen.

Caroline: Was empfiehlst du?

Rainer: Die Spezialität des Hauses sind die Rindsrouladen.

Caroline: Ich nehme die Rindsrouladen.

Rainer: Für mich bitte das Wiener Schnitzel mit Kartoffelsalat. Wolltest du das Geschenk nicht öffnen?

Caroline: Doch, natürlich. (*She opens the present.*) Rainer! Diese Ohrringe wollte ich schon so lange.

Rainer: Das wußte ich, mein Schatz.

Caroline: Woher wußtest du das?

Rainer: Na, wir waren schon oft genug zusammen bummeln. Und jedes Mal hast du diese Ohrringe bewundert.

Caroline: Das ist das beste Geschenk meines Lebens. Das war nicht nötig.

Rainer: Doch. Du bist die Frau meiner Träume.

Rainer: *I'd like to make reservations for tonight at 8:00 p.m. for two people. In the name "Schäfer."*

Simple Past of **sein**,
haben, and **werden**

The Simple Past of Regular
(Weak) Verbs

Time Expressions for the Past

The Simple Past of Irregular
(Strong) Verbs

Rainer:	*To honor the day, we'll have a bottle of champagne. After all, it's not your birthday every day.*
Rainer:	*To your health, Caroline.*
Caroline:	*Cheers!*
Rainer:	*Happy birthday!*
Caroline:	*Have you been to this restaurant before?*
Rainer:	*No, but I've always wanted to eat here. It belongs to the brother of a colleague.*
Caroline:	*What do you recommend?*
Rainer:	*The specialty of the house is the Rindsrouladen.*
Caroline:	*I'll have the Rindsrouladen.*
Rainer:	*The Wiener Schnitzel with potato salad for me. Didn't you want to open your present?*
Caroline:	*Yes, of course. Rainer! I've wanted these earrings for so long.*
Rainer:	*I knew that, my darling.*
Caroline:	*How did you know?*
Rainer:	*Well, we've been window-shopping often enough. And every time, you have admired those earrings.*
Caroline:	*This is the best present of my life. That wasn't necessary.*
Rainer:	*Yes, it was. You are the woman of my dreams.*

(II)

⊕ Culture Note

There is good reason why the German cuisine is considered meat-and-potatoes
fare. There are many excellent meat dishes. **Rindsrouladen**, for example, are a
German specialty. They are made with thinly sliced beef, rolled up with spring
onions, green peppers, and mustard. They are usually served with mashed potatoes
and a green salad or a vegetable medley. And the famous **Wiener Schnitzel** is a
breaded veal cutlet, often served with nothing but **Kartoffelsalat** (*potato salad*).

The Simple Past
of Modal Verbs

Expressing Possession: the Genitive

The Simple Past
of Mixed Verbs

Prepositions with
the Genitive

✎ Conversation Practice 1

Complete the sentences below. If you're unsure of the answer, listen to the conversation on your audio one more time.

1. **Auf dein** _____ **, Caroline.**

2. _____ **Wohl!**

3. _____ **empfehlen Sie?**

4. **Die Spezialität** _____ **sind die Rindsrouladen.**

5. **Ich** _____ **die Rindsrouladen.**

6. **Alles Gute zum** _____ **.**

7. **Wolltest du das** _____ **nicht öffnen?**

8. **Diese Ohrringe** _____ **ich schon so lange.**

9. **Das wußte ich, mein** _____ **.**

ANSWER KEY
1. Wohl; 2. Zum; 3. Was; 4. des Hauses; 5. nehme; 6. Geburtstag; 7. Geschenk; 8. wollte; 9. Schatz

Grammar Builder 1
▶ 8B Grammar Builder 1 (CD 8, Track 15)

EXPRESSING POSSESSION: THE GENITIVE

German uses the genitive case to show possession.

Das ist der Bruder eines Kollegen.
That is a colleague's brother./That is the brother of a colleague.

Eines Kollegen is in the genitive case and translates as *a colleague's* or *of a colleague*. Notice the similarity between the genitive ending **-es** on **eines** and

English apostrophe-*s*. In the genitive, not only do the articles change, but an **-s** or **-es** is also added to masculine and neuter singular nouns. Here are the genitive forms of articles, nouns, and adjectives.

MASCULINE	FEMININE	NEUTER	PLURAL
des Vaters	der Mutter	des Kindes	der Väter, der Mütter, der Kinder
eines Vaters	einer Mutter	eines Kindes	-
meines Vaters	meiner Mutter	meines Kindes	meiner Väter, meiner Mütter, meiner Kinder
keines Vaters	keiner Mutter	keines Kindes	keiner Väter, keiner Mütter, keiner Kinder
des netten Vaters	der netten Mutter	des netten Kindes	der netten Väter, der netten Mütter, der netten Kinder

Note that singular masculine and neuter nouns add an ending, but feminine nouns do not: **der Vater → des Vaters**, but **die Frau → der Frau**. Masculine and neuter nouns ending in **-t, -d, -s, -f**, and **-g** add an **-e-** before the **-s** to facilitate pronunciation—for example: **der Tag → des Tages**.

Zur Feier des Tages trinken wir Champagner.
As a celebration of the day, we'll have champagne.

The **n**-nouns, such as **der Herr** (*man, mister, sir*) and **der Patient** (*patient*), add an **-n** ending in the genitive, without the **-s**. For example: **der Kollege → des Kollegen**.

Das ist der Bruder eines Kollegen.
That is the brother of a colleague.

The genitive answers the question **Wessen?** (*Whose?*)

Wessen Bruder gehört das Restaurant?
Whose brother does the restaurant belong to?

Es gehört dem Bruder einer Kollegin.
It belongs to the brother of a colleague.

Das ist das beste Geschenk meines Lebens.
This is the best present of my life.

Du bist die Frau meiner Träume.
You are the woman of my dreams.

Possession can also be expressed by adding **-s** to proper names.

Das ist Rainers Freundin.
This is Rainer's girlfriend.

Das sind Carolines Ohrringe.
These are Caroline's earrings.

Ⅱ

✎ Work Out 1

Complete the sentences with the genitive phrases in parentheses.

1. **Das ist die Freundin** _____ . (*of a colleague*)

Simple Past of **sein**,
haben, and **werden**

The Simple Past of Regular
(Weak) Verbs

Time Expressions for the Past

The Simple Past of Irregular
(Strong) Verbs

2. Wo ist _____ Restaurant? *(Mr. Schneider's)*

3. Du bist der Mann _____ . *(of my dreams)*

4. Zur Feier _____ gehen wir essen.

   (your birthday)

5. Das ist der Kellner _____ . *(of the year)*

   ANSWER KEY
   1. eines Kollegen; 2. Herrn Schneiders; 3. meiner Träume; 4. deines Geburtstages; 5. des Jahres

🎧 Conversation 2

▶ 8C Conversation 2 (CD 8, Track 16 - German; Track 17; German and English)

Rainer and Caroline have finished their dinner.

Rainer:	Hat's geschmeckt?
Caroline:	Oh ja. Es war ausgezeichnet. Wie wär's mit einem Nachtisch oder einer Tasse Kaffee?
Rainer:	*(to the waiter)* Ich nehme eine Tasse Kaffee. Schwarz bitte.
Caroline:	Ich auch. Aber mit Milch und Zucker. Du warst so still während des Essens. Ist alles in Ordnung?
Rainer:	Ja, natürlich. Es ist nur …
Caroline:	Was ist denn?
Rainer:	Wie ich vorhin schon sagte, du bist die Frau meiner Träume.
Caroline:	Ja?
Rainer:	Und ich wollte einen perfekten Abend …
Caroline:	Ja?
Rainer:	Aber leider habe ich …
Caroline:	Was wolltest du denn sagen?
Rainer:	Leider habe ich meinen Geldbeutel zu Hause vergessen. Kannst du die Rechnung bezahlen?
Caroline:	*(laughing)* Aber selbstverständlich, Rainer. Und der Abend war trotz des vergessenen Geldbeutels perfekt.

The Simple Past
of Modal Verbs

Expressing Possession: the Genitive

The Simple Past
of Mixed Verbs

Prepositions with
the Genitive

Rainer:	*Did you enjoy it?*
Caroline:	*Oh, yes, it was excellent. How about some dessert or a cup of coffee?*
Rainer:	*I'll have a cup of coffee. Black, please.*
Caroline:	*Me, too. But with milk and sugar. You were so quiet during dinner. Is everything okay?*
Rainer:	*Yes, of course. It's just …*
Caroline:	*What's up?*
Rainer:	*As I said earlier, you are the woman of my dreams.*
Caroline:	*Yes?*
Rainer:	*And I wanted a perfect evening …*
Caroline:	*Yes?*
Rainer:	*But unfortunately, I …*
Caroline:	*What did you want to say?*
Rainer:	*Unfortunately, I forgot my wallet at home. Could you take care of the check?*
Caroline:	*But of course, Rainer. And the evening was perfect despite the forgotten wallet.*

✎ Conversation Practice 2

Fill in the blanks in the following sentences with the missing words. If you're unsure of the answer, listen to the conversation on your audio one more time.

1. Hat's _____?

2. Es war _____. Wie wär's mit einem Nachtisch

   _____ einer Tasse Kaffee?

3. Ich nehme eine Tasse Kaffee. _____ bitte.

4. Du warst so _____ während des Essens. Ist _____ in Ordnung?

5. Was ist _____?

6. Du bist die Frau _____.

7. Kannst du _____ bezahlen?

8. _____ selbstverständlich, Rainer.

ANSWER KEY

1. geschmeckt; 2. ausgezeichnet/oder; 3. Schwarz; 4. still/alles; 5. denn; 6. meiner Träume; 7. die Rechnung; 8. Aber

Grammar Builder 2

▶ 8D Grammar Builder 2 (CD 8, Track 18)

PREPOSITIONS WITH THE GENITIVE

There are four prepositions that are followed by the genitive case.

wegen	Wir sind wegen der Spezialitäten in diesem Restaurant.
because (of)	*We are in this restaurant for (lit., because of) its specialties.*
während	Wir haben während des Essens telefoniert.
during	*We made calls during dinner.*
(an)statt	Sie hat das Wiener Schnitzel statt der Rindsrouladen gegessen.
instead of	*She ate the Wiener Schnitzel instead of the Rindsrouladen.*
trotz	Er hat die Ohrringe trotz des Preises gekauft.
despite	*He bought the earrings despite their price.*

You will notice that, in spoken German, these prepositions are often followed by the dative case. So you may also hear **Wir haben während** <u>dem</u> **Essen telefoniert.**

⏸

The Simple Past
of Modal Verbs

Expressing Possession: the Genitive

The Simple Past
of Mixed Verbs

Prepositions with
the Genitive

✎ Work Out 2

Fill in the blanks with the genitive of the phrase in parentheses.

1. Während _____ rief meine Mutter an. (das Essen)

2. Ich hatte trotz _____ zu viel Arbeit. (deine Hilfe)

3. Der Kellner brachte einen Rotwein statt _____.

   (ein Weißwein)

4. Trotz _____ war das Restaurant leer.

   (das gute Essen)

5. Ich konnte wegen _____ nicht pünktlich kommen.

   (der Verkehr)

   ANSWER KEY
   1. des Essens/dem Essen; 2. deiner Hilfe; 3. eines Weißweins; 4. des guten Essens; 5. des Verkehrs

✎ Drive It Home

A. Complete the sentences with the genitive case of the English in parentheses.

1. Das Ende _____ war traurig. (der Film)

2. Wir essen im Restaurant _____ . (mein Vater)

3. Die Stimme _____ war nicht laut genug. (die Kellnerin)

4. Alle Tische _____ waren voll. (das Restaurant)

5. Die Gläser _____ waren leer. (die Gäste)

B. Complete the sentences with the genitive preposition in parentheses.

1. _____ des Essens möchte ich nicht sprechen. (*during*)

2. Ich gehe _____ der hohen Preise gern in das Restaurant. (*despite*)

3. _____ der vielen Gäste war der Service gut. (*despite*)

4. Ich kann _____ meiner Erkältung nicht mitkommen. (*because of*)

5. _____ der Karte brachte der Kellner die Rechnung. (*instead of*)

ANSWER KEY

A. 1. des Films; 2. meines Vaters; 3. der Kellnerin; 4. des Restaurants; 5. der Gäste

B. 1. Während; 2. trotz; 3. Trotz; 4. wegen; 5. (An)statt

⊕ Culture Note

Even though Germans are known as a time-conscious people, when it comes to eating out, Germans like to take their time. In most restaurants in Germany, Austria, and Switzerland, it is customary to seat yourself, and, once you are seated, it may take the Kellner (*waiter*) or Kellnerin (*waitress*) several minutes to greet you and bring the menu. The idea is to allow the guests to settle in and chat for a few minutes before ordering. Once you have ordered, the food is usually served as it is ready rather than to all parties at the same time. After the main course, people tend to stay and chat, sometimes over dessert or coffee. It is not at all unusual to spend well over an hour for lunch. A Kellner or Kellnerin will not expect a large tip, as gratuity is automatically included in the price of the meal. While additional tipping is customary, you usually just add a Euro or two, rounding up to the next five- or ten-Euro amount. Guten Appetit! (*Enjoy your meal!*)

How Did You Do?

You should now be able to:

☐ Express possession with the genitive case
(Still unsure? Jump back to page 103.)

☐ Use prepositions with the genitive case
(Still unsure? Jump back to page 108.)

✎ Word Recall

Unscramble the words.

1. nhegRncu _____

2. lselbteen _____

3. alGs _____

4. egewn _____

5. sseen _____

6. ekucZr _____

7. lbeGa _____

8. timmSt os _____

9. rsegetn _____

10. zhrtUei _____

ANSWER KEY

1. Rechnung; 2. bestellen; 3. Glas; 4. wegen; 5. essen; 6. Zucker; 7. Gabel; 8. Stimmt so; 9. gestern; 10. Uhrzeit

Don't forget to practice and reinforce what you've learned by visiting **www.livinglanguage.com/ languagelab** for flashcards, games, and quizzes for Unit 2!

Unit 2 Essentials

Vocabulary Essentials

Test your knowledge of the key material in this unit by filling in the blanks in the following charts. Once you've completed these pages, you'll have tested your retention, and you'll have your own reference for the most essential vocabulary.

AT A RESTAURANT

	I'd like to reserve a table for two people.
	For what time?
	For 7:00 p.m.
	What's the name?
	(In the name of) Schneider.
	Could we have a table in the garden?
	Unfortunately, there is no more room in the garden.
	Could we have a menu, please?
	What can I get you?
	What do you recommend?
	I'll have …
	We are missing … at our table.
	Enjoy your meal!, Bon Appetit!
	Please bring me another glass of red wine.
	The check, please.
	One check? (lit., All together?)
	Is the tip included?
	Keep the change. (lit., That's correct.)

TIME EXPRESSIONS FOR THE PAST

	yesterday
	the day before yesterday
	last
	last week
	last month
	last year
	earlier
	an hour ago
	many years ago

Grammar Essentials
THE SIMPLE PAST OF SEIN, HABEN, AND WERDEN

HABEN *(TO HAVE)*			
ich hatte	*I had*	wir hatten	*we had*
du hattest	*you had*	ihr hattet	*you had*
er/sie/es hatte	*he/she/it had*	sie/Sie hatten	*they, you had*

SEIN *(TO BE)*			
ich war	*I was*	wir waren	*we were*
du warst	*you were*	ihr wart	*you were*
er/sie/es war	*he/she/it was*	sie/Sie waren	*they, you were*

WERDEN *(TO BECOME)*			
ich wurde	*I became*	wir wurden	*we became*
du wurdest	*you became*	ihr wurdet	*you became*
er/sie/es wurde	*he/she/it became*	sie/Sie wurden	*they, you became*

THE SIMPLE PAST OF REGULAR (WEAK) VERBS

verb stem + -t- + -e, -est, -e, -en, -et, -en

KOCHEN *(TO COOK)*		
ich	stem + t + e	kochte
du	stem + t + est	kochtest
er/sie/es	stem + t + e	kochte
wir	stem + t + en	kochten
ihr	stem + t + et	kochtet
sie/Sie	stem + t + en	kochten

THE SIMPLE PAST OF IRREGULAR (STRONG) VERBS

verb stem (+vowel change) + --, -st, --, -en, -t, -en

FAHREN *(TO DRIVE)*		
ich	stem-vowel change + -	fuhr
du	stem-vowel change + st	fuhrst
er/sie/es	stem-vowel change + -	fuhr
wir	stem-vowel change + en	fuhren
ihr	stem-vowel change + t	fuhrt
sie/Sie	stem-vowel change + en	fuhren

THE SIMPLE PAST OF MODAL VERBS

verb stem + -t- + -e, -est, -e, -en, -et, -en.

DÜRFEN *(TO BE ALLOWED TO)*	
ich	durfte

KÖNNEN *(TO BE ABLE TO)*	
ich	konnte

MÖCHTEN *(TO LIKE TO)*	
ich	mochte

MÜSSEN *(TO HAVE TO)*	
ich	musste

WOLLEN *(TO WANT TO)*	
ich	wollte

THE SIMPLE PAST OF MIXED VERBS

verb stem (+ vowel change) + -t- + -e, -est, -e, -en, -et, -en

BRINGEN *(TO BRING)*	
ich	brachte

DENKEN *(TO THINK)*	
ich	dachte

KENNEN *(TO KNOW)*	
ich	kannte

RENNEN *(TO RUN)*	
ich	rannte

WISSEN *(TO KNOW)*	
ich	wusste

THE GENITIVE CASE OF ARTICLES, NOUNS, AND ADJECTIVES

MASCULINE	FEMININE	NEUTER	PLURAL
des Vaters	der Mutter	des Kindes	der Väter, der Mütter, der Kinder
eines Vaters	einer Mutter	eines Kindes	-
meines Vaters	meiner Mutter	meines Kindes	meiner Väter, meiner Mütter, meiner Kinder
keines Vaters	keiner Mutter	keines Kindes	keiner Väter, keiner Mütter, keiner Kinder
des netten Vaters	der netten Mutter	des netten Kindes	der netten Väter, der netten Mütter, der netten Kinder

PREPOSITIONS WITH THE GENITIVE CASE

wegen	Wir sind wegen der Spezialitäten in diesem Restaurant.
because	We are in this restaurant for (lit., because of) its specialties.
während	Wir haben während des Essens telefoniert.
during	We made calls during dinner.
(an)statt	Sie hat das Wiener Schnitzel statt der Rindsrouladen gegessen.
instead of	She ate the Wiener Schnitzel instead of the Rindsrouladen.
trotz	Er hat die Ohrringe trotz des Preises gekauft.
despite	He bought the earrings despite their price.

Unit 2 Quiz

Let's put the most essential German words and grammar points you've learned so far to practice. It's important to be sure that you've mastered this material before you move on. Score yourself at the end of the review and see if you need to go back for more practice, or if you're ready to move on to Unit 3.

Complete the following story using the simple past of the verbs in parentheses, and/or the genitive case, if appropriate.

Mein Sohn und ich (1)_____ (fahren) gestern in die Stadt. Wir (2)_____ (wollen) einkaufen gehen. Es (3)_____ (werden) sehr spät. Mein Sohn (4)_____ (fragen): "Können wir ins Restaurant gehen?" Ich (5)_____ (denken): "Das ist eine gute Idee!" und (6)_____ (antworten): "Ja, sehr gerne." Wir (7)_____ (suchen) ein gutes Restaurant, und (8)_____ (finden) ein gutes, aber auch sehr teures Restaurant. Mein Sohn (9)_____ (sagen) ganz aufgeregt: "Das ist das Restaurant (10)_____ (ein Freund)." Wir (11)_____ (haben) sehr großen Hunger, und so (12)_____ (gehen) wir trotz (13)_____ (der Preis) in das Restaurant. Der Kellner (14)_____ (bringen) sofort die Speisekarte. Ich (15)_____ (bestellen) den Rostbraten, mein Sohn (16)_____ (nehmen) das Schnitzel. Das Essen (17)_____ (sein) ausgezeichnet. Nach dem Essen (18)_____ (geben) es noch Nachtisch. Das Essen (19)_____ (kosten) so viel, ich (20)_____ (müssen) mit Kreditkarte bezahlen. Trotzdem ein schöner Abend mit meinem Sohn!

How Did You Do?

Give yourself a point for every correct answer, then use the following key to tell whether you're ready to move on:

0–7 points: It's probably a good idea to go back through the lesson again. You may be moving too quickly, or there may be too much "down time" between your contact with German. Remember that it's better to spend 30 minutes with German three or four times a week than it is to spend two or three hours just once a week. Find a pace that's comfortable for you, and spread your contact hours out as much as you can.

8–12 points: You would benefit from a review before moving on. Go back and spend a little more time on the specific points that gave you trouble. Reread the Grammar Builder sections that were difficult, and do the Work Outs one more time. Don't forget about the online supplemental practice material, either. Go to **www.livinglanguage.com/languagelab** for games and quizzes that will reinforce the material from this unit.

13–17 points: Good job! There are just a few points that you could consider reviewing before moving on. If you haven't worked with the games and quizzes on **www.livinglanguage.com/languagelab**, please give them a try.

18–20 points: Great! You're ready to move on to the next unit.

points

ANSWER KEY
1. fuhren; 2. wollten; 3. wurde; 4. fragte; 5. dachte; 6. antwortete; 7. suchten; 8. fanden; 9. sagte; 10. eines Freundes; 11. hatten; 12. gingen; 13. des Preises; 14. brachte; 15. bestellte; 16. nahm; 17. war; 18. gab; 19. kostete; 20. musste

Unit 3:
Professional Lives

If you are on a business trip, words and expressions about work and the workplace are very important. Or, you may be studying at a German school and want to know how to talk about your academic subjects. By the end of this unit you'll be able to:

☐ Talk about your work

☐ Talk about school

☐ Use the passive voice

☐ Use impersonal expressions as alternatives to the passive voice

☐ Form compound nouns

☐ Discuss your job and/or your studies

☐ Use the imperative

☐ Use sentences with wenn (*if, when*)

☐ Use sentences with dass (*that*) and ob (*whether*)

Lesson 9: Words

By the end of this lesson you'll be able to:

☐ Talk about your work

☐ Talk about school

☐ Use the passive voice

Let's first look at the basic vocabulary around your professional life.

Word Builder 1

⊳ 9A Word Builder 1 (CD 8, Track 19)

der Beruf	*profession, job*
beruflich	*professionally*
der Angestellte	*employee*
der Arbeiter	*worker*
der Vorgesetzte	*superior*
die Beförderung	*promotion*
die Arbeitsstelle	*workplace, job*
die Stellenanzeige	*job announcement, help-wanted ad*
die Berufschancen	*professional outlook (chances)*
die Berufserfahrung	*professional experience*
die Karriere	*career*
die Arbeitszeit	*work hours, working hours*
die Überstunden	*overtime*
die Teilzeitbeschäftigung	*part-time employment*
die Vollzeitbeschäftigung	*full-time employment*
die Arbeitslosenrate	*unemployment rate*
das Gehalt	*salary*
die Gehaltserhöhung	*raise*
die Rente	*retirement*
einstellen	*to hire*
befördern	*to promote*

| entlassen | to let go, to fire |
| arbeitslos | unemployed |

✎ Word Practice 1

Which word fits best?

1. A person working for somebody else is _____.
a. die Rente
b. der Angestellte
c. das Gehalt

2. If you've already worked several years, you have _____.
a. Berufserfahrung
b. Teilzeitbeschäftigung
c. Rente

3. If you do not have a job you are

_____.

a. reich
b. befördert
c. arbeitslos

4. The money you get paid for your work is _____.
a. das Gehalt
b. die Beförderung
c. die Stellenanzeige

5. If you are looking for a job, you search through _____.
a. die Karriere
b. die Stellenanzeigen
c. die Überstunden

ANSWER KEY
1. b; 2. a; 3. c; 4. a; 5. b

Grammar Builder 1

▶ 9B Grammar Builder 1 (CD 8, Track 20)

THE PASSIVE VOICE 1

All of the German sentences you've heard or read so far have been in the active voice. This means that the subject of the sentence performs the action of the verb.

Der Chef befördert den Angestellten.
The boss promotes the employee.

In the passive voice, the subject does not perform the action; instead, it is the person or object acted on. It is *passive*. The verb comes in a special form called the *passive voice*.

Der Angestellte wird befördert.
The employee is being promoted.

In English, the passive voice uses a form of *be* and the past participle (*promoted, taken, seen*, etc.) of the main verb. The German passive is formed with the verb **werden** (*to become*) and the past participle of the main verb. Here are the present tense forms of **werden**.

ich	werde	wir	werden
du	wirst	ihr	werdet
er/sie/es	wird	sie/Sie	werden

In the passive voice, the person or thing performing the action (technically known as the agent) may or may not be mentioned. In English, the agent is introduced in a *by* phrase, and in German, in a **von** phrase.

Der Angestellte wird befördert. (*no agent*)
The employee is being promoted.

Der Angestellte wird <u>vom Chef</u> befördert. (*agent* = **der Chef**)
The employee is being promoted <u>by the boss</u>.

Take a look at some more examples of passive sentences.

Werden Sie befördert?
Will you be promoted?

Ich werde entlassen.
I'll be let go.

Viele Arbeiter werden von InterCorp neu eingestellt.
Many workers are being newly employed by InterCorp.

The passive voice is often used with modal verbs. In this case, the modal verb is the main verb; it's conjugated and takes the position of the main verb, just like in English. Both the passive verb and **werden** are in the infinitive at the end of the sentence.

Kann er entlassen werden?
Can he be fired?

Ich will besser bezahlt werden.
I want to be paid better.

✎ Work Out 1

Rewrite the sentences below in the passive voice.

1. **Die Firma stellt neue Arbeiter ein.** _____

   _____

2. **Die andere Firma entlässt viele Angestellte.** _____

   _____

3. **Ich will meinen neuen Assistenten besser bezahlen.** _____

   _____

4. **Wir reservieren einen Tisch für Sie.** _____

   _____

5. **Mein Mann bestellt den Wein.** _____

   _____

ANSWER KEY

1.Neue Arbeiter werden (von der Firma) eingestellt. 2.Viele Angestellte werden (von der anderen Firma) entlassen. 3.Mein neuer Assistent wird (von mir) besser bezahlt werden wollen. 4.Ein Tisch wird (von uns) für Sie reserviert. 5.Der Wein wird (von meinem Mann) bestellt.

Word Builder 2

▶ 9C Word Builder 2 (CD 8, Track 21)

die Schule	school
die Universität	university
die Ausbildung	professional training, apprenticeship
das Praktikum	internship
das Volontariat	internship (newspaper)
der Schüler	pupil

der Mitschüler	classmate
der Kommilitone/die Kommilitonin	fellow university student (male/female)
der Auszubildende	apprentice
der Azubi	apprentice
das Fach	subject
das Lieblingsfach	favorite subject
das Zeugnis	report card
die Beurteilung	evaluation
der Hauptschulabschluß	school-leaving exam (lower level)
die Realschulprüfung	middle school exam
das Abitur	high school exam
studieren	to study (at a university)

✎ Word Practice 2

Match the German in column A with the English in column B.

1. der Schüler	a. *high school exam*
2. das Abitur	b. *university*
3. die Universität	c. *pupil*
4. die Schule	d. *classmate*
5. studieren	e. *to study*
6. der Mitschüler	f. *internship*
7. die Ausbildung	g. *professional training*
8. das Praktikum	h. *school*

ANSWER KEY
1. c; 2. a; 3. b; 4. h; 5. e; 6. d; 7. g; 8. f

Grammar Builder 2

▶ 9D Grammar Builder 2 (CD 8, Track 22)

THE PASSIVE VOICE 2

The passive voice can be formed in all tenses. The verb **werden** changes to express different tenses, and the past participle of the main verb remains the same.

PRESENT TENSE

Ich werde befördert.
I am being promoted.

Die Angestellten werden entlassen.
The employees are being let go.

FUTURE TENSE

Even though it is possible to form the future tense in the passive voice (with an extra **werden**), the present tense is much more common.

Ich werde befördert (werden).
I will be promoted.

Die Angestellten werden entlassen (werden).
The employees will be let go.

SIMPLE PAST TENSE

Remember your simple past forms of **werden: wurde, wurdest, wurde, wurden, wurdet, wurden**.

Ich wurde befördert.
I was promoted.

Die Angestellten wurden entlassen.
The employees were let go.

PRESENT PERFECT

Werden forms the present perfect with the conjugated form of **sein** plus the past participle **worden**. Note that in the present perfect, the conjugated form of **sein** takes the second position in the sentence, and the past participle of the main verb and the past participle of **werden** —**worden**—follow at the very end of the sentence.

Ich bin befördert worden.
I have been promoted.

Die Angestellten sind entlassen worden.
The employees have been let go.

Ⓘ

✎ Work Out 2

Rewrite each sentence below in the passive voice, keeping the tense of the active sentence.

1. **Die Firma hat neue Arbeiter eingestellt.** _____

_____

2. **Die andere Firma hat viele Angestellte entlassen.** _____

_____

3. Ich wollte meinen neuen Assistenten besser bezahlen. _____

_____

4. Wir werden einen Tisch für Sie reservieren. _____

_____

5. Mein Mann hat den Wein bestellt. _____

_____

ANSWER KEY

1. Neue Arbeiter sind (von der Firma) eingestellt worden. 2. Viele Angestellte sind (von der anderen Firma) entlassen worden. 3. Mein neuer Assistant ist (von mir) besser bezahlt werden wollen. 4. Ein Tisch wird (von uns) für Sie reserviert (werden). 5. Der Wein ist (von meinem Mann) bestellt worden.

🖊 Drive It Home

Rewrite these sentences in the passive voice, first in the present tense, then the future, and then the simple past tense.

1. Ich bin entlassen worden.

a. Present tense: _____

b. Future tense: _____

c. Simple past: _____

2. Die Zeugnisse sind geschrieben worden.

a. Present tense: _____

b. Future tense: _____

c. Simple past: _____

3. **Du bist befördert worden.**

   a. Present tense: _____

   b. Future tense: _____

   c. Simple past: _____

4. **Sie sind angerufen worden.**

   a. Present tense: _____

   b. Future tense: _____

   c. Simple past: _____

5. **Die Rechnung ist schon bezahlt worden.**

   a. Present tense: _____

   b. Future tense: _____

   c. Simple past: _____

ANSWER KEY

1. a. **Ich werde entlassen.** b. **Ich werde entlassen werden.** c. **Ich wurde entlassen.**
2. a. **Die Zeugnisse werden geschrieben.** b. **Die Zeugnisse werden geschrieben werden.**
   c. **Die Zeugnisse wurden geschrieben.**
3. a. **Du wirst befördert.** b. **Du wirst befördert werden.** c. **Du wurdest befördert.**
4. a. **Sie werden angerufen.** b. **Sie werden angerufen werden.** c. **Sie wurden angerufen.**
5. a. **Die Rechnung wird bezahlt.** b. **Die Rechnung wird bezahlt werden.** c. **Die Rechnung wurde bezahlt.**

How Did You Do?

Let's make sure you know how to:

☐ Talk about your work
   (Still unsure? Jump back to page 121.)

☐ Talk about school
   (Still unsure? Jump back to page 125.)

☐ Use the passive voice

(Still unsure? Jump back to page 123 and page 127.)

✎ Word Recall

Translate each of the following into German.

1. *unemployed* _____

2. *profession, job* _____

3. *internship* _____

4. *report card* _____

5. *full-time employment* _____

6. *high school exam* _____

7. *employee* _____

8. *to promote* _____

9. *worker* _____

10. *promotion* _____

11. *job announcement, help-wanted ad* _____

12. *part-time employment* _____

13. *professional training, apprenticeship* _____

14. *raise* _____

15. *to let go, to fire* _____

16. *subject* _____

17. *retirement* _____

18. *university* _____

19. *to hire* _____

20. *salary* _____

ANSWER KEY

1. arbeitslos; 2. der Beruf; 3. das Praktikum; 4. das Zeugnis; 5. die Vollzeitbeschäftigung; 6. das Abitur; 7. der Angestellte; 8. befördern; 9. der Arbeiter; 10. die Beförderung; 11. die Stellenanzeige; 12. die Teilzeitbeschäftigung; 13. die Ausbildung; 14. die Gehaltserhöhung; 15. entlassen; 16. das Fach; 17. die Rente; 18. die Universität; 19. einstellen; 20. das Gehalt

Lesson 10: Phrases

By the end of this lesson you should be able to:

☐ Use impersonal expressions as alternatives to the passive voice

☐ Form compound nouns

Phrase Builder 1

▶ 10A Phrase Builder 1 (CD 8, Track 23)

die gleitende Arbeitszeit	*flexible working hours*
von ... bis arbeiten	*to work from ... to*
laut Statistik	*according to/based on statistics*
Überstunden machen	*to work overtime*
Karriere machen	*to advance (to make a career)*
sich Urlaub nehmen	*to take a vacation/time off*
die (Berufs)Erfahrung sammeln	*to collect (professional) experience*
freiberuflich arbeiten	*to freelance*
freiberuflich tätig sein	*to freelance*

selbstständig sein	to be self-employed
arbeitslos sein	to be unemployed
in Rente gehen	to retire
in Pension gehen	to retire

✎ Phrase Practice 1

Translate the following phrases from English to German or vice versa.

1. *to be self-employed* _____

2. *to work from ... to* _____

3. *to work overtime* _____

4. freiberuflich tätig sein _____

5. Karriere machen _____

6. in Pension gehen _____

ANSWER KEY

1. **selbständig sein;** 2. **von ... bis arbeiten;** 3. **Überstunden machen;** 4. *to freelance;* 5. *to advance;* 6. *to retire*

Grammar Builder 1

▶ 10B Grammar Builder 1 (CD 8, Track 24)

ALTERNATIVES TO THE PASSIVE VOICE

Let's take a look at a few constructions that can be used instead of the passive voice, which you've just learned.

MAN + ACTIVE VERB

The construction using **man** is the most common way to express the passive, particularly if the agent has not been named in the passive sentence. It's very much like impersonal *they* in English.

Der Arbeiter wurde entlassen.	**Man hat den Arbeiter entlassen.**
The worker was let go.	*They let the worker go.*
Die Schüler wurden gelobt.	**Man hat die Schüler gelobt.**
The students were praised.	*They praised the students.*

SEIN + ZU + INFINITIVE

Passive constructions with **können** and **müssen** can be replaced with **sein** + **zu** + infinitive. You will come across both versions in many newspaper articles.

Das kann so nicht gesagt werden.	**Das ist so nicht zu sagen.**
That cannot be said like that.	*That can't be said like that. (lit., That is not to be said like that.)*
So viele Entlassungen können nicht aufrecht erhalten werden.	**So viele Entlassungen sind nicht aufrecht zu erhalten.**
So many firings cannot continue/be kept up.	*This many firings are not to continue. / So many firings are not to continue.*

SICH LASSEN + INFINITIVE

This can replace **können** and a passive infinitive. You will hear this often if the speaker does not want to name a specific agent.

Das kann besser gemacht werden.	**Das läßt sich besser machen.**
That can be done better.	*That can be done better.*
Diese Meinung kann nicht bewiesen werden.	**Diese Meinung lässt sich nicht beweisen.**
This opinion cannot be backed up.	*This opinion cannot be backed up.*

✎ Work Out 1

Rewrite the following story using the alternatives to the passive discussed above. Watch your tenses.

Gestern haben Schneiders angerufen. Herr Schneider ist befördert worden (man). Das muss gross gefeiert werden (sein + zu + *infinitive*). Es wurde mir gesagt, dass ich Wein mitbringen soll (man). Ich habe eine Flasche Weißwein mitgebracht. Das Essen wurde um 20 Uhr serviert (man). Es schmeckte hervorragend.

_____

_____

_____

_____

_____

_____

ANSWER KEY

Gestern haben Schneiders angerufen. Man hat Herrn Schneider befördert. Das ist groß zu feiern. Man hat mir gesagt, dass ich Wein mitbringen soll. Ich habe eine Flasche Weißwein mitgebracht. Man hat das Essen um 20 Uhr serviert. Es schmeckte hervorragend.

Phrase Builder 2

▶ 10C Phrase Builder 2 (CD 8, Track 25)

ein guter Schüler sein	*to be a good (school) student*
ein guter Student sein	*to be a good (college) student*
ein schlechter Schüler sein	*to be a bad (school) student*
ein schlechter Student sein	*to be a bad (college) student*

die Hausaufgaben machen	to do homework
eine Pause machen	to take a break
eine Ausbildung machen	to apprentice (to do an apprenticeship)
ein Volontariat machen	to intern at a newspaper
die Realschulprüfung machen	to take the middle school exam
das Abitur machen	to take the high school exam
einen Magister machen	to study for a Master's degree
einen Magister haben	to have a Master's degree
einen Doktor machen	to study for a Ph.D.
einen Doktor haben	to have a Ph.D.
viel zu tun haben	to have a lot to do
viel zu lernen haben	to have a lot to learn
eine (Ausbildungs)Stelle suchen	to look for a job (apprenticeship)
sich auf eine Stelle bewerben	to apply for a job/position
den Lebenslauf schreiben	to prepare one's résumé
eine Familie gründen	to start a family

✎ Phrase Practice 2

Supply the translations below.

viel zu lernen haben	1.
den Magister machen	2.
3.	to start a family
4.	to do homework
eine Pause machen	5.
6.	to prepare one's résumé

ANSWER KEY
1. *to have a lot to learn*; 2. *to study for a master's degree*; 3. eine Familie gründen; 4. Hausaufgaben machen; 5. *to take a break*; 6. den Lebenslauf schreiben

Grammar Builder 2
▶ 10D Grammar Builder 2 (CD 8, Track 26)

COMPOUND NOUNS

The German language likes putting long nouns together to make even longer ones. If a new noun is made of one or more nouns, it is called a compound noun— for example, **die Realschule** with **die Prüfung** makes **die Realschulprüfung** (*middle school exam,* from *middle school + exam*).

Note that English has similar compounds, for example *middle school exam,* but in German, compounds are written together as one word. The gender of the last noun in the string determines the gender of the whole compound.

das Leben + <u>der</u> **Lauf** = <u>der</u> **Lebenslauf** (*résumé, curriculum vitae*)

das Haus + <u>die</u> **Aufgabe** = <u>die</u> **Hausaufgabe** (*homework*)

die Arbeitslosen + <u>die</u> **Rate** = <u>die</u> **Arbeitslosenrate** (*unemployment rate*)

Many compounds have a kind of possessive "glue" in them, either the **-s-** of the genitive or the **-n-** of **n**-nouns.

das Gehalt + **die Erhöhung** = **die Gehalt<u>s</u>erhöhung** (*raise*)

die Arbeit + **die Stelle** = **die Arbeit<u>s</u>stelle** (*workplace*)

die Arbeit + **los** + **die Rate** = **die Arbeit<u>s</u>los<u>en</u>rate** (*unemployment rate*)

German also creates compounds from noun + adjective or adjective + adjective pairs.

der Zucker + süß = zuckersüß (*sugary sweet*)

süß + sauer = süßsauer (*sweet-and-sour*)

All the letters in the members of a compound remain, even if they are identical, in order to keep the old word stem intact. So you'll sometimes see three consonants in a row, for example.

das Schiff + die Fahrt = die Schifffahrt (*cruise*)

schnell + lebig = schnelllebig (*fast-paced*)

der Schluss + der Satz = der Schlusssatz (*final sentence*)

An alternative is to use a hyphen: **der Schluss-Satz**. If the hyphenated compound consists of two nouns, both are capitalized.

(II)

✎ Work Out 2

A. Create the compound.

1. **die Arbeit + der Kollege =** _____

2. **die Pause + das Brot =** _____

3. **die Zeitung + der Artikel =** _____

Lesson 11: Sentences

By the end of this lesson you should be able to:

☐ Discuss your job and/or your studies

☐ Use the imperative

Sentence Builder 1

▶ 11A Sentence Builder 1 (CD 8, Track 27)

Ich suche eine neue Stelle.	*I am looking for a new job.*
Ich möchte mich beruflich verbessern.	*I want to get ahead in my profession.*
Wollen Sie Karriere machen oder eine Familie gründen?	*Do you want to have a career or start a family?*
Kann man denn nicht beides machen?	*Can't one/you do both?*
Heutzutage muss man viele Überstunden machen.	*These days, you have to work overtime a lot.*
Wo haben Sie Ihre Berufserfahrung gesammelt?	*Where have you gained your professional experience?*
Ich war freiberuflich tätig.	*I freelanced.*
Bitte bringen Sie Ihren Lebenslauf mit.	*Please bring your résumé along.*

⏸

✎ Sentence Practice 1

Translate from English to German.

1. *He freelanced.* _____

   _____

2. *Now he is looking for a new job.* _____

   _____

3. *I'd rather have a career than start a family.* _____

   _____

4. *But you can do both.* _____

   _____

5. *I cannot work overtime today.* _____

   _____

ANSWER KEY
1. Er war freiberuflich tätig. 2. Jetzt sucht er eine neue Stelle. 3. Ich will lieber Karriere machen als eine Familie gründen. 4. Aber man kann doch beides machen. 5. Ich kann heute keine Überstunden machen.

Grammar Builder 1

▶ 11B Grammar Builder 1 (CD 8, Track 28)

THE IMPERATIVE 1

The imperative forms are used to give commands, instructions, suggestions, and requests. English has only one imperative, because there is only one word for *you*.

But German has three words for *you*—Sie, du, and ihr—and therefore has three imperative forms.

du-*form:*	Unterbrich mich nicht, Martin!
	Don't interrupt me, Martin!
Sie-*form:*	Unterbrechen Sie mich nicht, mein Herr!
	Don't interrupt me, sir!
ihr-*form:*	Unterbrecht mich nicht, Kinder!
	Don't interrupt me, children!

If you want to soften the request, add bitte.

Bitte unterbrechen Sie mich nicht, mein Herr!
Please don't interrupt me, sir!

Let's first look at the singular informal du and formal Sie imperative forms.

DU-FORM

The du-form is basically the stem of the verb, which you get by taking off the infinitive ending -en: sagen minus -en becomes sag. Do not use the pronoun du.

Schreib deinen Lebenslauf.
Write your résumé.

Irregular (strong) verbs, such as unterbrechen (*to interrupt*) and bewerben (*to apply*), which take vowel changes in the second and third person singular in the present tense, take the same vowel change in the imperative.

Du unterbrichst mich.
You are interrupting me.

Unterbrich mich nicht, Martin!
Don't interrupt me, Martin!

Du bewirbst dich auf diese Stelle.
You are applying for this job.

Bewirb dich auf diese Stelle.
Apply for this job.

However, verbs with vowel changes from a to ä in the second and third person singular present, such as laufen (*to run*) and fahren (*to drive*), do not add the umlaut in the imperative.

Du fährst schnell.
You are driving fast.

Fahr nicht so schnell!
Don't drive so fast!

Verbs with a stem ending in -t, -d, or -g, such as wart(en) or antwort(en), always add an -e in the imperative.

Warte auf mich!
Wait for me!

Antworte mir!
Answer me!

SIE-FORM

The imperative form is identical to the Sie-form of the present tense. You have to use the personal pronoun Sie, but note that subject (Sie) and verb (e.g., unterbrechen) trade places.

Unterbrechen Sie mich nicht, mein Herr!
Don't interrupt me, sir!

Bewerben Sie sich doch!
Apply! (Why don't you apply?)

Note that the verb sein (*to be*) is the only irregular imperative form.

Bitte seien Sie pünktlich, Herr Müller.
Please be punctual, Mr. Müller.

Bitte sei leise, Klaus!
Please be quiet, Klaus!

✎ Work Out 1

Rewrite the sentences in the imperative.

1. **Du gehst jetzt in die Schule.** _____

_____

2. **Sie bringen den Lebenslauf mit.** _____

_____

3. Sie kommen pünktlich. _____

_____

4. Du machst Überstunden. _____

_____

5. Du suchst eine Stelle. _____

_____

ANSWER KEY

1. Geh jetzt in die Schule! 2. Bringen Sie den Lebenslauf mit! 3. Kommen Sie pünktlich! 4. Mach Überstunden! 5. Such eine Stelle!

Sentence Builder 2

▷ 11C Sentence Builder 2 (CD 8, Track 29)

Meine Tochter geht auf das Gymnasium.	*My daughter goes to high school.*
Ohne Abitur findet man keine Stelle.	*Without the high school exit exam, one/you won't find a job.*
Wo sind Sie zur Schule gegangen?	*Where did you go to school?*
Eine gute Ausbildung ist wichtig.	*A good education is important.*
Nach dem Abitur mache ich erst mal Pause.	*After my high school exit exam, I'll first take a break.*
Ich möchte einen Doktor in Psychologie machen.	*I want to get a Ph.D. in psychology.*
Ich muss meinen Lebenslauf schreiben.	*I have to prepare my résumé.*
Ich möchte mich als Auszubildender bei Ihrer Firma bewerben.	*I want to apply for an apprenticeship with your company.*

⏸

✎ Sentence Practice 2

Complete the sentences below.

1. Eine gute _____ ist wichtig.

2. Wo geht Ihre Tochter _____ ?

3. Meine Tochter geht nicht auf das _____ .

4. Aber ohne Abitur findet man keine _____ .

5. Sie muss ihren Lebenslauf _____ .

6. Sie möchte sich als Auszubildender bei Ihrer Firma _____ .

ANSWER KEY
1. Ausbildung; 2. zur Schule; 3. Gymnasium; 4. Stelle; 5. schreiben; 6. bewerben

Grammar Builder 2

▶ 11D Grammar Builder 2 (CD 8, Track 30)

THE IMPERATIVE 2

Let's take a look at the plural command forms.

IHR-FORM

For commands or suggestions to a group of people you'd address with ihr, simply use
the regular present tense form for the second person plural. Do not use the pronoun.

Unterbrecht mich nicht, Kinder!
Don't interrupt me, children!

Macht die Hausaufgaben!
Do your homework!

If you want to make suggestions and include yourself, use the German verb lassen (*to let*) similarly to the way you would use the English verb *let's* in comparable sentences.

Lass uns eine neue Stelle suchen.
Let's look for a new job.

You can also simply use the **wir**-form of the verb and switch subject and verb.

Suchen wir eine neue Stelle.
Let's look for a new job.

The verb **sein** (*to be*) is irregular in the plural imperative as well.

Seid nicht so laut, Kinder!
Don't be so loud, children!

(II)

✎ Work Out 2

Rewrite these imperatives in the plural.

1. **Schreib deinen Lebenslauf!** _____

   _____

2. **Sei nicht böse!** _____

   _____

3. **Laß uns Biologie studieren!** _____

   _____

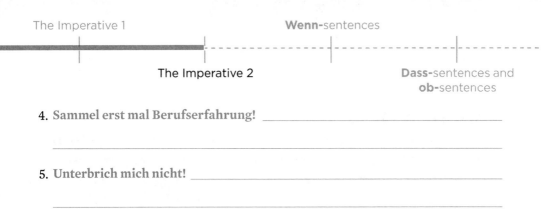
4. **Sammel erst mal Berufserfahrung!** _____

_____

5. **Unterbrich mich nicht!** _____

_____

ANSWER KEY

1. Schreibt euren Lebenslauf! 2. Seid nicht böse! 3. Laßt uns Biologie studieren! 4. Sammelt erst mal Berufserfahrung! 5. Unterbrecht mich nicht!

✎ Drive It Home

Complete the sentences with the imperative of the verb in parentheses. Use the form indicated by the pronoun.

1. _____ still! (sein, du)

2. _____ bitte mit! (kommen, du)

3. _____ auf mich! (warten, du)

4. _____ Sie bitte Ihren Lebenslauf! (schreiben, Sie)

5. _____Sie bitte pünktlich. (sein, Sie)

6. _____ Sie mich bitte zurück. (rufen, Sie)

7. _____ mich mitspielen. (lassen, ihr)

8. _____ keine Überstunden. (machen, ihr)

9. _____ nicht so viel Geld aus. (geben, ihr)

ANSWER KEY

1. Sei; 2. Komm; 3. Warte; 4. Schreiben; 5. Seien; 6. Rufen; 7. Lasst; 8. Macht; 9. Gebt

⊕ Culture Note

A typical school career starts with **die Grundschule** (*elementary school, first grade through fourth grade*) and goes to either **die Hauptschule** (*junior high school, fifth grade through ninth grade*), **die Realschule** (*middle school, fifth grade through tenth grade*), or the **Gymnasium** (*high school, fifth grade through twelfth grade*). Students graduating from the **Hauptschule** usually go on to **die Berufsschule** (*vocational school*) to learn a trade, those graduating from the **Realschule** often choose administrative careers, and only those graduating with the **Abitur** from the **Gymnasium** can go on to the **Universität**. This threefold school system has been criticized for locking children into a certain career based on their academic performance at too early an age—in grade school. Therefore, **Gesamtschulen** (*comprehensive schools*), which keep all students together until the tenth grade and thus eliminate the **Hauptschule** altogether, have become more and more popular. These days, job opportunities for students without the **Abitur** are becoming rather scarce.

How Did You Do?

Before you move on, make sure you are able to:

☐ Discuss your job and/or your studies
   (Still unsure? Jump back to page 141.)

☐ Use the imperative
   (Still unsure? Jump back to page 142 and page 147.)

✎ Word Recall

Unscramble the words.

1. tleSel _____

2. labeLufens _____

3. nebreweb _____

4. levi uz utn ahenb _____

5. ückzruesß _____

6. runfufreBserahg _____

7. enteR _____

8. rufiefrlbiech _____

9. rKiraere _____

ANSWER KEY
1. Stelle; 2. Lebenslauf; 3. bewerben; 4. viel zu tun haben; 5. zuckersüß; 6. Berufserfahrung;
7. Rente; 8. freiberuflich; 9. Karriere

Lesson 12: Conversations

By the end of this lesson you'll know how to:

☐ Use sentences with wenn (*if, when*)

☐ Use sentences with dass (*that*) and ob (*whether*)

Conversation 1

▶ 12A Conversation 1 (CD 9, Track 1 - German; Track 2; German and English)

Martin and Maria Huber are sitting at the breakfast table, reading the newspaper.

Maria: Hör mal zu: «Schon wieder sind Hunderte von Arbeitnehmern entlassen worden. Die Arbeitslosenrate ist auf fast zehn Prozent gestiegen.»

Martin: Ja, heutzutage sind die Berufsaussichten schlecht. Man kann nicht mehr so einfach Karriere machen. Wenn man kein Abitur hat, bekommt man keine Ausbildungsstelle. Ohne gute Ausbildung wird man nicht eingestellt. Und wenn man nicht ständig Überstunden macht, wird man nicht befördert. Heute heißt es entweder Familie gründen oder Karriere machen.

Maria: Na, ich weiß nicht. War das nicht schon immer so?

Martin: Aber nein. Ich habe eine Familie und eine erfolgreiche Karriere.

Maria: Ja, das stimmt. Aber sag mal ganz ehrlich, hast du nicht mehr Zeit im Büro als mit deiner Familie verbracht?

Martin: Äh …

Maria: Man muss einen Partner haben, wenn man Karriere erfolgreich mit einem Familienleben vereinbaren will.

Martin: Aber du hast doch auch eine Karriere.

Maria: Ja, aber um die Kinder muss ich mich kümmern.

Martin: Aber Maria, das lässt sich so nicht sagen.

Maria: Ach nein? Wann hast du dir das letzte Mal Urlaub genommen, wenn die Kinder krank waren?

Martin: Ich … ah … hmmm …

Maria: Na bitte.

Maria: Listen to this: "Once again, hundreds of employees have been laid off. The unemployment rate has risen to almost ten percent."

Martin: Yes, these days job opportunities are scarce. It is not that easy to have a career. If you don't have the Abitur, you won't get an apprenticeship. Without a good education, you won't be employed. And if you don't work overtime constantly, you will not get promoted. Today it is either family or career.

Maria: Well, I don't know. Hasn't it always been like that?

Martin: Well, no. I have a family and a successful career.

Maria: Yes, that's true. But be honest, didn't you spend more time in the office than with your family?

Martin:	Uh …
Maria:	One has to have a partner to combine a career with family life successfully.
Martin:	But you have a career, too.
Maria:	Yes, but I am the one who takes care of the children.
Martin:	But Maria, you can't say that!
Maria:	Oh no? When was the last time you took time off when the kids were sick?
Martin:	I … uh … hmmm …
Maria:	See!

Take It Further

Ach is a versatile interjection, similar to the English *oh*. The English *well* can be translated into the German **Na**. **Na also!** is equivalent to the English *See!* or *There you have it!*

✎ Conversation Practice 1

Fill in the blanks in the following sentences with the missing words. If you're unsure of the answer, listen to the conversation on your audio one more time.

1. Die _____ ist auf fast zehn Prozent

   gestiegen.

2. Man kann nicht mehr _____ Karriere machen.

3. Ohne gute _____ wird man nicht eingestellt.

4. Heute heißt es _____ Familie gründen _____

   Karriere machen.

5. _____ , ich weiß nicht.

6. War das nicht _____ so?

7. Man muss einen Partner haben, _____ man Karriere

   erfolgreich mit einem Familienleben vereinbaren will.

8. Na _____ .

ANSWER KEY
1. Arbeitslosenrate; 2. so einfach; 3. Ausbildung; 4. entweder/oder; 5. Na; 6. schon immer; 7. wenn;
8. bitte

Grammar Builder 1
▶ 12B Grammar Builder 1 (CD 9, Track 3)

WENN-SENTENCES

In German, wenn-sentences introduce a condition on which the main clause
depends. In English, these sentences can be expressed with either *if*- or *when*-clauses.

Wenn die Kinder krank sind, muss ich Urlaub nehmen.
When/If the kids are sick, I have to take time off.

If the wenn-sentence is mentioned first, subject and verb change places in the
main clause. Compare the following sentences.

<u>Man muss</u> einen Partner haben, wenn man erfolgreich sein will.
You have to have a partner when/if you want to be successful.

Wenn man erfolgreich sein will, <u>muss man</u> **einen Partner haben.**

If/When you want to be successful, you have to have a partner.

✎ Work Out 1

Connect the following sentences with wenn.

1. **Die Kinder sind krank. Ich muss Urlaub nehmen.** _____

    _____

2. **Man braucht eine gute Ausbildung. Man will eine gute Stelle.** _____

    _____

3. **Du musst lernen. Du willst ein gutes Zeugnis.** _____

    _____

4. **Sie wollen befördert werden. Sie müssen Überstunden machen.** _____

    _____

5. **Du brauchst meine Hilfe. Du willst erfolgreich sein.** _____

    _____

ANSWER KEY

1. Wenn die Kinder krank sind, muss ich Urlaub nehmen. 2. Man braucht eine gute Ausbildung, wenn man eine gute Stelle will. 3. Du musst lernen, wenn du ein gutes Zeugnis willst. 4. Wenn Sie befördert werden wollen, müssen Sie Überstunden machen. 5. Du brauchst meine Hilfe, wenn du erfolgreich sein willst.

🔊 Conversation 2

▶ 12C Conversation 2 (CD 9, Track 4 - German; Track 5; German and English)

Susi is applying for a job as an editor with a newspaper. She has an interview with Lars Hochut.

Lars Hochut:	**Ihr Lebenslauf ist sehr beeindruckend.**
Susi:	**Danke.**
Lars Hochut:	**Warum wollen Sie denn bei uns arbeiten?**
Susi:	**Ich glaube, dass meine Ausbildung mich gut auf diese Stelle vorbereitet hat.**
Lars Hochut:	**Wo haben Sie denn Ihre Berufserfahrung gesammelt?**
Susi:	**Nach meinem Studium habe ich bei der Hohenloher Tageszeitung ein Volontariat gemacht. Und dann bin ich zur Assistentin des Herausgebers befördert worden.**
Lars Hochut:	**Die Stelle einer Redakteurin ist viel Arbeit. Sie wissen, dass Sie manchmal Überstunden machen müssen.**
Susi:	**Ja.**
Lars Hochut:	**Aber wir haben gleitende Arbeitszeit. Wenn Sie abends spät arbeiten, können Sie am nächsten Tag später ins Büro kommen.**
Susi:	**Die Stelle interessiert mich sehr. Ich möchte mich beruflich verbessern.**
Lars Hochut:	**Gut. Wir melden uns.**

Lars Hochut:	*Your résumé is very impressive.*
Susi:	*Thank you.*
Lars Hochut:	*Why do you want to work for us?*
Susi:	*I think my education has prepared me well for this position.*
Lars Hochut:	*Where did you get your job experience?*
Susi:	*After my studies I did an internship with the Hohenloher newspaper. And then I was promoted to assistant to the publisher.*

Lars Hochut: *The position of editor is a lot of work. You know that you have to*
                work overtime sometimes.

Susi: *Yes.*

Lars Hochut: *But we have flexible working hours. If you work late at night, you*
                can come in later the next day.

Susi: *I am very interested in this position. I want to get ahead in my*
                profession.

Lars Hochut: *Good. We will contact you.*

Ⅱ

Culture Note

Almost every larger company in Germany offers gleitende Arbeitszeit. This
means that as long as the employees are at their workplace during the so-called
Kernzeit (*core/base hours*), usually between 9:00 *a.m.* and 2:00 *p.m.*, they can
choose whether they'd like to work early or late in the day.

Conversation Practice 2

Fill in the blanks in the following dialogue with the missing words. If you're
unsure of the answer, listen to the conversation on your audio one more time.

1. **Ihr Lebenslauf ist sehr** _____ .

2. _____ .

3. **Wo haben Sie denn Ihre** _____**gesammelt?**

4. _____ **habe ich bei der Hohenloher**

   Tageszeitung ein Volontariat gemacht.

5. **Sie wissen,** _____ **Sie manchmal Überstunden machen müssen.**

6. **Aber wir haben** _____ **Arbeitszeit.**

7. _____ , können Sie am nächsten

Tag später ins Büro kommen.

ANSWER KEY
1. beeindruckend; 2. Danke; 3. Berufserfahrung 4. Nach meinem Studium; 5. dass; 6. gleitende;
7. Wenn Sie abends spät arbeiten

Grammar Builder 2
▶ 12D Grammar Builder 2 (CD 9, Track 6)

DASS-SENTENCES AND OB-SENTENCES

Dass introduces a clause that is dependent on a main clause and cannot stand
alone. It is equivalent to the English *that*. Unlike in English, it is not possible to
drop dass. In written German, a comma is used before the dass clause.

Ich weiss, dass ich viel arbeiten muss.
I know (that) I have to work a lot.

Ich glaube, dass ich die richtige Ausbildung habe.
I believe I have the right education.

Ob-sentences also introduce a dependent clause; ob is equivalent to the English *if*
or *whether*.

Ich weiß nicht, ob ich die richtige Ausbildung habe.
I don't know whether I have the right education.

Ich bin nicht sicher, ob ich Karriere machen oder eine Familie gründen will.
I'm not sure whether I want to have a career or start a family.

Note that the verb in the dass- and ob-clause always takes the final position in the
sentence.

Ⅱ

✎ Work Out 2

Put the two sentences together with **dass** or **ob**.

1. **Ich habe eine gute Ausbildung. Ich hoffe,** _____

   _____ .

2. **Die Stelle ist frei. Ich weiß nicht,** _____

   _____ .

3. **Ich bewerbe mich. Du weißt,** _____

   _____ .

4. **Ich bin befördert worden. Haben Sie gehört,** _____

   _____ ?

5. **Er arbeitet hier. Ich bin nicht sicher,** _____

   _____ .

ANSWER KEY
1. **Ich hoffe, dass ich eine gute Ausbildung habe.** 2. **Ich weiß nicht, ob die Stelle frei ist.** 3. **Du weißt, dass ich mich bewerbe.** 4. **Haben Sie gehört, dass ich befördert worden bin?** 5. **Ich bin nicht sicher, ob er hier arbeitet.**

✎ Drive It Home

Fill in the blanks with **wenn**, **dass**, or **ob**, as indicated in the parentheses. Then try to translate each sentence.

1. _____ **man eine gute Stelle will, muss man eine gute Ausbildung haben.**

   (wenn) _____

2. **Man muss Überstunden machen, _____ man befördert werden will.**

   (wenn) _____

3. **_____ ich dich zurückrufen soll, musst du mir deine Nummer geben.**

   (wenn) _____

4. **Ich kümmere mich darum, _____ Sie keine Zeit haben. (wenn)**

   _____

5. **Wissen Sie, _____ es schon 17 Uhr ist? (dass)**

   _____

6. **Ich glaube, _____ er erst später ins Büro kommt. (dass)**

   _____

7. **Wollen Sie, _____ ich Überstunden mache? (dass)**

   _____

8. **Wissen Sie, _____ Sie befördert werden? (ob)**

   _____

9. **Ich frage mich, _____ die Arbeitslosenzahlen steigen werden. (ob)**

   _____

10. **Ich weiß nicht, _____ ich heute Abend Zeit habe. (ob)**

    _____

ANSWER KEY

1. If you want a good job, you've got to get a good apprenticeship/training. 2. You've got to put in overtime if you want to be promoted. 3. If I'm supposed to call you back, you've got to give me your telephone number. 4. I'll take care of it, if you have no time. 5. Do you know that it's already 5:00 p.m.? 6. I believe he only comes to the office later. 7. Do you want me to put in overtime? 8. Do you know whether you'll be promoted? 9. I wonder whether the unemployment rate will increase. 10. I don't know whether I'll have time this evening.

How Did You Do?

Before you move on to the next unit, make sure you know how to:

☐ Use sentences with **wenn** (*if, when*)
(Still unsure? Jump back to page 154.)

☐ Use sentences with **dass** (*that*) and **ob** (*whether*)
(Still unsure? Jump back to page 158.)

✎ Word Recall

Fill in the blanks with the missing translations.

sich bewerben	1.
die Ausbildung	2.
3.	*subject*
4.	*to fire, to let go*
die Gehaltserhöhung	5.
6.	*to study*
in Pension gehen	7.
freiberuflich arbeiten	8.
9.	*employee*
10.	*to retire*

ANSWER KEY

1. *to apply;* 2. *professional training;* 3. **das Fach;** 4. **entlassen;** 5. *raise;* 6. **studieren;** 7. *to retire;* 8. *to freelance;* 9. **der Angestellte;** 10. **in Pension/Rente gehen**

Don't forget to practice and reinforce what you've learned by visiting **www.livinglanguage.com/ languagelab** for flashcards, games, and quizzes for Unit 3!

Unit 3 Essentials

Vocabulary Essentials

Test your knowledge of the key material in this unit by filling in the blanks in the following charts. Once you've completed these pages, you'll have tested your retention, and you'll have your own reference for the most essential vocabulary.

	I am looking for a new job/position.
	I want to get ahead in my profession. (lit., I want to better myself professionally.)
	I want to apply with your company.
	Did you bring your résumé?
	A good education is important.
	I have a Ph.D.
	Where did you go to school?
	Where have you collected/gotten your professional experience?
	I freelanced.
	I have been employed at Bosch for a long time.
	I was promoted.
	I was let go.

Grammar Essentials

THE PASSIVE VOICE

werden + past participle of the main verb

PRESENT TENSE	FUTURE TENSE	PAST TENSE	PRESENT PERFECT
Ich werde befördert. *I am being promoted.*	Ich werde befördert (werden). *I will be promoted.*	Ich wurde befördert. *I was promoted.*	Ich bin befördert worden. *I have been promoted.*

ALTERNATIVES TO THE PASSIVE

MAN + ACTIVE VERB	
Der Arbeiter wurde entlassen.	Man hat den Arbeiter entlassen.
The worker was let go.	*One/They let the worker go.*

SEIN + ZU + INFINITIVE	
Das kann so nicht gesagt werden.	Das ist so nicht zu sagen.
That cannot be said like that.	*That can't be said like that.*

SICH LASSEN + INFINITIVE	
Das kann besser gemacht werden.	Das läßt sich besser machen.
That can be done better.	*That can be done better.*

COMPOUNDS

das Leben + der Lauf = der Lebenslauf (*résumé, curriculum vitae*)

die Arbeit + die Stelle = die Arbeitsstelle (*workplace*)

der Zucker + süß = zuckersüß (*sugar sweet*)

THE IMPERATIVE

du-*form:*	Unterbrich mich nicht, Martin!
	Don't interrupt me, Martin!
Sie-*form:*	Unterbrechen Sie mich nicht, mein Herr!
	Don't interrupt me, sir!
ihr-*form:*	Unterbrecht mich nicht, Kinder!
	Don't interrupt me, children!

COMPLEX SENTENCES WITH WENN, DASS, AND OB

Man muss einen Partner haben, wenn man erfolgreich sein will.

You have to have a partner when/if you want to be successful.

Wenn man erfolgreich sein will, muss man einen Partner haben.

If/When you want to be successful, you have to have a partner.

Ich weiss, dass ich viel arbeiten muss.

I know (that) I have to work a lot.

Ich weiß nicht, ob ich die richtige Ausbildung habe.

I don't know whether I have the right education.

Unit 3 Quiz

A. Rewrite the sentences in the passive voice.

1. **Mein Chef hat mich befördert.** _____

   _____

2. **Ich schicke den Lebenslauf.** _____

   _____

3. **Wir bezahlen die Rechnung.** _____

   _____

B. Rewrite the sentences using man.

1. **Auf Deutsch wird das anders gesagt.** _____

   _____

2. **Hier darf nicht geraucht werden.** _____

   _____

3. **Hier kann geparkt werden.** _____

   _____

C. Complete the sentences with the correct form of sich lassen.

1. **Dieser Erfolg** _____ **feiern.**

2. **Diese Erfolge** _____ **nicht wiederholen.**

D. Form the compound nouns.

1. die Arbeit + die Stunde _____

2. das Gehalt + die Erhöhung _____

3. die Zeitung + der Artikel _____

4. die Firma + die Leitung _____

E. Use the imperative.

1. _____ ihr bitte mit. (ihr-*form of* kommen)

2. _____ doch endlich still! (du-*form of* sein)

3. _____ Sie doch etwas länger. (Sie-*form of* bleiben)

4. _____ mir bitte meinen Schlüssel zurück. (du-*form of* geben)

F. Complete the sentences with wenn, dass, or ob.

1. _____ man Erfolg haben will, muss man hart arbeiten.

2. Ich weiss nicht, _____ er heute oder morgen kommt.

3. Haben Sie schon gehört, _____ ich eine neue Stelle habe?

4. Ich muss Überstunden machen, _____ ich das Projekt fertig machen will.

How Did You Do?

Give yourself a point for every correct answer, then use the following key to tell whether you're ready to move on:

0–7 points: It's probably a good idea to go back through the unit again. You may be moving too quickly, or there may be too much "down time" between your contact with German. Remember that it's better to spend 30 minutes with German three or four times a week than it is to spend two or three hours just once a week. Find a pace that's comfortable for you, and spread your contact hours out as much as you can.

8–12 points: You would benefit from a review before moving on. Go back and spend a little more time on the specific points that gave you trouble. Reread the Grammar Builder sections that were difficult, and do the Work Outs one more time. Don't forget about the online supplemental practice material, either. Go to **www.livinglanguage.com/languagelab** for games and quizzes that will reinforce the material from this unit.

13–17 points: Good job! There are just a few points that you could consider reviewing before moving on. If you haven't worked with the games and quizzes on **www.livinglanguage.com/languagelab**, please give them a try.

18–20 points: Great! You're ready to move on to the next unit.

points

Unit 4:
Spare Time Activities

Welcome to the final unit of *Advanced German*! By the end of this unit you'll be able to:

☐ Talk about sports activities

☐ Talk about your hobbies and spare time activities

☐ Use relative clauses

☐ Talk about the weather

☐ Use infinitives with **zu**

☐ Use **weil**-sentences

☐ Use subordinate clauses with question words such as **wer** (*who*) or **warum** (*why*)

☐ Use the **würde**-form (*would*)

☐ Use the subjunctive of modal verbs

☐ Articulate and reply to apologies

Subordinate Clauses with
Question Pronouns

The Subjunctive of Modal Verbs

Polite Speech: The **würde-**form and the
subjunctive of **haben** and **sein**

Apologies

Lesson 13: Words

By the end of this lesson you'll be able to:

☐ Talk about sports activities

☐ Talk about your hobbies and spare time activities

☐ Use relative clauses

Word Builder 1

▶ 13A Word Builder 1 (CD 9, Track 7)

der Sport	sports
(Freizeit)Sportler	(hobby) athlete
das Sportstudio	sports center
der Fitnessclub	fitness club
das Schwimmbad	public pool
das Skigebiet	ski resort
der Verein	club
das Mitglied	member
Rad fahren	to bicycle
Motorrad fahren	to ride a motorcycle
Ski fahren	to ski
snowboarden	to snowboard
schwimmen	to swim
tauchen	to (scuba) dive
Karate	karate
Yoga	yoga

joggen	*to jog*
wandern	*to hike*
Berg steigen	*to go mountain climbing*

⏸

✎ Word Practice 1

Complete the sentences with the German word that fits best.

1. Swimming, skiing, and hiking are all _____ .
a. **Yoga**
b. **Sport**
c. **Schwimmbad**

2. In the winter many people go _____ .
a. **Ski fahren**
b. **Berg steigen**
c. **Rad fahren**

3. One of the most popular ways to stay fit is _____ .
a. **tauchen**
b. **Motorrad fahren**
c. **joggen**

4. If you belong to a club you are considered a _____ .
a. **Sportler**
b. **Mitglied**
c. **Verein**

5. You can go swimming in the ocean, the lake, the river, and the

_____ .

a. **Schwimmbad**
b. **Yogastudio**
c. **Berg**

ANSWER KEY
1. b; 2. a; 3. c; 4. b; 5. a

Subordinate Clauses with
Question Pronouns

The Subjunctive of Modal Verbs

- -

Polite Speech: The **würde**-form and the
subjunctive of **haben** and **sein**

Apologies

Grammar Builder 1

▶ 13B Grammar Builder 1 (CD 9, Track 8)

RELATIVE CLAUSES 1

Relative clauses give additional information about a noun. For example:

Der Mann, der joggt, **ist sehr sportlich.**
The man who is jogging is very athletic.

The pronoun **der** (*who*) is used to refer back to the noun **der Mann** (*the man*), which the relative clause describes further: **der joggt** (*who is jogging*). In other words, *who* is the relative pronoun *relating* back to the noun mentioned in the main clause: **Der Mann ist sehr sportlich.** (*The man is very athletic.*)

Other relative pronouns in English are *that* and *which*. In English, these relative pronouns can sometimes be omitted. In German, they cannot.

Die Frau, die eine rote Mütze trägt, fährt Ski.
The woman (who is) wearing a red cap is skiing.

Das Snowboard, das du benutzt, gehört mir.
The snowboard (that) you're using belongs to me.

Notice that the relative pronoun agrees with the noun it refers to, and it's usually identical to the definite article. The verb stands in the last position in a relative clause.

Der **Fitnessclub,** der (*m. sg.*) **neu aufgemacht hat, ist prima.**
The fitness club, which recently opened, is great.

Die **Tasse,** die (*f. sg.*) **auf dem Tisch steht, habe ich getöpfert.**
The cup that is on the table was made by me.

<u>Das</u> **Motorrad,** <u>das</u> (*n. sg.*) **in der Garage steht, war sehr teuer.**
The motorbike that is standing in the garage was very expensive.

Make sure not to mix up **dass** and **das**. Even though they are pronounced the same, they are spelled differently and have very different meanings. **Das** is the definite article for singular neuter nouns and also a relative pronoun.

Das Motorrad, das in der Garage steht, war sehr teuer.
The motorbike that is standing in the garage was very expensive.

Dass, on the other hand, does not refer to a noun but to the information conveyed by the entire sentence.

Bist du sicher, dass das Motorrad noch in der Garage steht?
Are you sure (that) the motorbike is still in the garage?

(II)

🖉 **Work Out 1**

Complete the sentences with the appropriate relative pronoun.

1. **Das Motorrad, _____ ich fahre, ist weiß.**

2. **Der Fitnessclub, _____ neu aufgemacht hat, ist immer voll.**

3. **Das Schwimmbad, _____ in der Innenstadt liegt, ist immer kalt.**

4. **Ich kann in Schuhen, _____ neu sind, nicht joggen.**

5. **Der Mann, _____ Karate unterrichtet, ist sehr sportlich.**

   ANSWER KEY
   1. das; 2. der; 3. das; 4. die; 5. der

Subordinate Clauses with
Question Pronouns

The Subjunctive of Modal Verbs

Polite Speech: The **würde-**form and the
subjunctive of **haben** and **sein**

Apologies

Word Builder 2

▶ 13C Word Builder 2 (CD 9, Track 9)

die Freizeitbeschäftigung	leisure time activity
das Hobby	hobby
fotografieren	to photograph
malen	to paint
zeichnen	to draw
töpfern	to make pottery
stricken	to knit
häkeln	to crochet
kochen	to cook
backen	to bake
die Musik	music
die Gitarre	guitar
das Klavier	piano

⑪

✎ Word Practice 2

Complete each sentence with the German word that fits best.

1. Beethoven played _____.
a. **Gitarre**
b. **Klavier**
c. **Tennis**

2. Jimi Hendrix played _____.
a. **Gitarre**
b. **Klavier**
c. **Tennis**

3. _____ is taking pictures.
a. **töpfern**
b. **malen**
c. **fotografieren**

4. _____ is using paint on canvas.
a. **töpfern**
b. **malen**
c. **fotografieren**

5. **Stricken, häkeln, töpfern,** and even **fotografieren** can be considered _____.
a. **Musik**
b. **Hobbies**
c. **Sport**

ANSWER KEY
1. b; 2. a; 3. c; 4. b; 5. b

Grammar Builder 2

▶ 13D Grammar Builder 2 (CD 9, Track 10)

RELATIVE CLAUSES 2

A relative pronoun can be the subject or the object of the relative clause. So far we've only dealt with relative pronouns in the subject case (nominative). If the relative pronoun refers to an object in the relative clause, it has to change accordingly. Let's compare the following two sentences.

Der **Mann,** der **Karate unterrichtet, ruft dich.**
The man who is teaching karate is calling you.

Der **Mann,** den **du rufst, unterrichtet Karate.**
The man who(m) you are calling is teaching karate.

Just as the English relative pronoun can change from *who* to *whom* in the second
sentence to signify the change from subject to object in the relative clause, the
German relative pronoun changes from **der** to **den**. In English, *whom* is a bit
formal, and *who* is often used. But in German, the accusative form is always used
to refer to a direct object. Let's look at another example.

Der **Fußball,** den **du hältst, gehört mir.**
The soccer ball (that) you're holding belongs to me.

In the relative clause, the subject is **du**, and **der Fußball**, represented by the relative
pronoun **den**, is the direct object: **Du hältst den Fußball.** (*You are holding the soccer
ball.*) **Der Fußball, den du hältst …** (*The soccer ball that you are holding …*) So the
relative pronoun needs to be in the masculine singular accusative form: **den**.

A relative clause can begin with a preposition followed by a relative pronoun. The
case of the relative pronoun is dictated by the preposition.

Das ist der Fitnessclub, bei dem **ich Mitglied bin.**
This is the fitness club where/at which I am a member.

In the example above, because **bei** takes the dative case, **dem** is used to refer
back to **der Fitnessclub**. If the noun were feminine, the relative pronoun would
be **der**, which is the feminine dative form.

Ⓘ

✎ Work Out 2

Insert the appropriate relative pronoun. If there's a preposition, remember which case it takes!

1. Der Fußball, mit _____ ich am liebsten spiele, ist schwarz.

2. Das Bild, _____ ich male, wird verkauft.

3. Der Pullover, _____ ich stricke, ist bald fertig.

4. Das Fahrrad, mit _____ ich fahre, gehört meiner Freundin.

5. Die Kekse, _____ du gegessen hast, habe ich gebacken.

ANSWER KEY
1. dem; 2. das; 3. den; 4. dem; 5. die

✎ Drive It Home

Fill in the correct relative pronoun using the cues for case in parentheses.

1. Das Snowboard, _____ dort steht, gehört mir. (*nominative*)

2. Die Tennisschuhe, _____ zu groß sind, sind neu. (*nominative*)

3. Der Fitnessclub, _____ gestern eröffnet hat, ist schon ausgebucht. (*nominative*)

4. Das Skigebiet, _____ ich meine, ist in Österreich. (*accusative*)

5. Der Berg, auf _____ ich steigen möchte, ist gefährlich. (*accusative*)

6. Die Gitarre, _____ du spielst, gehört mir. (*accusative*)

7. Das Auto, mit _____ du in das Skigebiet fahren willst, ist nicht gut für den Winter. (*dative*)

8. Der Karatelehrer, bei _____ Sie Unterricht nehmen, ist sehr gut. (*dative*)

9. Die Karatelehrerin, bei _____ Sie Unterricht nehmen, ist sehr gut. (*dative*)

ANSWER KEY

1. das; 2. die; 3. der; 4. das; 5. den; 6. die; 7. dem; 8. dem 9. der

How Did You Do?

By now you should be able to:

☐ Talk about sports activities
(Still unsure? Jump back to page 169.)

☐ Talk about your hobbies and spare time activities
(Still unsure? Jump back to page 173.)

☐ Use relative clauses
(Still unsure? Jump back to page 171 and page 174.)

✎ Word Recall

Match the German in column A with the English translation in column B.

1. häkeln	a. *to hike*
2. das Mitglied	b. *to ride a bike*
3. der Freizeitsportler	c. *to knit*
4. Rad fahren	d. *to cook*
5. töpfern	e. *music*
6. wandern	f. *member*
7. stricken	g. *hobby athlete*
8. die Musik	h. *to make pottery*
9. Motorrad fahren	i. *to crochet*
10. kochen	j. *to ride a motorcycle*

ANSWER KEY

1. i; 2. f; 3. g; 4. b; 5. h; 6. a; 7. c; 8. e; 9. j; 10. d

Lesson 14: Phrases

By the end of this lesson you will be able to:

- ☐ Talk about the weather
- ☐ Use infinitives with **zu**
- ☐ Use **weil**-sentences

Phrase Builder 1

▶ 14A Phrase Builder 1 (CD 9, Track 11)

Sport treiben	*to do sports*
einem Verein beitreten	*to join a club*
Fußball spielen	*to play soccer*
Handball spielen	*to play handball*
Basketball spielen	*to play basketball*
Volleyball spielen	*to play volleyball*
Tennis spielen	*to play tennis*
Squash spielen	*to play squash*
Golf spielen	*to play golf*
einen Marathon laufen	*to run a marathon*
(keine) Lust haben	*to (not) feel like it*
fit bleiben	*to stay in shape*
das Wetter	*weather*
bei gutem Wetter	*in good weather*
bei schlechtem Wetter	*in bad weather*
bei Regenwetter	*in rainy weather*

Subordinate Clauses with
Question Pronouns

The Subjunctive of Modal Verbs

Polite Speech: The **würde**-form and the
subjunctive of **haben** and **sein**

Apologies

bei Schneewetter	in snowy weather
Es regnet.	It is raining.
Es schneit.	It is snowing.
Die Sonne scheint.	The sun is shining.

⏸

✎ Phrase Practice 1

Complete the phrases below to match the translations in parentheses.

1. bei _____ Wetter (*in bad weather*)

2. Fußball _____ (*to play soccer*)

3. _____ schneit. (*It's snowing.*)

4. keine _____ haben (*to not feel like it*)

5. Sport _____ (*to do sports*)

ANSWER KEY
1. schlechtem; 2. spielen; 3. Es; 4. Lust; 5. treiben

Grammar Builder 1

▶ 14B Grammar Builder 1 (CD 9, Track 12)

INFINITIVES WITH ZU

Infinitive constructions with **zu** never have their own subject, and instead relate
back to the subject of the main clause. They're similar to *to* or *-ing* constructions
in English, but they can be translated in a few different ways.

Hast du Lust, mit mir joggen zu gehen?
Do you feel like going for a jog with me?

Glaubst du, schnell genug zu laufen?
Do you believe you run fast enough?

Note that separable verbs place the **zu** between the separable prefix and the stem.

Hast du Lust mitzuspielen.
Do you want to play along?

Bei Regenwetter habe ich keine Lust hinauszugehen.
In rainy weather I don't feel like going out.

Constructions with **um** followed by **zu** and the infinitive are comparable to the English *in order to.*

Ich muss nicht schnell laufen, um mit dir zu joggen.
I don't have to run fast in order to jog with you.

Ohne … zu and **anstatt … zu** are other infinitive constructions.

Er spielt im Verein Tennis, ohne beizutreten.
He plays tennis at the club without joining.

Die Kinder spielen Fußball, anstatt Hausaufgaben zu machen.
The kids are playing soccer instead of doing their homework.

(II)

Subordinate Clauses with
Question Pronouns

The Subjunctive of Modal Verbs

Polite Speech: The **würde**-form and the
subjunctive of **haben** and **sein**

Apologies

✎ Work Out 1

Answer the questions with an infinitive construction.

1. *Do you feel like playing tennis? (no)* _____

   _____

2. *Do you believe you play the piano well? (yes)* _____

   _____

3. *Do you feel like dancing? (yes)* _____

   _____

4. *Do you prefer to play golf instead of working? (yes)* _____

   _____

5. *Do you run fast enough to run with me? (yes)* _____

   _____

ANSWER KEY
1. Nein, ich habe keine Lust, Tennis zu spielen. 2. Ja, ich glaube gut Klavier zu spielen. 3. Ja, ich
habe Lust zu tanzen. 4. Ja, ich spiele lieber Golf, anstatt zu arbeiten. 5. Ja, ich laufe schnell genug,
um mit dir/Ihnen zu laufen.

Phrase Builder 2

▶ 14C Phrase Builder 2 (CD 9, Track 13)

einem Hobby nachgehen	*to have a hobby, to pursue a hobby*
Gitarre spielen	*to play the guitar*
Klavier spielen	*to play the piano*
Briefmarken sammeln	*to collect stamps*
im Garten arbeiten	*to work in the garden*
Blumen pflanzen	*to plant flowers*

einen Kuchen backen	*to bake a cake*
dick machen	*to be fattening*
Tango tanzen	*to dance the tango*
Ballettunterricht nehmen	*to take ballet classes*
stricken lernen	*to learn (how) to knit*
Leute kennenlernen	*to meet people*
Es macht Spaß.	*It is fun.*

✎ Phrase Practice 2

Complete the phrases so they match the translation in parentheses.

1. dick _____ *(to be fattening)*

2. Blumen _____ *(to plant flowers)*

3. _____ kennenlernen *(to meet people)*

4. Es _____ Spaß. *(It is fun.)*

5. stricken _____ *(to learn to knit)*

ANSWER KEY
1. machen; 2. pflanzen; 3. Leute; 4. macht; 5. lernen

Grammar Builder 2

▶ 14D Grammar Builder 2 (CD 9, Track 14)

WEIL-SENTENCES

Weil-sentences introduce the reason for a particular action in the main clause with **weil** (*because*). In other words, **weil** answers the question **warum?** (*why?*)

Warum sollte ich Sport treiben?
Why should I play sports?

Du solltest Sport treiben, weil es gesund ist.
You should play sports because it's healthy.

Ich will nicht Tennis spielen, weil ich müde bin.
I don't want to play tennis, because I am tired.

Remember that in the subordinate clause, the verb is moved to the end. And finally, as you may have noticed, all subordinate clauses in German have to be separated from the main clause by a comma.

Ⓘ

✎ Work Out 2

Connect the sentences using weil.

1. **Ich lerne stricken. Es macht Spaß.** _____

_____

2. **Ich gehe gern tanzen. Ich lerne Leute kennen.** _____

_____

3. **Wir essen nie Kuchen. Es macht dick.** _____

_____

4. **Er sammelt Briefmarken. Er hat viel Zeit.** _____

_____

5. Sie sind müde. Sie arbeiten zu viel. _____

ANSWER KEY
1. Ich lerne stricken, weil es Spaß macht. 2. Ich gehe gern tanzen, weil ich Leute kennenlerne.
3. Wir essen nie Kuchen, weil es dick macht. 4. Er sammelt Briefmarken, weil er viel Zeit hat. 5. Sie
sind müde, weil Sie zu viel arbeiten.

✎ Drive It Home

Complete the sentences with the infinitive with **zu**.

1. **Hast du Lust, mit mir** _____ **?** *(to hike)*

2. **Hast du Lust, mit mir** _____ **?** *(to jog)*

3. **Hast du Lust, mich** _____ **?** *(to call)*

4. **Haben Sie Lust, mit uns** _____ **?** *(to ski)*

5. **Haben Sie Lust, mit uns** _____ **?** *(to cook)*

6. **Haben Sie Lust, mit uns** _____ **?** *(to go shopping)*

ANSWER KEY
1. zu wandern; 2. zu joggen; 3. anzurufen; 4. Ski zu fahren; 5. zu kochen; 6. einzukaufen

Now complete the sentences with **weil** and then translate.

1. **Ich bin müde,** _____ **ich spät ins Bett gehe.**

_____

2. **Sie sind erfolgreich,** _____ **Sie viel arbeiten.**

_____

3. **Er ist schlank, _____ er viel Sport treibt.**

   _____

4. **Wir gehen Ski fahren, _____ es schneit.**

   _____

ANSWER KEY

1. *I'm tired because I go to bed late.* 2. *You're successful because you work a lot.* 3. *He's slim because he plays a lot of sports.* 4. *We're going skiing because it's snowing.*

How Did You Do?

Before you move on, make sure you know how to:

☐ Talk about the weather
   (Still unsure? Jump back to page 178.)

☐ Use infinitives with **zu**
   (Still unsure? Jump back to page 179.)

☐ Use **weil**-sentences
   (Still unsure? Jump back to page 182.)

✎ Word Recall

Time to review the vocabulary you learned so far in this unit.

Complete the paragraph below with the most appropriate words and phrases from the word bank.

jogge, spät, spielt, schwimmt, zu nehmen, Lust, pünktlich, mit dem Fahrrad, treibt, wandern

Meine Familie (1)_____ viel Sport. Mein Sohn (2) _____ gern Fußball, mein Mann (3)_____ gern, meine beiden Töchter (4)_____ gern und ich (5)

_____ oft und gern. Und wir haben alle immer (6)
_____ Ski zu fahren. Mein Sohn fährt manchmal (7)_____
_____ in die Schule. Aber oft hat er keine Zeit das
Fahrrad (8)_____, weil er zu (9)_____
aufsteht. Dann muss er sich beeilen, um (10) _____ in die
Schule zu kommen.

ANSWER KEY
1. treibt; 2. spielt; 3. schwimmt; 4. wandern; 5. jogge; 6. Lust; 7. mit dem Fahrrad; 8. zu nehmen;
9. spät; 10. pünktlich

Lesson 15: Sentences

By the end of this lesson you'll be able to:

☐ Use subordinate clauses with question words such as **wer** (_who_) or **warum** (_why_)

☐ Use the **würde**-form (_would_)

Sentence Builder 1

▶ 15A Sentence Builder 1 (CD 9, Track 15)

Treiben Sie Sport?	_Do you play sports?_
Ich spiele Tennis.	_I play tennis._
Meine Kinder möchten gern Fußball spielen.	_My children would like to play soccer._
Ich habe früher Golf gespielt.	_I used to play golf._
Wenn Sie Golf spielen wollen, müssen Sie dem Verein beitreten.	_If you want to play golf, you have to join the club._

Subordinate Clauses with
Question Pronouns

The Subjunctive of Modal Verbs

Polite Speech: The **würde-**form and the
subjunctive of **haben** and **sein**

Apologies

Gibt es hier einen Fitnessclub in der Nähe?	Is there a fitness club nearby?
Wo kann ich hier in der Nähe joggen gehen?	Where can I go for a jog around here?
Gibt es hier ein Schwimmbad?	Is there a public pool around here?
Haben Sie Lust, Squash zu spielen?	Do you feel like playing squash?
Leider habe ich keine Zeit, um heute wandern zu gehen.	Unfortunately, I don't have time to go hiking today.

(II)

✎ Sentence Practice 1

Translate from English to German.

1. *Do you play sports?* _____

_____

2. *I used to play tennis.* _____

_____

3. *Do you feel like playing golf?* _____

_____

4. *Where can I go hiking around here?* _____

_____

5. *Is there a public pool nearby?* _____

_____

ANSWER KEY
1. Treiben Sie Sport? 2. Ich habe früher Tennis gespielt. 3. Haben Sie Lust Golf zu spielen?
4. Wo kann ich hier in der Nähe wandern gehen? 5. Gibt es hier in der Nähe ein Schwimmbad?

Grammar Builder 1

▶ 15B Grammar Builder 1 (CD 9, Track 16)

SUBORDINATE CLAUSES WITH QUESTION PRONOUNS

It is also possible to form subordinate clauses with question words such as warum (*why*), wer (*who*), wann (*when*), wie (*how*), and wo (*where*).

Ich weiß nicht, wo man hier Squash spielen kann.
I don't know where you can play squash around here.

Wissen Sie, wann das Schwimmbad aufmacht?
Do you know when the pool opens?

Können Sie mir zeigen, wie man strickt?
Can you show me how to knit?

Es ist mir egal, warum man Sport treiben soll.
I don't care why you are supposed to play sports.

As with all of the subordinate clauses you've learned so far (wenn, dass, and ob sentences and relative clauses), the verb moves to the final position in subordinate clauses with question words, as well.

Wer will Fußball spielen?
Who wants to play soccer?

Ich weiß nicht, wer Fußball spielen will.
I don't know who wants to play soccer.

⏸

✎ Work Out 1

Complete each sentence with a subordinate clause starting with a question word.

1. **Wo kann man hier joggen? Wissen Sie,** _____

   _____ ?

2. **Wann wollen Sie Golf spielen? Es ist mir egal,** _____

   _____ .

3. **Warum brauche ich einen neuen Tennisschläger? Ich weiß nicht,** _____

   _____ .

4. **Wie komme ich am besten zum Schwimmbad? Können Sie mir sagen,** _____

   _____ ?

5. **Wer hat Zeit, Fußball zu spielen? Ich weiß nicht,** _____

   _____ .

ANSWER KEY

1. Wissen Sie, wo man hier joggen kann? 2. Es ist mir egal, wann Sie Golf spielen wollen. 3. Ich weiß nicht, warum ich einen neuen Tennisschläger brauche. 4. Können Sie mir sagen, wie ich am besten zum Schwimmbad komme? 5. Ich weiß nicht, wer Zeit hat, Fußball zu spielen.

Sentence Builder 2

▶ 15C Sentence Builder 2 (CD 9, Track 17)

Haben Sie ein Hobby?	*Do you have a hobby?*
Ich arbeite gern in meinem Garten.	*I enjoy working in my garden.*
Meine Mutter töpfert.	*My mother does pottery.*
Sie macht Vasen aus Ton.	*She makes vases from clay.*
Können Sie stricken?	*Do you know how to knit?*
Nein, aber ich häkle gern.	*No, but I enjoy crocheting.*

Ich bin Hobbyfotograf.	*I am an amateur photographer.*
Ich wäre gern Amateur-Filmemacher.	*I'd like to be an amateur filmmaker.*
Das ist aber ein teures Hobby.	*That's an expensive hobby.*

✎ Sentence Practice 2

Complete the sentences below with the most appropriate word from the word bank.

gern, teures, stricken, Hobby, Amateur-Filmemacher

1. Haben Sie ein _____ ?

2. Ich töpfere _____ .

3. Kann Ihre Mutter _____ ?

4. Ich bin _____ .

5. Das ist aber ein _____ Hobby.

ANSWER KEY
1. Hobby; 2. gern; 3. stricken; 4. Amateur-Filmemacher; 5. teures

Grammar Builder 2
▷ 15D Grammar Builder 2 (CD 9, Track 18)

POLITE SPEECH: THE WÜRDE-FORM AND THE SUBJUNCTIVE OF HABEN AND SEIN

The subjunctive, the form expressing hypothetical conditions, is not very common in everyday German speech, except in polite requests. All you need to know are hätte, wäre, and würde, which are the subjunctive forms of haben, sein, and werden, respectively. They are used very much like the English *would*. Let's take a look.

WÜRDE + INFINITIVE

In polite speech, most verbs take the subjunctive of werden, which is würde, and
the infinitive of the main verb. This is similar to the English *would*. A request like
Hilf mir bitte! (*Help me!*) becomes more polite by saying, **Würdest du mir bitte
helfen?** (*Would you help me, please?*)

Würden Sie mir sagen, wie ich zum Golfplatz komme?
Would you please tell me how to get to the golf course?

Würdest du mir zeigen, wie man strickt?
Would you show me how to knit?

Here are the subjunctive forms of werden.

WERDEN *(WOULD)* - SUBJUNCTIVE			
ich würde	*I would*	**wir würden**	*we would*
du würdest	*you would*	**ihr würdet**	*you would*
er/sie/es würde	*he/she/it would*	**sie/Sie würden**	*they/you would*

THE SUBJUNCTIVE OF HABEN AND SEIN

Haben and sein do not use the würde-form. Their subjunctive forms, hätte and
wäre, are rather common.

Hätten Sie Zeit, mit mir Tennis zu spielen?
Would you have time to play tennis with me?

Wie wäre es, wenn wir heute joggen gehen?
How about going jogging today? (lit., How would it be if we go jogging today?)

Here are the subjunctive forms of **haben** and **sein**.

HABEN *(TO HAVE)* - SUBJUNCTIVE			
ich hätte	*I would have*	**wir hätten**	*we would have*
du hättest	*you would have*	**ihr hättet**	*you would have*
er/sie/es hätte	*he/she/it would have*	**sie/Sie hätten**	*they/you would have*

SEIN *(TO BE)* - SUBJUNCTIVE			
ich wäre	*I would be*	**wir wären**	*we would be*
du wärst	*you would be*	**ihr wärt**	*you would be*
er/sie/es wäre	*he/she/it would be*	**sie/Sie wären**	*they/you would be*

Ⓘ

✎ Work Out 2

Make these requests more polite by using the subjunctive.

1. Zeigen Sie mir bitte, wie ich zum Schwimmbad komme. _____

   _____

2. Haben Sie Lust, mit mir Golf zu spielen? _____

   _____

3. Sind Sie bitte so freundlich! _____

   _____

4. Beeilen Sie sich bitte! _____

   _____

Polite Speech: The **würde**-form and the
subjunctive of **haben** and **sein**   Apologies

5. **Hilf mir bitte!** _____

_____

ANSWER KEY

1. Würden Sie mir bitte zeigen, wie ich zum Schwimmbad komme? 2. Hätten Sie Lust, mit mir Golf
zu spielen? 3. Wären Sie bitte so freundlich! 4. Würden Sie sich bitte beeilen? 5. Würdest du mir
bitte helfen?

✎ Drive It Home

Complete each sentence by translating the clues into German.

1. **Kannst du mir sagen,** _____ **hier wohnt?** (*who*)

2. **Wissen Sie,** _____ **hier Yoga unterrichtet?** (*who*)

3. **Können Sie mir bitte sagen,** _____ **das Schwimmbad ist?** (*where*)

4. **Ich habe vergessen,** _____ **meine Schlüssel sind.** (*where*)

5. **Ich weiß nicht,** _____ **mein Termin ist.** (*when*)

6. **Sag mir doch bitte,** _____ **du nach Hause kommen wirst.** (*when*)

7. _____ **Sie mir bitte den Weg ins Yogastudio zeigen?** (*would*)

8. _____ **du das bitte wiederholen?** (*would*)

9. _____ **Sie Lust mit mir joggen zu gehen?** (*would have*)

10. _____ **du Zeit, mich zurückzurufen?** (*would have*)

11. _____ **Sie so freundlich, mir zu helfen?** (*would be*)

12. _____ **ihr so lieb, mich nach Hause zu fahren?** (*would be*)

ANSWER KEY

1. wer; 2. wer; 3. wo; 4. wo; 5. wann; 6. wann; 7. Würden; 8. Würdest; 9. Hätten; 10. Hättest; 11. Wären;
12. Wärt

How Did You Do?

Make sure you know how to:

☐ Use subordinate clauses with question words such as **wer** (*who*) or **warum** (*why*)
(Still unsure? Jump back to page 188.)

☐ Use the **würde**-form (*would*)
(Still unsure? Jump back to page 190.)

✎ Word Recall

Translate the following into German.

1. *to play golf* _____

2. *because* _____

3. *club* _____

4. *to join* _____

5. *to go jogging* _____

6. *sport* _____

7. *who (nominative)* _____

8. *to cook* _____

9. *why* _____

10. *weather* _____

ANSWER KEY
1. Golf spielen; 2. weil; 3. Verein; 4. beitreten; 5. joggen gehen; 6. Sport; 7. wer; 8. kochen; 9. warum;
10. Wetter

Subordinate Clauses with
Question Pronouns

The Subjunctive of Modal Verbs

Polite Speech: The **würde**-form and the
subjunctive of **haben** and **sein**

Apologies

Lesson 16: Conversations

By the end of this lesson you'll be able to:

☐ Use the subjunctive of modal verbs

☐ Articulate and reply to apologies

ᴖ Conversation 1

▶ 16A Conversation 1 (CD 9, Track 19 - German; Track 20 - German and English)

Dan Andrews has just moved to Germany. He is chatting with a neighbor.

Dan:	Ich kenne mich hier noch nicht so gut aus. Was kann man denn hier in der Freizeit machen?
Roswitha:	Das kommt darauf an, was Sie gerne machen. Treiben Sie Sport?
Dan:	Ja, ich spiele Golf.
Roswitha:	Wenn Sie Golf spielen wollen, müssen Sie einem Club beitreten.
Dan:	Wissen Sie, ob es hier in der Nähe einen Golfclub gibt?
Roswitha:	Es gibt einen Golfclub in Büttchen. Büttchen ist das Dorf, das in der Nähe des Flughafens liegt. Sie könnten mit meinem Mann Golf spielen. Er ist Mitglied.
Dan:	Spielen Sie auch Golf?
Roswitha:	Nein, ich spiele nicht Golf, weil ich nicht genug Zeit habe. Ich jogge lieber. Das hält mich fit.
Dan:	So ein Zufall, ich laufe auch gern. Hätten Sie Lust, mit mir joggen zu gehen?
Roswitha:	Ich weiß nicht …
Dan:	Sie könnten mir zeigen, wo man hier am besten joggen gehen kann.
Roswitha:	Ja, das stimmt.
Dan:	Wie wär's mit Samstag?

Roswitha: **Das wäre gut. Am Samstag könnte sich mein Mann um die Kinder kümmern.**

Dan: **Gut.**

Roswitha: **Wenn es regnet, verschieben wir unseren Lauf.**

Dan: *I don't know my way around here yet. What can you do here in your leisure time?*

Roswitha: *That depends on what you enjoy doing. Do you play sports?*

Dan: *Yes, I play golf.*

Roswitha: *If you want to play golf, you need to join a club.*

Dan: *Do you know if there's a golf club near here?*

Roswitha: *There is a golf club in Büttchen. That's the village that's near the airport. You could go with my husband. He's a member.*

Dan: *Do you play golf, too?*

Roswitha: *No, I don't play golf, because I don't have enough time. I'd rather jog. That keeps me in shape.*

Dan: *What a coincidence—I enjoy running too. Would you feel like going jogging with me?*

Roswitha: *I don't know …*

Dan: *You could show me where you can go jogging around here.*

Roswitha: *Yes, that's true.*

Dan: *How about Saturday?*

Roswitha: *That would be good. On Saturday my husband could take care of the kids.*

Dan: *Good.*

Roswitha: *If it's raining, we'll postpone our run.*

Subordinate Clauses with
Question Pronouns

The Subjunctive of Modal Verbs

Polite Speech: The **würde**-form and the
subjunctive of **haben** and **sein**

Apologies

✎ Conversation Practice 1

Complete the dialogue sentences below. If you're unsure of the answer, listen to
the conversation on your audio one more time.

1. Was kann man denn hier _____ machen?

2. _____ Sie Sport?

3. Ja, ich _____ Golf.

4. _____, ob es hier in der Nähe einen Golfclub gibt?

5. Ich jogge _____.

6. _____, mit mir joggen zu gehen?

7. _____ mit Samstag?

ANSWER KEY
1. in der Freizeit; 2. Treiben; 3. spiele; 4. Wissen Sie; 5. lieber; 6. Hätten Sie Lust; 7. Wie wär's

Grammar Builder 1

▶ 16B Grammar Builder 1 (CD 9, Track 21)

THE SUBJUNCTIVE OF MODAL VERBS

As you already know, modal verbs are used frequently in polite requests. To make
these requests extra polite, use their subjunctive form. Compare these two pairs
of sentences; the second sentence of each pair uses the subjunctive.

Darf ich Sie etwas fragen?
Can I ask you something?

Dürfte ich Sie etwas fragen?
May I ask you something?

Kann ich Sie fotografieren?
Can I photograph you?

Könnte ich Sie fotografieren?
Could I photograph you?

Even though wollen has its own subjunctive form, which can be used in polite speech, möchten often takes its place.

Wollen Sie heute noch Tennis spielen?
Do you want to play tennis today?

Wollten Sie heute noch Tennis spielen?
Would you want to play tennis today?

Möchten Sie heute noch Tennis spielen?
Would you like to play tennis today?

Let's look at the full subjunctive conjugation of each modal.

	TO BE ABLE TO	TO HAVE TO	TO BE ALLOWED TO
ich	könnte	müsste	dürfte
du	könntest	müsstest	dürftest
er/sie/es	könnte	müsste	dürfte
wir	könnten	müssten	dürften
ihr	könntet	müsstet	dürftet
sie/Sie	könnten	müssten	dürften

Polite Speech: The **würde**-form and the
subjunctive of **haben** and **sein**

Apologies

	TO WANT TO	TO LIKE TO	TO BE SUPPOSED TO
ich	wollte	möchte	sollte
du	wolltest	möchtest	solltest
er/sie/es	wollte	möchte	sollte
wir	wollten	möchten	sollten
ihr	wolltet	möchtet	solltet
sie/Sie	wollten	möchten	sollten

✎ Work Out 1

Rephrase these requests using the subjunctive.

1. **Können Sie mir helfen?** _____

2. **Darf ich Sie etwas fragen?** _____

3. **Müssen wir nicht einen Schläger mitbringen?** _____

_____

4. **Wir sollen langsamer laufen.** _____

5. **Können Sie mir zeigen, wie man strickt?** _____

_____

ANSWER KEY
1. **Könnten Sie mir helfen?** 2. **Dürfte ich Sie etwas fragen?** 3. **Müssten wir nicht einen Schläger mitbringen?** 4. **Wir sollten langsamer laufen.** 5. **Könnten Sie mir zeigen, wie man strickt?**

Conversation 2

16C Conversation 2 (CD 9, Track 22 - German; Track 23 - German and English)

Roswitha and Dan never went jogging that Saturday. Let's find out what happened.

Dan:	Wo waren Sie denn gestern? Ich habe bei Ihnen geklingelt.
Roswitha:	Das ist mir aber peinlich. Leider ist etwas dazwischen gekommen. Ich musste meinen Sohn zum Arzt bringen, weil er krank war. Tut mir leid.
Dan:	Macht nichts. Darf ich fragen, wie es ihm jetzt geht?
Roswitha:	Ach, viel besser. Es ist erstaunlich, wie schnell Kinder gesund werden. Er ist schon wieder im Garten und geht seinem Hobby nach.
Dan:	Was macht er denn gern?
Roswitha:	Gartenarbeit. Er pflanzt gerade Blumen.
Dan:	Haben Sie auch ein Hobby?
Roswitha:	Ja, ich backe gern. Deshalb muss ich ja joggen. *(They both laugh.)* Sie sollten meinen Marmorkuchen probieren. Wie wär's mit einer Tasse Kaffee und einem Stück Kuchen, der gar nicht dick macht?
Dan:	Nicht's wäre mir lieber. Aber leider muss ich ins Büro.
Roswitha:	An einem Sonntag?
Dan:	Leider ja. Tut mir leid.
Roswitha:	Kein Problem. Hätten Sie heute Nachmittag Zeit?
Dan:	Ja, gern.
Roswitha:	Prima, dann lernen Sie auch meinen Mann kennen. Er freut sich schon, mit Ihnen Golf zu spielen.

Dan:	*Where were you yesterday? I rang your doorbell.*
Roswitha:	*That's embarrassing. Unfortunately, something came up. I had to take my son to the doctor, because he was sick. I'm sorry.*
Dan:	*No harm done. May I ask how he's doing now?*

Roswitha:	Oh, much better. It's amazing how quickly children recuperate. He's in the backyard already, pursuing his hobby.
Dan:	What does he like to do?
Roswitha:	Garden work. He's planting flowers just now.
Dan:	Do you have a hobby, too?
Roswitha:	Yes, I enjoy baking. That's why I have to go jogging. You should try my marble cake. How about a cup of coffee and a piece of cake, which is not at all fattening?
Dan:	There's nothing I'd rather do. But unfortunately, I have to go to the office.
Roswitha:	On a Sunday?
Dan:	Unfortunately, yes. I'm sorry.
Roswitha:	No problem. Would you have time this afternoon?
Dan:	Yes, I'd like that.
Roswitha:	Great, then you'll meet my husband. He's looking forward to a round of golf with you.

⑪

Take It Further 1

Germans don't *ring a doorbell*; they just *ring*.

Ich habe bei Ihnen geklingelt.
I rang your doorbell.

You could also use läuten.

Ich habe zwei mal geläutet.
I rang your doorbell twice.

✎ Conversation Practice 2

Fill in the blanks in the following sentences with the missing words. If you're unsure of the answer, listen to the conversation on your audio one more time.

1. Ich habe _____ geklingelt.

2. _____ ist etwas dazwischen gekommen.

3. Macht _____.

4. _____ mit einer Tasse Kaffee und einem Stück Kuchen?

5. Nicht's _____ mir lieber.

6. Aber _____ muss ich ins Büro.

7. _____ Problem.

8. _____ Sie heute Nachmittag Zeit?

ANSWER KEY

1. bei Ihnen; 2. Leider; 3. nichts; 4. Wie wär's; 5. wäre; 6. leider; 7. Kein; 8. Hätten

Grammar Builder 2

▶ 16D Grammar Builder 2 (CD 9, Track 24)

APOLOGIES

You're bound to find yourself in a situation where an apology will save the day. Here are the essentials of apologizing.

(Es) tut mir leid.
I'm sorry.

Entschuldigung.
Sorry./Forgive me.

Subordinate Clauses with
Question Pronouns

The Subjunctive of Modal Verbs

Polite Speech: The **würde-**form and the
subjunctive of **haben** and **sein**

Apologies

Verzeihung.
Forgive me.

Leider kann ich heute nicht.
Unfortunately, I can't make it today.

Leider ist etwas dazwischen gekommen.
Unfortunately, something came up.

Das wollte ich nicht.
I didn't mean for that to happen.

Das war nicht meine Absicht.
This was not my intention.

Das ist mir aber peinlich.
That is embarrassing.

Wie kann ich das wieder gut machen?
How can I make this up to you?

Reacting graciously if somebody else apologizes will help you make friends.

Das macht nichts.
It doesn't matter.

Kein Problem.
No problem.

Schon gut.
It's okay.

Nichts passiert.
No harm done.

Ⓘ

✎ Work Out 2

Translate the following into German.

1. *I am sorry.* _____

2. *It's okay.* _____

3. *Unfortunately, something came up.* _____

_____

4. *How can I make this up to you?* _____

_____

5. *No harm done.* _____

ANSWER KEY
1. (Es) tut mir leid./Entschuldigung. 2. Schon gut. 3. Leider ist etwas dazwischen gekommen.
4. Wie kann ich das wieder gut machen? 5. Nichts passiert.

✎ Drive It Home

Complete the sentences with the subjunctive of the modal verb in parentheses.

1. _____ ich Sie später anrufen? (dürfen)

2. Sie _____ mehr Sport treiben. (sollen)

3. Wir _____ auch noch etwas länger bleiben. (können)

4. Das _____ sich machen lassen. (müssen)

5. Du _____ dich wirklich entschuldigen. (sollen)

6. Das _____ Sie auch interessieren. (können)

7. _____ Sie mit mir Tennis spielen? (mögen)

8. _____ ich dich etwas fragen? (dürfen)

ANSWER KEY
1. **Dürfte**; 2. **sollten**; 3. **könnten**; 4. **müsste**; 5. **solltest**; 6. **könnte**; 7. **Möchten**; 8. **Dürfte**

How Did You Do?

Herzlichen Glückwunsch! *Congratulations!* You've done a great job in this course and have just completed its fourth and final unit. You've learned a lot of practical vocabulary and useful basic grammar, which now you are all ready to put to use. Before you move on, make sure you know how to:

☐ Use the subjunctive of modal verbs
(Still unsure? Jump back to page 197.)

☐ Articulate and reply to apologies
(Still unsure? Jump back to page 202.)

✎ Word Recall

Match the German word or phrase in column A with the appropriate English translation in column B.

1. Schon gut.   a. *Forgive me.*

2. Das ist mir aber peinlich.   b. *Is there … ?*

3. der Sportler   c. *No harm done.*

4. Verzeihung.   d. *It's okay.*

5. klingeln   e. *athlete*

6. Handball spielen   f. *I didn't mean for that to happen.*

7. Nichts passiert.   g. *Do you feel like … ?*

8. **Gibt es hier … ?**
9. **Hätten Sie Lust … ?**
10. **Das wollte ich nicht.**

h. *That is embarrassing.*
i. *to ring the doorbell*
j. *to play handball*

ANSWER KEY
1. d; 2. h; 3. e; 4. a; 5. i; 6. j; 7. c; 8. b; 9. g; 10. f.

Don't forget to practice and reinforce what you've learned by visiting **www.livinglanguage.com/languagelab** for flashcards, games, and quizzes for Unit 4!

Unit 4 Essentials

Vocabulary Essentials

Test your knowledge of the key material in this unit by filling in the blanks in the following charts. Once you've completed these pages, you'll have tested your retention, and you'll have your own reference for the most essential vocabulary.

TALKING ABOUT HOBBIES

	Do you play sports?
	I play tennis.
	I used to play golf.
	Is there a fitness club nearby?
	Where can you go for a jog around here?
	Is there a public pool around here?
	Do you feel like playing squash?
	Do you have a hobby?
	I enjoy working in my garden.
	Would you help me?
	I am an amateur photographer.
	That's an expensive hobby.
	Would you feel like a cup of coffee?

	I'm sorry.
	Sorry./Forgive me.
	Forgive me.
	Unfortunately, I can't make it today.
	Unfortunately, something came up.
	This was not my intention.
	How can I make this up to you?
	It doesn't matter.
	No problem.

Grammar Essentials

RELATIVE CLAUSES

MASCULINE	FEMININE	NEUTER
Der Fitnessclub, der neu aufgemacht hat, ist prima.	**Die Frau, die eine rote Mütze trägt, fährt Ski.**	**Das Snowboard, das du benutzt, gehört mir.**
The fitness club, which recently opened, is great.	*The woman who is wearing a red cap is skiing.*	*The snowboard (that) you are using is mine.*

SUBJECT	ACCUSATIVE OBJECT	DATIVE OBJECT
Der Mann, der Karate unterrichtet, ruft dich.	**Der Mann, den du rufst, unterrichtet Karate.**	**Der Mann, bei dem du Karate lernst, ruft dich.**
The man who is teaching karate is calling you.	*The man whom you are calling is teaching karate.*	*The man with whom you study karate is calling you.*

INFINITIVES WITH ZU

Hast du Lust, mit mir joggen zu gehen?
Do you feel like going for a jog with me?
Hast du Lust mitzuspielen.
Do you want to play along?

UM ... ZU	OHNE ... ZU	ANSTATT ... ZU
Ich muss nicht schnell laufen, um mit dir zu joggen.	Er spielt im Verein Tennis, ohne beizutreten.	Die Kinder spielen Fußball, anstatt Hausaufgaben zu machen.
I don't have to run fast in order to jog with you.	*He plays tennis at the club without joining.*	*The kids are playing soccer instead of doing their homework.*

SUBORDINATE CLAUSES

Du solltest Sport treiben, weil es gesund ist.
You should play sports because it's healthy.
Ich weiß nicht, wer Fußball spielen will.
I don't know who wants to play soccer.

THE SUBJUNCTIVE

WERDEN, HABEN, AND SEIN			
	werden	haben	sein
ich	würde	hätte	wäre
du	würdest	hättest	wärst
er/sie/es	würde	hätte	wäre
wir	würden	hätten	wären
ihr	würdet	hättet	wärt
sie/Sie	würden	hätten	wären

MODALS

	TO BE ABLE TO	TO HAVE TO	TO BE ALLOWED TO
ich	könnte	müsste	dürfte
du	könntest	müsstest	dürftest
er/sie/es	könnte	müsste	dürfte
wir	könnten	müssten	dürften
ihr	könntet	müsstet	dürftet
sie/Sie	könnten	müssten	dürften

	TO WANT TO	TO LIKE TO	TO BE SUPPOSED TO
ich	wollte	möchte	sollte
du	wolltest	möchtest	solltest
er/sie/es	wollte	möchte	sollte
wir	wollten	möchten	sollten
ihr	wolltet	möchtet	solltet
sie/Sie	wollten	möchten	sollten

Unit 4 Quiz

Let's practice the most essential German words and grammar points you've learned in *Living Language Advanced German*. It's important to be sure that you've mastered this material. Score yourself at the end of the review and see if you need to review any of the lessons for more practice.

A. Combine the sentences with relative clauses.

1. **Der Sportler ist erfolgreich. Der Sportler joggt viel.** _____

_____

2. **Das Schwimmbad ist groß. Das Schwimmbad hat neu eröffnet.** _____

_____

3. **Die Yogalehrerin hat viele Schüler. Die Yogalehrerin ist nett.** _____

_____

4. **Der Kollege läuft schneller als ich. Ich gehe mit dem Kollegen joggen.** _____

_____

5. **Mein Freund hat Geburtstag. Ich besuche meinen Freund.** _____

_____

B. Combine the sentences using weil.

1. Ich gehe nicht schwimmen. Ich habe eine Erkältung. _____

_____

2. Er treibt so viel Sport. Er will abnehmen. _____

_____

3. Wir gehen jeden Winter Skifahren. Es macht uns viel Spaß. _____

_____

C. Complete the sentences using the appropriate question word.

1. Wo sind meine Schlüssel? Ich weiß nicht, _____

_____ .

2. Warum kommst du nicht mit? Sag mir doch bitte, _____

_____ .

3. Wie komme ich in die Innenstadt? Könnten Sie mir bitte sagen, _____

_____ ?

4. Hat er heute Zeit? Ich weiß nicht, _____

_____ .

D. Rephrase the following using more polite language.

1. Hast Du Lust mit mir Tennis zu spielen? _____

_____

2. Können Sie mir bitte helfen? _____

_____

3. Zeigen Sie mir bitte, wie man strickt. _____

_____

4. Darf ich Ihnen ein Kompliment machen? _____

_____

5. Geben Sie mir bitte meine Tasche. _____

_____

E. Complete the apologies.

1. Das _____ ich aber nicht.

2. Das tut mir _____.

3. _____ ist etwas dazwischen gekommen.

How Did You Do?

Congratulations! You've successfully completed *Living Language Advanced German.*

Give yourself a point for every correct answer.

0–7 points: It's probably a good idea to go back through the lesson again. You may be moving too quickly, or there may be too much "down time" between your contact with German. Remember that it's better to spend 30 minutes with German three or four times a week than it is to spend two or three hours just once a week. Find a pace that's comfortable for you, and spread your contact hours out as much as you can.

8–12 points: You would benefit from a review. Go back and spend a little more time on the specific points that gave you trouble. Reread the Grammar Builder sections that were difficult, and do the Work Outs one more time. Don't forget about the online supplemental practice material, either. Go to **www. livinglanguage.com/languagelab** for games and quizzes that will reinforce the material from this unit.

13-17 points: Good job! There are just a few points that you could consider reviewing before moving on. If you haven't worked with the games and quizzes on **www.livinglanguage.com/languagelab**, please give them a try.

18-20 points: Great! Your German has come a long way! Even though you've reached the end of this course, there's no reason to stop learning. Consider some of these activities to keep your German active, and to continue learning.

☐ Watch German language movies.

☐ Download a few German songs and pay attention to the lyrics.

☐ Bookmark an online German newspaper or magazine. Read a little bit every day.

☐ Buy a book in German and try to read every day.

☐ Check out chatrooms or other online communities in German.

Use your imagination, and tailor your exposure to German to your interests. Enjoy!

☐☐ **points**

ANSWER KEY

A. 1. Der Sportler, der viel joggt, ist erfolgreich. 2. Das Schwimmbad, das neu eröffnet hat, ist groß. 3. Die Yogalehrerin, die nett ist, hat viele Schüler. 4. Der Kollege, mit dem ich joggen gehe, läuft schneller als ich. 5. Mein Freund, den ich besuche, hat Geburtstag.
B. 1. Ich gehe nicht schwimmen, weil ich eine Erkältung habe. 2. Er treibt so viel Sport, weil er abnehmen will. 3. Wir gehen jeden Winter Skifahren, weil es uns viel Spaß macht.
C. 1. Ich weiß nicht, wo meine Schlüssel sind. 2. Sag mir doch bitte, warum du nicht mitkommst. 3. Könnten Sie mir bitte sagen, wie ich in die Innenstadt komme? 4. Ich weiß nicht, ob er heute Zeit hat.
D. 1. Hättest Du Lust mit mir Tennis zu spielen? 2. Könnten Sie mir bitte helfen? 3. Würden Sie mir bitte zeigen, wie man strickt? 4. Dürfte ich Ihnen ein Kompliment machen? 5. Würden Sie mir bitte meine Tasche geben?
E. 1. wollte; 2. leid; 3. Leider

Pronunciation Guide

Vowels

LETTER	PRONUNCIATION	EXAMPLES
a	*(long) ah in father*	sagen, Datum, Laden, Tafel
	(short) o in hot	kann, Mann, Pfanne, was?
ä	*(long) ai in fair*	spät, Erklärung, Währung, Ernährung
	(short) e in bet	Männer
e	*(long) ay in may*	geben, stehen
	(short) e in bent	Adresse, Moment, wetten, rennen
	at the end of a word, e in pocket	beide, heute, Karte, seine
	followed by another e *or* h, *a in care*	Heer, mehr
i	*(long) ee in see*	Miete, dienen, Liebe, Dieb
	(short) i in ship	mit, Sitte, Witz, mittags
o	*(long) o in lone*	oben, Obst, Boden, holen
	(short) o in off	oft, kommen, Stoff, Loch
ö	*(long) like the German* e in geben, *but with rounded lips*	König, Löwe, hören, böse
	(short) like a short u with rounded lips, as in pup	können, Töchter, möchte, Röcke
u	*(long) oo in noon*	Blume, Huhn, Hut, gut

LETTER	PRONUNCIATION	EXAMPLES
	(short) u in bush	muss, dumm, bummeln, Russland
ü	(long) ee in see but with rounded lips	über, drüben, früher, Frühstück
	(short) like short i but with rounded lips	Stück, Brücke, dünn, müssen
y	same as short ü	typisch, Lyrik
ai	y in by	Mai
ei	y in by	Ei, Heimat
ie	ee in see	sieht, mieten, vier
au	ou in house	Haus, Maus, Baum, Pflaume
äu	oy in boy	Häuser, träumen
eu	oy in boy	Leute, heute

Consonants

LETTER	PRONUNCIATION	EXAMPLES
b	b in before	Bett, Gabe
	at the end of a word, p in trap	Grab, Trab
c	before a, o, and u, k in kilt	Cato
	before e, i, ä, ö, and y, ts in cats	Cäsar
d	d in date	Datum, Norden
	at the end of a word, t in but	Bad, Hund
f	f in fuss	Fliege, Fluss
g	g in garden	Garten

LETTER	PRONUNCIATION	EXAMPLES
	in foreign words, s in pleasure	Genie
h	*h in help*	hundert, Heimat, Geheimnis, behalten
	silent	Schuh, fröhlich
j	*y in your*	Jahr, jemand
k	*k in keep*	Katze, Kind, Keller, Kunde
l	*l in land*	Land, Wolf, Leben
m	*m in mother*	Meile, Maler
n	*n in never*	nur, Neffe
p	*p in park*	Preis, Papier
q	*q in quiet*	Quelle, Qualität
r	*r in risk, but rolled and more strongly pronounced*	Rede, reine
s	*before a vowel, z in zoo*	süß, Sahne
	at the end of a word or syllable, s in son	Maus, Eis
ß	*ss in less*	süß, Straße
t	*t in tea, even when followed by* h	Tanz, Tasse, Theater, Thron
v	*f in fair*	Vogel, Vater
	when used in a word with Latin roots, v in victory	Vase, Vulkan
w	*v in vain*	Wein, Waffe
x	*x in next*	Axt, Hexe
z	*ts in cats*	Zahn, Zauber

Special Sounds and Spelling Combinations

LETTER	PRONUNCIATION	EXAMPLES
ch	*hard ch similar to Scottish ch in loch, after* a, o, u, *and* au	machen, auch, Loch, Buch
	soft ch like the initial h in Hughes, after e, i, eu, äu, ä, ö, *and* ü	China, Kirche, mich, sicher
	ch in character	Christ, Chor, Charakter
	when followed by s, x *in next*	Fuchs, Wachs
ig	*at the end of a word, like* ch *in* ich	ewig, König
	when followed by lich *or* e, *like a hard* g *or* k	wenigstens, richtige, königlich
sch	*sh in shoe*	Kirsche, Schuh, amerikanisch
tsch	*ch in choose*	Rutsch, tschüss
sp	*sh + p*	Spanien, Spiegel
st	*sh + t*	stehen, Stahl
ng	*ng in sing*	bringen, anfangen
tz	*ts in cats*	Mütze, Blitz
er	*at the end of a word, a in father*	kleiner, schöner, Vater, Wetter

Grammar Summary

1. CASES

CASE: PRINCIPAL USE	EXAMPLE
Nominative: Subject	**Der Lehrer** ist hier.
	The teacher is here.
Accusative: Direct object	Sie sieht **den Lehrer.**
	She sees the teacher.
Dative: Indirect object	Er gibt **dem Lehrer** einen Apfel.
	He gives an apple to the teacher.
Genitive: Possession	Ich weiss den Namen **des Lehrers** nicht.
	I don't know the teacher's name.

2. DEFINITE ARTICLES (*THE*)

	NOM.	ACC.	DAT.	GEN.
m.	der	den	dem	des
f.	die	die	der	der
n.	das	das	dem	des
pl.	die	die	den	der

3. INDEFINITE ARTICLES (*A, AN*)

	NOM.	ACC.	DAT.	GEN.
m.	ein	einen	einem	eines
f.	eine	eine	einer	einer
n.	ein	ein	einem	eines

4. THE NEGATIVE KEIN (*NOT A, NOT ANY, NO*)

	NOM.	ACC.	DAT.	GEN.
m.	kein	keinen	keinem	keines
f.	keine	keine	keiner	keiner
n.	kein	kein	keinem	keines
pl.	keine	keine	keinen	keiner

5. PERSONAL PRONOUNS

NOM.	ACC.	DAT.	GEN.
ich	mich	mir	meiner
du	dich	dir	deiner
er	ihn	ihm	seiner
sie	sie	ihr	ihrer
es	es	ihm	seiner
wir	uns	uns	unser
ihr	euch	euch	eurer
Sie	Sie	Ihnen	Ihrer
sie	sie	ihnen	ihrer

6. DEMONSTRATIVES (*THIS*)

	NOM.	ACC.	DAT.	GEN.
m.	dieser	diesen	diesem	dieses
f.	diese	diese	dieser	dieser
n.	dieses	dieses	diesem	dieses
pl.	diese	diese	diesen	dieser

7. POSSESSIVE ADJECTIVES

M./N. SG. NOM.	F. SG. NOM.	PL. NOM.	
mein	meine	meine	*my*
dein	deine	deine	*your (infml.)*
sein	seine	seine	*his, its*
ihr	ihre	ihre	*her*
unser	unsere	unsere	*our*
euer	eure	eure	*your (infml. pl.)*
Ihr	Ihre	Ihre	*your (fml.)*
ihr	ihre	ihre	*their*

8. POSSESSIVE PRONOUNS

M. NOM.	F. NOM.	N. NOM.	
meiner	meine	meines	*mine*
deiner	deine	deines	*yours (infml.)*
seiner	seine	seines	*his*
ihrer	ihre	ihres	*hers*
unser	unsere	unseres	*ours*
euer	eure	eures	*yours (infml.)*
Ihrer	Ihre	Ihres	*yours (fml.)*
ihrer	ihre	ihres	*theirs*

9. RELATIVE PRONOUNS

	NOM. *(WHO)*	ACC. *(WHOM)*	DAT. *(TO WHOM)*	GEN. *(WHOSE)*
m.	der	den	dem	dessen
f.	die	die	der	deren
n.	das	das	dem	dessen
pl.	die	die	denen	deren

10. STRONG ADJECTIVE ENDINGS (WITHOUT ARTICLE OR PRONOUN)

	NOM.	ACC.	DAT.	GEN.
m.	roter Wein	roten Wein	rotem Wein	roten Weines
f.	rote Tinte	rote Tinte	roter Tinte	roter Tinte
n.	rotes Licht	rotes Licht	rotem Licht	roten Lichtes
pl.	rote Weine	rote Weine	roten Weinen	roter Weine

11. WEAK ADJECTIVE ENDINGS (WITH THE DEFINITE ARTICLE)

	NOM.	ACC.	DAT.	GEN.
m.	der rote Wein	den roten Wein	dem roten Wein	des roten Weines
f.	die rote Tinte	die rote Tinte	der roten Tinte	der roten Tinte
n.	das rote Licht	das rote Licht	dem roten Licht	des roten Lichtes
pl.	die roten Weine	die roten Weine	den roten Weinen	der roten Weine

12. MIXED ADJECTIVE ENDINGS (WITH EIN WORDS, KEIN WORDS, OR POSSESSIVES)

	NOM.	ACC.	DAT.	GEN.
m.	ein roter Wein	einen roten Wein	einem roten Wein	eines roten Weines
f.	seine rote Tinte	seine rote Tinte	seiner roten Tinte	seiner roten Tinte
n.	kein rotes Licht	kein rotes Licht	keinem roten Licht	keines roten Lichtes
pl.	meine roten Weine	meine roten Weine	meinen roten Weinen	meiner roten Weine

13. DEGREES OF ADJECTIVES

POSITIVE	COMPARATIVE	SUPERLATIVE
schlecht (*bad*)	schlechter (*worse*)	schlechtest (*worst*)
alt (*old*)	älter (*older*)	ältest (*oldest*)

14. IRREGULAR ADJECTIVES

POSITIVE	COMPARATIVE	SUPERLATIVE
gut	besser	der (die, das) beste, am besten
groß	größer	der (die, das) größte, am größten
hoch	höher	der (die, das) höchste, am höchsten
nahe	näher	der (die, das) nächste, am nächsten
viel	mehr	der (die, das) meiste, am meisten
gern	lieber	der (die, das) liebste, am liebsten

15. IRREGULAR ADVERBS

Common adverbs with irregular comparatives and superlatives

POSITIVE	COMPARATIVE	SUPERLATIVE
viel	mehr	am meisten
gern	lieber	am liebsten
bald	eher	am ehesten

16. ACCUSATIVE PREPOSITIONS

durch	*through, by*
für	*for*
gegen	*against, toward*
ohne	*without*
um	*round, about, at (time)*

17. DATIVE PREPOSITIONS

aus	*from, out of*
außer	*besides, except*
bei	*at, by, near, with*
mit	*with*
nach	*after, to (a place)*
seit	*since*
von	*of, from, by*
zu	*to, at*

18. "TWO-WAY" PREPOSITIONS

an	*at, to*
auf	*on, upon, in*
hinter	*behind*
in	*in, into, at*
neben	*beside, near*
über	*over, across*
unter	*under, among*
vor	*before, ago*
zwischen	*between*

19. GENITIVE PREPOSITIONS

statt, anstatt	*instead of*
trotz	*in spite of*
während	*during*
wegen	*because of*

sein
to be

ich	wir
du	ihr
er/sie/es	sie/Sie

Present		Imperative	
bin	sind		seien wir!
bist	seid	sei!	seid!
ist	sind		seien Sie!

Present Perfect		Simple Past	
bin gewesen	sind gewesen	war	waren
bist gewesen	seid gewesen	warst	wart
ist gewesen	sind gewesen	war	waren

Future		Past Perfect	
werde sein	werden sein	war gewesen	waren gewesen
wirst sein	werdet sein	warst gewesen	wart gewesen
wird sein	werden sein	war gewesen	waren gewesen

Subjunctive (II)		Past Subjunctive	
wäre	wären	wäre gewesen	wären gewesen
wärest	wäret	wärest gewesen	wäret gewesen
wäre	wären	wäre gewesen	wären gewesen

Conditional		Special Subjunctive (I)	
würde sein	würden sein	sei	seien
würdest sein	würdet sein	seist	seiet
würde sein	würden sein	sei	seien

haben
to have

ich	wir
du	ihr
er/sie/es	sie/Sie

Present		Imperative	
habe	haben		haben wir!
hast	habt	hab!	habt!
hat	haben		haben Sie!

Present Perfect		Simple Past	
habe gehabt	haben gehabt	hatte	hatten
hast gehabt	haben gehabt	hattest	hattet
hat gehabt	haben gehabt	hatte	hatten

Future		Past Perfect	
werde haben	werden haben	hatte gehabt	hatten gehabt
wirst haben	werdet haben	hattest gehabt	hattet gehabt
wird haben	werden haben	hatte gehabt	hatten gehabt

Subjunctive (II)		Past Subjunctive	
hätte	hätten	hätte gehabt	hätten gehabt
hättest	hättet	hättest gehabt	hättet gehabt
hätte	hätten	hätte gehabt	hätten gehabt

Conditional		Special Subjunctive (I)	
würde haben	würden haben	habe	haben
würdest haben	würdet haben	habest	habet
würde haben	würden haben	habe	haben

fragen
to ask

ich	wir
du	ihr
er/sie/es	sie/Sie

Present		Imperative	
frage	fragen		fragen wir!
fragst	fragt	frag(e)!	fragt!
fragt	fragen		fragen Sie!

Present Perfect		Simple Past	
habe gefragt	haben gefragt	fragte	fragten
hast gefragt	habt gefragt	fragtest	fragtet
hat gefragt	haben gefragt	fragte	fragten

Future		Past Perfect	
werde fragen	werden fragen	hatte gefragt	hatten gefragt
wirst fragen	werdet fragen	hattest gefragt	hattet gefragt
wird fragen	werden fragen	hatte gefragt	hatten gefragt

Subjunctive (II)		Past Subjunctive	
fragte	fragten	hätte gefragt	hätten gefragt
fragtest	fragtet	hättest gefragt	hättet gefragt
fragte	fragten	hätte gefragt	hätten gefragt

Conditional		Special Subjunctive (I)	
würde fragen	würden fragen	frage	fragen
würdest fragen	würdet fragen	fragest	fraget
würde fragen	würden fragen	frage	fragen

kommen
to come

ich	wir
du	ihr
er/sie/es	sie/Sie

Present		Imperative	
komme	kommen		kommen wir!
kommst	kommt	komm(e)!	kommt!
kommt	kommen		kommen Sie!

Present Perfect		Simple Past	
bin gekomnen	sind gekomnen	kam	kamen
bist gekomnen	seid gekomnen	kamst	kamt
ist gekomnen	sind gekomnen	kam	kamen

Future		Past Perfect	
werde kommen	werden kommen	war gekommen	waren gekommen
wirst kommen	werdet kommen	warst gekommen	wart gekommen
wird kommen	werden kommen	war gekommen	waren gekommen

Subjunctive (II)		Past Subjunctive	
käme	kämen	wäre gekommen	wären gekommen
kämest	kämet	wärest gekommen	wäret gekommen
käme	kämen	wäre gekommen	wären gekommen

Conditional		Special Subjunctive (I)	
würde kommen	würden kommen	komme	kommen
würdest kommen	würdet kommen	kommest	kommet
würde kommen	würden kommen	komme	kommen

20. COMMON IRREGULAR VERBS

INFINITIVE	PRESENT	SIMPLE PAST	PAST PARTICIPLE
backen (*to bake*)	backt	backte	gebacken
befehlen (*to order*)	befiehlt	befahl	befohlen
beginnen (*to begin*)	beginnt	begann	begonnen
beißen (*to bite*)	beißt	biss	gebissen
bewegen (*to move*)	bewegt	bewog	bewogen
biegen (*to bend, turn*)	biegt	bog	ist gebogen
bieten (*to offer*)	bietet	bot	geboten
binden (*to tie*)	bindet	band	gebunden
bitten (*to request*)	bittet	bat	gebeten
blasen (*to blow*)	bläst	blies	geblasen
bleiben (*to stay*)	bleibt	blieb	ist geblieben
brechen (*to break*)	bricht	brach	gebrochen
brennen (*to burn*)	brennt	brannte	gebrannt
bringen (*to bring*)	bringt	brachte	gebracht
denken (*to think*)	denkt	dachte	gedacht
dürfen (*may*)	darf	durfte	gedurft
empfehlen (*to recommend*)	empfiehlt	empfahl	empfohlen
essen (*to eat*)	isst	aß	gegessen
fahren (*to go, drive*)	fährt	fuhr	ist gefahren
fallen (*to fall*)	fällt	fiel	ist gefallen
fangen (*to catch*)	fängt	fing	gefangen

INFINITIVE	PRESENT	SIMPLE PAST	PAST PARTICIPLE
finden (*to find*)	findet	fand	gefunden
fliegen (*to fly*)	fliegt	flog	ist geflogen
fließen (*to flow*)	fließt	floss	geflossen
frieren (*to freeze*)	friert	fror	ist gefroren
geben (*to give*)	gibt	gab	gegeben
gehen (*to go, walk*)	geht	ging	ist gegangen
genießen (*to enjoy*)	genießt	genoss	genossen
geschehen (*to happen*)	geschieht	geschah	ist geschehen
gewinnen (*to win*)	gewinnt	gewann	gewonnen
gießen (*to pour*)	gießt	goss	gegossen
gleichen (*to resemble*)	gleicht	glich	geglichen
gleiten (*to glide*)	gleitet	glitt	ist geglitten
graben (*to dig*)	gräbt	grub	gegraben
greifen (*to grasp*)	greift	griff	gegriffen
haben (*to have*)	hat	hatte	gehabt
halten (*to hold*)	hält	hielt	gehalten
hängen (*to be hanging*)	hängt	hing	gehangen
heißen (*to be called*)	heißt	hieß	gehießen
helfen (*to help*)	hilft	half	geholfen
kennen (*to know*)	kennt	kannte	gekannt
kommen (*to come*)	kommt	kam	ist gekommen
können (*can*)	kann	konnte	gekonnt
lassen (*to let*)	lässt	ließ	gelassen

INFINITIVE	PRESENT	SIMPLE PAST	PAST PARTICIPLE
laufen (to run)	läuft	lief	ist gelaufen
leihen (to lend)	leiht	lieh	geliehen
lesen (to read)	liest	las	gelesen
liegen (to lie, be lying)	liegt	lag	gelegen
lügen (to lie, tell lies)	lügt	log	gelogen
mögen (to like)	mag	mochte	gemocht
müssen (must)	muss	musste	gemusst
nehmen (to take)	nimmt	nahm	genommen
nennen (to name)	nennt	nannte	genannt
raten (to advise)	rät	riet	geraten
reißen (to rip)	reißt	riss	gerissen
reiten (to ride)	reitet	ritt	ist geritten
rennen (to run)	rennt	rannte	ist gerannt
riechen (to smell)	riecht	roch	gerochen
rufen (to call, shout)	ruft	rief	gerufen
scheinen (to seem, shine)	scheint	schien	geschienen
schießen (to shoot)	schießt	schoss	geschossen
schlafen (to sleep)	schläft	schlief	geschlafen
schlagen (to hit, beat)	schlägt	schlug	geschlagen
schließen (to shut)	schließt	schloss	geschlossen
schneiden (to cut)	schneidet	schnitt	geschnitten
schreiben (to write)	schreibt	schrieb	geschrieben
schreien (to yell)	schreit	schrie	geschrieen

INFINITIVE	PRESENT	SIMPLE PAST	PAST PARTICIPLE
schwimmen (to swim)	schwimmt	schwamm	ist geschwommen
sehen (to see)	sieht	sah	gesehen
sein (to be)	ist	war	ist gewesen
senden (to send)	sendet	sandte	gesandt
singen (to sing)	singt	sang	gesungen
sinken (to sink)	sinkt	sank	ist gesunken
sitzen (to sit, be sitting)	sitzt	saß	gesessen
sollen (should)	soll	sollte	gesollt
sprechen (to speak)	spricht	sprach	gesprochen
springen (to jump)	springt	sprang	ist gesprungen
stehen (to stand)	steht	stand	gestanden
stehlen (to steal)	stiehlt	stahl	gestohlen
steigen (to rise, mount)	steigt	stieg	ist gestiegen
sterben (to die)	stirbt	starb	ist gestorben
stinken (to stink)	stinkt	stank	gestunken
stoßen (to push, kick)	stößt	stieß	gestoßen
tragen (to wear, carry)	trägt	trug	getragen
treffen (to meet)	trifft	traf	getroffen
treiben (to drive, force)	treibt	trieb	getrieben
trinken (to drink)	trinkt	trank	getrunken
tun (to do)	tut	tat	getan

INFINITIVE	PRESENT	SIMPLE PAST	PAST PARTICIPLE
verbergen (to hide, conceal)	verbirgt	verbarg	verborgen
verderben (to ruin, spoil)	verdirbt	verdarb	verdorben
vergessen (to forget)	vergisst	vergaß	vergessen
verlassen (to leave, quit someone/thing)	verlässt	verließ	verlassen
verlieren (to lose)	verliert	verlor	verloren
vermeiden (to avoid)	vermeidet	vermied	vermieden
verschwinden (to disappear)	verschwindet	verschwand	ist verschwunden
verzeihen (to excuse, to forgive)	verzeiht	verzieh	verziehen
wachsen (to grow, get bigger)	wächst	wuchs	ist gewachsen
waschen (to wash)	wäscht	wusch	gewaschen
wenden (to turn)	wendet	wandte	gewandt
werden (to get, become)	wird	wurde	ist geworden
werfen (to throw)	wirft	warf	geworfen
wiegen (to weigh)	wiegt	wog	gewogen
wissen (to know)	weiß	wusste	gewusst
wollen (to want)	will	wollte	gewollt
ziehen (to pull)	zieht	zog	gezogen
zwingen (to force, compel)	zwingt	zwang	gezwungen

Glossary

Note that the following abbreviations will be used in this glossary: (m.) = masculine, (f.) = feminine, (sg.) = singular, (pl.) = plural, (fml.) = formal/polite, (infml.) = informal/familiar. If a word has two grammatical genders, (m./f.) or (f./m.) is used.

German-English

A

abbiegen *to turn*
  links abbiegen *to turn left*
  rechts abbiegen *to turn right*
Abend (m.) (Abende) *evening*
  am Abend *in the evening*
  gestern Abend *last night*
  Guten Abend. *Good evening.*
  heute Abend *tonight, this evening*
Abendessen (n.) (Abendessen) *dinner*
abends *in the evening*
aber *but*
  Aber gern! *With pleasure!*
  Das klingt aber gut. *That sounds good.*
  schon, aber … *yes, but …*
abfahren *to leave*
Abitur (n.) (Abiture) *high school exam*
  das Abitur machen *to take the high school exam*
abnehmen *to remove, to decrease, to lose weight*
absagen *to cancel*
abschicken *to send off, to mail*
Absicht (f.) (Absichten) *intention*
ach *oh*
  Ach so. *I see.*
acht *eight*
achtundzwanzig *twenty-eight*
achtzehn *eighteen*
achtzig *eighty*
Adresse (f.) (Adressen) *address*
Afrika (n.) *Africa*
Äh … *Uh …*
Aha! *I see.*
akademisch *academic*

akademische Viertel (n.) *academic quarter*
alle *all*
allergisch *allergic*
  gegen Katzen allergisch sein *to be allergic to cats*
alles *everything*
  Alles Gute zum Geburtstag! *Happy birthday!*
  Alles zusammen? *One check? (at a restaurant)*
  Das ist alles. *That's everything.*
  Ist alles in Ordnung? *Is everything okay?*
als *as, than, when*
also *so, therefore*
  Na also! *See!/There you have it!*
alt *old*
  Ich bin zwanzig Jahre alt. *I am twenty years old.*
  Wie alt sind Sie? *How old are you?*
Alter (n.) (Alter) *age*
  im Alter von *at the age of*
am (an + dem) *at/to/on the, at the side of the*
  am Abend *in the evening*
  am größten *biggest* (adverb)
  am höchsten *highest* (adverb)
  am meisten *most* (adverb)
  am Montag *on Monday*
  am Morgen *in the morning*
  am Nachmittag *in the afternoon*
  am Stück *in one piece*
Amateur-Filmemacher/-in (m./f.) (Amateur-Filmemacher/-innen) *amateur filmmaker*
Amerika (n.) *America*
Amerikaner/-in (m./f.) (Amerikaner/-innen) *American*
Ampel (f.) (Ampeln) *traffic light*
  an der Ampel *at the traffic light*
an *at, at the side of, to, on*
andere *other, another*
  die anderen *the others*

ändern *to change, to alter*
anders *differently*
anfangen *to begin*
Angebot (n.) (Angebote) *offer*
  im Angebot *on sale*
Angestellte (m./f.) (Angestellten) *employee*
ankommen *to arrive*
anlegen *to put, to lay on*
  einen Verband anlegen *to put on a bandage*
Annonce (f.) (Annoncen) *classified ad*
anprobieren *to try on*
Anrufbeantworter (m.)
  (Anrufbeantworter) *answering machine*
anrufen *to call (on the telephone)*
ans (an + das) *at/to/on the, at the side of the*
ansagen *to announce*
anstatt *instead of*
anstecken *to infect*
  sich anstecken *to catch something (somebody else's illness)*
ansteckend *contagious*
Antwort (f.) (Antworten) *answer*
  Wie lautet die richtige Antwort? *What's the right answer?*
antworten *to answer*
Anwalt/Anwältin (m./f.) (Anwälte/ Anwältinnen) *lawyer*
anziehen *to dress, to wear, to put on*
Anzug (m.) (Anzüge) *suit*
Apfel (m.) (Äpfel) *apple*
Apfelsaft (m.) (Apfelsäfte) *apple juice*
Apotheke (f.) (Apotheken) *pharmacy*
Apparat (m.) (Apparate) *apparatus*
  am Apparat *on the phone, speaking*
  Honberg am Apparat. *Honberg speaking.*
  Wer ist am Apparat? *Who is speaking?*
Appetit (m.) (no pl.) *appetite*
  Guten Appetit! *Enjoy your meal!*
April (m.) (Aprile) *April*
Arbeit (f.) (Arbeiten) *work*
arbeiten *to work*
  freiberuflich arbeiten *to freelance*
Arbeiter/-in (m./f.) (Arbeiter/-innen) *worker*
Arbeitnehmer/-in (m./f.) (Arbeitnehmer/-innen) *employee*
Arbeitskollege/Arbeitskollegin (m./f.) (Arbeitskollegen/ Arbeitskolleginnen) *colleague*

arbeitslos *unemployed*
Arbeitslose (m./f.) (Arbeitslosen) *unemployed (people)*
Arbeitslosenquote (f.) (Arbeitslosenquoten) *unemployment rate*
Arbeitsplatz (m.) (Arbeitsplätze) *workplace*
Arbeitsstelle (f.) (Arbeitsstellen) *workplace, job*
Arbeitszeit (f.) (Arbeitszeiten) *work hours, working hours*
  gleitende Arbeitszeit *flexible working hours*
Arbeitszimmer (n.) (Arbeitszimmer) *office*
Architekt/-in (m./f.) (Architekten/ Architektinnen) *architect*
ärgern *to annoy*
  sich ärgern *to be annoyed*
arm *poor*
Arm (m.) (Arme) *arm*
Artikel (m.) (Artikel) *article*
Arzt/Ärztin (m./f.) (Ärzte/Ärztinnen) *doctor*
Aspirin (n.) (no pl.) *aspirin*
Assistent/-in (m./f.) (Assistenten/ Assistentinnen) *assistant*
Au ja. *Oh yes.*
auch *too, also, as well, even*
auf *on, on top of, onto*
  Auf welchen Namen? *Under which name? (reservation)*
  Auf Wiederhören. *Until next time. (on the phone)*
  Auf Wiedersehen. *Goodbye.*
  Auf Wiedersehen bis dann. *Good-bye until then.*
  warten auf *to wait for*
Aufgabe (f.) (Aufgaben) *job, task*
aufgeregt *excited; excitedly*
auflegen *to hang up*
  den Hörer auflegen *to hang up the receiver*
aufmachen *to open*
aufpassen *to watch, to keep an eye on*
  Pass auf! *Pay attention!*
  Pass gut auf dich auf! *Take good care of yourself!/Be careful!*
aufrecht *upright*
aufrunden *to round up (the amount)*
aufs (auf + das) *on/onto the, on top of the*
aufstehen *to get up*
  früh aufstehen *to get up early*

spät aufstehen *to get up late*
Auge (n.) (Augen) *eye*
August (m.) (Auguste) *August*
aus *from, out of*
Ausbildung (f.) (Ausbildungen) *professional training, apprenticeship, education*
  eine Ausbildung machen *to apprentice*
Ausbildungsstelle (f.) (Ausbildungsstellen) *apprenticeship*
Ausdruck (m.) (Ausdrücke) *expression*
Ausfahrt (f.) (Ausfahrten) *exit, departure*
ausgebucht *booked out*
ausgehen *to go out*
ausgezeichnet *excellent*
auskennen *to know one's way around*
  sich auskennen *to know one's way around*
aussehen *to look, to appear*
  Sie sehen schlecht aus. *You look bad/sick.*
außer *except for*
außerdem *in addition*
auswaschen *to wash out*
  Wunde (f.) auswaschen *to clean the wound*
Auszubildende (m./f.)
  (Auszubildenden) *apprentice*
Auto (n.) (Autos) *car*
  das Auto nehmen *to take the car*
  mit dem Auto *by car*
Autobahn (f.) (Autobahnen) *highway (interstate)*
Azubi (m./f.) (Azubis) *apprentice*

B

backen *to bake*
Bäcker/-in (m./f.) (Bäcker/Bäckerinnen) *baker*
Bäckerei (f.) (Bäckereien) *bakery*
Bad (n.) (Bäder) *bathroom*
Badezimmer (n.) (Badezimmer) *bathroom*
Bahnhof (m.) (Bahnhöfe) *train station*
bald *soon*
  Bis bald. *See you soon.*
Balkon (m.) (Balkone) *balcony*
Ball (m.) (Bälle) *ball*
Ballettunterricht (m.) (no pl.) *ballet classes*
Banane (f.) (Bananen) *banana*
Bank (f.) (Banken) *bank (financial institution)*
Bank (f.) (Bänke) *bench*
Basketball (m.) (no pl.) *basketball (game)*
  Basketball spielen *to play basketball*

Bauch (m.) (Bäuche) *belly, stomach*
Bauchschmerzen (pl.) *stomachache*
Bauchweh (n.) (no pl.) *stomachache*
beantworten *to reply to*
Bedienung (f.) (no pl.) *waitress*
beeilen *to hurry, to hasten*
  sich beeilen *to hurry*
beeindruckend *impressive*
befördern *to promote*
Beförderung (f.) (Beförderungen) *promotion*
beginnen *to begin*
behandeln *to treat*
bei *with, by, at*
  bei gutem Wetter *in good weather*
  bei Regenwetter *in rainy weather*
  bei schlechtem Wetter *in bad weather*
  bei Schneewetter *in snowy weather*
beide *both*
beim (bei + dem) *at/by the*
Bein (n.) (Beine) *leg*
beitreten *to join*
  einem Verein beitreten *to join a club*
bekommen *to get, to receive*
  ein Kind bekommen *to have a baby*
  eine Erkältung bekommen *to catch a cold*
belegen *to cover*
  belegte Brote (pl.) *open-faced sandwiches*
beliebt *popular*
benutzen *to use*
Berg (m.) (Berge) *mountain*
  Berg steigen *to go mountain climbing*
Beruf (m.) (Berufe) *occupation, profession, job*
  von Beruf *by profession*
beruflich *job-oriented, professionally*
  Sie sind beruflich hier. *You are here on business.*
Berufsaussicht (f.) (Berufsaussichten) *professional outlook*
Berufschance (f.) (Berufsschancen) *job opportunity, chance*
Berufserfahrung (f.) (Berufserfahrungen) *professional experience*
Berufsschule (f.) (Berufsschulen) *vocational school*
Beschäftigung (f.)
  (Beschäftigungen) *employment*
beschreiben *to describe*
besetzt *busy (phone line), being used*

Besprechung (f.) (Besprechungen) *meeting*
besser *better*
beste *best* (adjective)
  am besten *best* (adverb)
Besteck (n.) (Bestecke) *silverware*
bestellen *to order*
  einen Tisch bestellen *to reserve a table, to make reservations*
bestimmen *to decide, to determine*
bestimmt *certain, definite; certainly, definitely*
  Bestimmt! *Sure!*
Besuch (m.) (Besuche) *visit*
  zu Besuch sein *to be on a visit*
besuchen *to visit*
Bett (n.) (Betten) *bed*
  ins Bett gehen *to go to bed*
Beurteilung (f.) (Beurteilungen) *evaluation*
beweisen *to prove*
bewerben *to apply*
  sich auf eine Stelle bewerben *to apply for a job, to apply for a position*
bewundern *to admire*
bezahlen *to pay*
Bier (n.) (Biere) *beer*
Bild (n.) (Bilder) *photo, picture*
billig *cheap*
Biologie (f.) (no pl.) *biology*
bis *until*
  Bis bald. *See you soon.*
  Bis zum nächsten Mal. *Till next time.*
  von … bis *from … to*
bitte *please, you're welcome*
  Bitte sehr. *Here you go.*
  Wie bitte? *Excuse me/I'm sorry?*
blau *blue*
bleiben *to stay, to remain*
  fit bleiben *to stay in shape*
Blitz (m.) (Blitze) *lightning*
Blume (f.) (Blumen) *flower*
  Vielen Dank für die Blumen! *Thanks for the compliment! (lit., Thanks for the flowers. [often used ironically])*
Bluse (f.) (Blusen) *blouse*
böse *angry, bad*
Boss (m.) (Bosse) *boss*
Boutique (f.) (Boutiquen) *boutique*
brauchen *to need*
braun *brown*

Bravo! *Well done!*
brechen *to break*
Brief (m.) (Briefe) *letter*
Briefmarke (f.) (Briefmarken) *stamp*
bringen *to bring*
Brot (n.) (Brote) *bread*
  belegte Brote (pl.) *open-faced sandwiches*
  ein Laib Brot *a loaf of bread*
Brötchen (n.) (Brötchen) *breakfast roll*
Bruder (m.) (Brüder) *brother*
Brüderchen (n.) (Brüderchen) *little brother*
Brunch (m.) (Brunches/Brunche) *brunch*
Buch (n.) (Bücher) *book*
Buchhalter/-in (m./f.) (Buchhalter/-innen) *accountant*
Buchseite (f.) (Buchseiten) *book page*
Büro (n.) (Büros) *office*
  im Büro *in an office, at the office*
  ins Büro *to the office*
bummeln *to stroll*
  bummeln gehen *to go (window-)shopping*
Bus (m.) (Busse) *bus*
  den Bus nehmen *to take the bus*
  mit dem Bus *by bus*
Bushaltestelle (f.) (Bushaltestellen) *bus stop*
Butter (f.) (no pl.) *butter*

C

Champagner (m.) (no pl.) *champagne*
Chance (f.) (Chancen) *chance*
Chef/-in (m./f.) (Chefs/Chefinnen) *boss*
Computer (m.) (Computer) *computer*
Computermaus (f.) (Computermäuse) *computer mouse*
Couch (f.) (Couches) *couch*
Cousin/Cousine (m./f.) (Cousins/Cousinen) *cousin*

D

da *there, then*
dabei *at the same time, with it, near, near by*
dadurch *thereby, through it*
dafür *for it, for that, instead*
dagegen *against it, on the other hand*
dahin *to there, to that place*
Dame (f.) (Damen) *lady*
Damenpullover (m.) (Damenpullover) *woman's sweater*

damit *with it*

danach *afterwards*

Dank (m.) (no pl.) *thanks* (pl.)

  Vielen Dank. *Many thanks.*

  Vielen Dank für die Blumen! *Thanks for the compliment!* (lit., *Thanks for the flowers. [often used ironically]*)

danken *to thank*

  Danke. *Thank you.*

  Danke schön. *Thank you.*

dann *then*

  Na dann … *Well, in that case …*

daran (dran) *on it, alongside it, by it*

darauf *on that, on there, on it*

  Das kommt darauf an. *That depends.*

darin (drin) *in it*

darüber *over it, about it, concerning that*

darum *about it, about that; therefore*

das *the* (n.) (nominative); *the* (n.) (accusative); *that, those* (demonstrative pronoun); *who* (n.), *whom* (n.) (relative pronoun)

  Das ist … *This is …*

  Das sind … *Those are …*

dass *that*

davor *in front of it, before that*

dazu *to it, for it*

dazwischen *in between*

dein *your* (sg. infml.)

dem *the* (m./n.) (dative); *to whom* (m./n.) (relative pronoun)

den *the* (m.) (accusative); *the* (pl.) (dative); *whom* (m.) (relative pronoun)

denen *to whom* (pl.) (relative pronoun)

denken *to think*

denn *because, since, then*

  Was ist denn los? *What's the matter?*

der *the* (m.) (nominative); *the* (f.) (dative); *of the* (f./pl.) (genitive); *who* (m.), *to whom* (f.) (relative pronoun)

deren *whose* (f./pl.) (relative pronoun)

des *of the* (m./n.) (genitive)

deshalb *therefore*

dessen *whose* (m./n.) (relative pronoun)

Deutsch (n.) (no pl.) *German* (language)

  auf Deutsch *in German*

Deutscher/Deutsche (m./f.) (Deutschen) *German* (person)

Deutschland (n.) (no pl.) *Germany*

Dezember (m.) (Dezember) *December*

dich *you* (sg. infml.) (accusative); *yourself* (sg. infml.)

dick *fat*

  dick machen *to be fattening*

die *the* (f./pl.) (nominative); *the* (f./pl.) (accusative); *who* (f./pl.), *whom* (f./pl.) (relative pronoun)

Diele (f.) (Dielen) *foyer*

Dienstag (m.) (Dienstage) *Tuesday*

dieser *this*

dir *you, to you* (sg. infml.) (dative)

direkt *straight, directly*

doch *"flavoring" word*

  Ja, doch! *Yes, absolutely!*

  Kommst du nicht mit? -Doch! *Aren't you coming along? -Yes, I am!*

  Nimm doch den Fisch. *Have the fish, why don't you?*

Doktor (m.) (Doktoren) *Ph.D.*

  einen Doktor machen *to study for a Ph.D.*

Donner (m.) (no pl.) *thunder*

Donnerstag (m.) (Donnerstage) *Thursday*

  jeden Donnerstag *every Thursday*

Dorf (n.) (Dörfer) *village*

dort *there*

dran (daran) *on it, alongside it, by it*

draußen *outside*

drei *three*

dreimal *three times*

dreißig *thirty*

  Es ist vier Uhr dreißig. *It is four thirty.*

dreiundzwanzig *twenty-three*

dreizehn *thirteen*

drin (darin) *in it*

dringend *urgent; urgently*

Drogerie (f.) (Drogerien) *drugstore*

du *you* (sg. infml.) (nominative)

dürfen *to be allowed to*

  Darf's sonst noch etwas sein? *Anything else?* (at a store)

  Was darf's (denn) sein? *What can I get you?*

durch *through, by*

E

eben *just, simply*

Ecke (f.) (Ecken) *corner*

  an der Ecke *at the corner*

  um die Ecke *around the corner*

egal *the same*
  Es ist mir egal. *I don't care./It makes no difference to me.*
Ehefrau (f.) **(Ehefrauen)** *wife*
Ehemann (m.) **(Ehemänner)** *husband*
ehrlich *honest*
eilig *urgent*
ein *a/an*
  ein bisschen *a little bit*
Einbahnstraße (f.) **(Einbahnstraßen)** *one-way street*
einfach *simple; simply, just*
Einfahrt (f.) **(Einfahrten)** *entrance*
einkaufen *to shop*
  einkaufen gehen *to go (grocery) shopping*
Einkaufsliste (f.) **(Einkaufslisten)** *shopping list*
einladen *to invite*
Einladung (f.) **(Einladungen)** *invitation*
einmal *once*
  noch einmal *once more*
eins *one*
einschlafen *to fall asleep*
einstellen *to hire*
einunddreißig *thirty-one*
einundzwanzig *twenty-one*
Eis (n.) (no pl.) *ice cream*
Elektriker/-in (m./f.) **(Elektriker/-innen)** *electrician*
elf *eleven*
Ellbogen (m.) **(Ellbogen)** *elbow*
Eltern (pl.) *parents*
E-Mail (f.) **(E-Mails)** *e-mail*
empfehlen *to recommend*
Ende (n.) **(Enden)** *end*
enden *to end*
endlich *finally*
  Na endlich! *Finally!/At last!*
eng *tight*
Enkel/-in (m./f.) **(Enkel/-innen)** *grandson/granddaughter*
Enkelkind (n.) **(Enkelkinder)** *grandchild*
entlassen *to let go, to fire*
Entlassung (f.) **(Entlassungen)** *layoff*
entschuldigen *to excuse*
  Entschuldige. *Excuse me.*
  sich entschuldigen *to apologize*
Entschuldigung (f.) **(Entschuldigungen)** *excuse*

Entschuldigung. *Excuse me./Sorry./Forgive me.*
entweder *either*
  entweder … oder … *either … or …*
er *he*
Erbsensuppe (f.) **(Erbsensuppen)** *pea soup*
Erfahrung (f.) **(Erfahrungen)** *experience*
erfolgreich *successful*
erhalten *to receive, to maintain*
erhöhen *to raise, to increase*
  erhöhte Temperatur (f.) *elevated temperature*
Erhöhung (f.) **(Erhöhungen)** *raise*
erkälten (reflexive) *to catch a cold*
  sich erkälten *to catch a cold*
Erkältung (f.) **(Erkältungen)** *cold*
  eine Erkältung bekommen *to catch a cold*
erklären *to explain*
eröffnen *to open*
  neu eröffnen *to reopen*
erreichen *to reach*
erst *only, not until, at first*
  erst mal *first*
  zum ersten Mal *for the first time*
erstaunlich *amazing*
es *it* (nominative); *it* (accusative)
essen *to eat*
  zu Mittag essen *to have lunch*
Essen (n.) **(Essen)** *meal*
Esstisch (m.) **(Esstische)** *dining table*
Esszimmer (n.) **(Esszimmer)** *dining room*
etwa *about, approximately, by chance*
etwas *something, some, somewhat*
  Darf's sonst noch etwas sein? *Anything else?* (at a store)
  noch etwas *some more*
  so etwas *something like that*
euch *you* (pl. infml.) (accusative); *you, to you* (pl. infml.) (dative); *yourselves* (pl. infml.)
euer *your* (pl. infml.)
Euro (m.) **(Euros)** *euro*

F

Fach (n.) **(Fächer)** *subject*
  Lieblingsfach (n.) *favorite subject*
fahren *to drive, to go, to leave, to take*
  die Tochter in die Schule fahren *to take the daughter to school*
  Fahrrad fahren *to ride a bicycle*

fahren mit … *to go by means of …*
  Rad fahren *to bicycle*
  Ski fahren *to go skiing*
Fahrgast (n.) (**Fahrgäste**) *passenger*
Fahrgeld (n.) (no pl.) *fare*
Fahrkarte (f.) (**Fahrkarten**) *ticket*
Fahrrad (n.) (**Fahrräder**) *bicycle*
  Fahrrad fahren *to ride a bicycle*
Fahrt (f.) (**Fahrten**) *trip*
  Gute Fahrt! *Drive safely!*
falsch *wrong*
Familie (f.) (**Familien**) *family*
  eine Familie gründen *to start a family*
  Familienfotos (pl.) *family photographs*
Familienleben (n.) (no pl.) *family life*
fantastisch *fantastic*
Farbe (f.) (**Farben**) *color*
fast *almost*
Februar (m.) (**Februare**) *February*
fehlen *to be missing, to be lacking*
feiern *to celebrate*
Fenster (n.) (**Fenster**) *window*
Ferien (pl.) *vacation*
Ferienwohnung (f.)
  (**Ferienwohnungen**) *vacation apartment*
Fernsehen (n.) (no pl.) *television*
  im Fernsehen *on TV*
Fernseher (m.) (**Fernseher**) *television (set)*
fertig *finished*
Fieber (n.) (**Fieber**) *fever*
  Fieber messen *to take someone's temperature*
  hohes Fieber *high fever*
Film (m.) (**Filme**) *movie*
finden *to find*
  Das finde ich auch. *I think so, too.*
Finger (m.) (**Finger**) *finger*
Firma (f.) (**Firmen**) *company*
Fisch (m.) (**Fische**) *fish*
fit *fit*
  fit bleiben *to stay in shape*
Fitnessclub (m.) (**Fitnessclubs**) *fitness club*
Flasche (f.) (**Flaschen**) *bottle*
  eine Flasche Mineralwasser *a bottle of mineral water*
  eine Flasche Wein *a bottle of wine*
Fleisch (n.) (no pl.) *meat*
Flughafen (m.) (**Flughäfen**) *airport*
folgen *to follow*

Foto (n.) (**Fotos**) *photograph*
  Familienfotos (pl.) *family photographs*
fotografieren *to photograph*
Frage (n.) (**Fragen**) *question, issue*
fragen *to ask, to wonder*
Fragestunde (f.) (**Fragestunden**) *question time*
Frankreich (n.) (no pl.) *France*
Franzose (m.) (**Franzosen**) *Frenchman*
Frau (f.) (**Frauen**) *woman, wife, Mrs., Ms.*
  meine Frau *my wife*
  Willst du meine Frau werden? *Will you marry me? (lit., Will you be my wife?)*
Fräulein (n.) (**Fräulein**) *Miss*
frei *vacant*
freiberuflich *freelance (adjective/adverb)*
  freiberuflich arbeiten *to freelance*
  freiberuflich tätig sein *to freelance*
Freitag (m.) (**Freitage**) *Friday*
Freizeit (f.) (no pl.) *leisure time*
Freizeitbeschäftigung (f.) (**Freizeitbeschäftigungen**) *leisure time activity*
fremd *foreign, strange*
freuen (reflexive) *to be glad*
  sich auf … freuen *to look forward to …*
Freund (m.) (**Freunde**) *friend (male), boyfriend*
Freundin (f.) (**Freundinnen**) *friend (female), girlfriend*
freundlich *kind, friendly*
frisch *fresh*
früh *early*
  früh aufstehen *to get up early*
früher *earlier*
Frühling (m.) (**Frühlinge**) *spring*
Frühstück (n.) (**Frühstücke**) *breakfast*
fühlen *to feel*
  sich fühlen *to feel*
  sich gesund fühlen *to feel healthy*
  sich krank fühlen *to feel sick*
  sich wohl fühlen *to feel well*
fünf *five*
fünfundzwanzig *twenty-five*
fünfzehn *fifteen*
  Es ist sechs Uhr fünfzehn. *It is 6:15.*
fünfzig *fifty*
  aus den Fünfzigern *from the fifties ('50s)*
für *for*
fürs (für + das) *for the*
Fuß (m.) (**Füße**) *foot*

zu Fuß gehen *to go by foot, to walk*
Fußball (m.) (no pl.) *soccer (game), soccer ball*
   Fußball spielen *to play soccer*
Fußgänger (m.) (Fußgänger) *pedestrian*
Fußgängerüberweg (m.)
   (Fußgängerüberwege) *crosswalk*
   Gehen Sie über den
      Fußgängerüberweg. *Take the crosswalk.*
Fußgängerzone (f.)
   (Fußgängerzonen) *pedestrian zone*

G

Gabel (f.) (Gabeln) *fork*
ganz *entire, whole, complete; completely*
   den ganzen Tag *all day*
   ganz neu *brand-new*
gar *fully, quite*
   gar nicht *not at all*
Garten (m.) (Gärten) *garden*
   im Garten arbeiten *to work in the garden*
Gartenarbeit (f.) (Gartenarbeiten) *garden work*
Gast (m.) (Gäste) *guest*
Gatte (m.) (Gatten) *husband*
geben *to give*
   eine Party geben *have a party*
   es gibt *there is/are*
   Was gibt's Neues? *What's new?*
Geburtstag (m.) (Geburtstage) *birthday*
   Alles Gute zum Geburtstag! *Happy birthday!*
gefährlich *dangerous*
gefallen *to please, to be to one's liking*
   Das gefällt mir. *I like it.*
   Das gefällt mir nicht. *I don't like it.*
gegen *against, toward*
   gegen Katzen allergisch sein *to be allergic to cats*
Gegenstand (m.) (Gegenstände) *thing*
gegenüber *across from*
Gehalt (n.) (Gehälter) *salary*
Gehaltserhöhung (f.)
   (Gehaltserhöhungen) *raise (in salary)*
gehen *to go*
   bummeln gehen *to go (window-)shopping*
   einkaufen gehen *to go (grocery) shopping*
   in Rente gehen *to retire*
   ins Bett gehen *to go to bed*
   schwimmen gehen *to go swimming*

spazieren gehen *to go for a walk*
   Wie geht es Ihnen? *How are you?* (fml.)
   Wie geht's? *How are you?* (infml.)
gehören *to belong to*
Gehweg (m.) (Gehwege) *sidewalk*
gelb *yellow*
Geld (n.) (Gelder) *money*
Geldbeutel (m.) (Geldbeutel) *wallet*
Gelee (m.) (Gelees) *jam, jelly*
Gemüse (n.) (no pl.) *vegetables*
Gemüseladen (m.) (Gemüseläden) *grocery store*
genehmigen *to approve*
   Genehmigt! *Accepted!, Approved!*
genug *enough*
gerade *at the moment, just*
geradeaus *straight (ahead)*
   geradeaus gehen *to continue straight ahead*
gern(e) *gladly, willingly, happily (expresses likes and preferences)*
   Aber gern! *With pleasure!*
   Gern geschehen! *You're welcome!/My pleasure!*
   gern haben *to like*
   gern Ski fahren *to enjoy skiing*
   Ich hätte gern … *I would like to have …*
   Ja, gern. *Yes, please.*
Gesamtschule (f.)
   (Gesamtschulen) *comprehensive school*
Geschäft (n.) (Geschäfte) *store*
Geschäftsmann (m.)
   (Geschäftsmänner) *businessman*
Geschäftsreise (f.) (Geschäftsreisen) *business trip*
geschehen *to happen*
   Gern geschehen! *You're welcome!/My pleasure!*
Geschenk (n.) (Geschenke) *gift*
   als Geschenk für … *as a gift for …*
geschieden *divorced*
   geschieden werden *to get divorced*
Geschwister (pl.) *siblings*
gestern *yesterday*
   gestern Abend *last night*
gestreift *striped*
gesund *healthy*
   sich gesund fühlen *to feel healthy*
Getränk (n.) (Getränke) *drink, beverage*
gewinnen *to win*

Gewürz (n.)(Gewürze) *spice*
Gitarre (f.)(Gitarren) *guitar*
  Gitarre spielen *to play the guitar*
Glas (n.)(Gläser) *glass*
  ein Glas Wein *a glass of wine*
glauben *to believe, to think*
  Ich glaube nicht. *I don't think so.*
gleich *same; right, just, immediately*
  gleich hier *right here*
gleitend *gliding, sliding*
  gleitende Arbeitszeit (f.) *flexible working
    hours*
Glück (n.)(no pl.) *luck*
  Viel Glück! *Good luck!*
Glückwunsch (m.)
  (Glückwünsche) *congratulation, wish*
  Herzlichen Glückwunsch! *Congratulations!*
Golf (m.) *golf*
  Golf spielen *to play golf*
Golfplatz (m.)(Golfplätze) *golf course*
Grad (m.)(Grade) *degree*
Gramm (n.)(Gramme; no pl. after
  numbers) *gram*
Gras (n.)(Gräser) *grass*
grau *gray*
Grippe (f.)(Grippen) *flu*
  Die Grippe geht um. *The flu is going around.*
  Grippe haben *to have the flu*
groß *big*
  am größten *biggest* (adverb)
  größer *bigger*
  größte *biggest* (adjective)
Größe (f.)(Größen) *size*
  welche Größe *what size*
Großeltern (pl.) *grandparents*
Großmutter (f.)(Großmütter) *grandmother*
Großvater (m.)(Großväter) *grandfather*
grün *green*
gründen *to found*
  eine Familie gründen *to start a family*
Grüß Gott. *Hello.*
Grundschule (f.)(Grundschulen) *elementary
  school (first grade through fourth grade)*
gucken *to look*
  Guck mal! *Look!*
Gürtel (m.)(Gürtel) *belt*
Gurke (f.)(Gurken) *cucumber*
gut *good, well*

gut kochen *to cook well*
gut passen *to fit well*
gut passen zu *to go well with*
gut stehen *to look good on (somebody)*
Alles Gute zum Geburtstag! *Happy birthday!*
Guten Abend. *Good evening.*
Guten Appetit! *Enjoy your meal!*
Guten Morgen. *Good morning.*
Guten Tag. *Hello./Good day.*
Gute Fahrt! *Drive safely!*
Mach's gut. *Take care.*
Pass gut auf dich auf! *Take good care of
  yourself!/Be careful!*
Schon gut. *It's okay.*
Sehr gut. *Very well.*
Wie kann ich das wieder gut machen? *How
  can I make this up to you?*
gutaussehend *handsome, good-looking*
Gymnasium (n.)(Gymnasien) *high school (fifth
  grade through twelfth grade)*

H

Haar (n.)(Haare) *hair*
haben *to have*
  gern haben *to like*
  Hunger haben *to be hungry*
  Ich hätte gern … *I would like to have …*
  keine Lust haben *to not feel like*
  lieb haben *to like (among family members)*
  Lust haben *to feel like*
  Recht haben *to be right*
  Schmerzen haben *to be in pain*
  zu etwas Lust haben *to feel like doing
    something*
häkeln *to crochet*
halb *half*
  Es ist halb acht. *It is half past seven.*
Hallo. *Hi.*
Halsschmerzen (pl.) *sore throat*
halten *to hold*
Haltestelle (f.)(Haltestellen) *stop (bus, tram,
  subway)*
Hand (f.)(Hände) *hand*
Handball (m.) (no pl.) *handball (game)*
  Handball spielen *to play handball*
Handschuhe (pl.) *gloves*
Handwerk (n.)(Handwerke) *trade*
Handy (n.)(Handys) *cell phone*

Handynummer (f.) (Handynummern) *cell phone number*
hängen *to hang*
hart *hard*
Hauptgericht (n.) (Hauptgerichte) *main course*
Hauptschulabschluß (m.) (Hauptschulabschlüsse) *school-leaving exam (lower level)*
Hauptschule (f.) (Hauptschulen) *junior high school (fifth grade through ninth grade)*
Hauptspeise (f.) (Hauptspeisen) *main course*
als Hauptspeise *as a main course*
Haus (n.) (Häuser) *house*
nach Hause *home*
zu Hause *home*
Hausaufgaben (pl.) *homework*
die Hausaufgaben machen *to do homework*
heiraten *to get married*
Heirate mich! *Marry me!*
heiß *hot*
Es ist heiß. *It is hot.*
heißen *to be named, to be called*
Ich heiße ... *My name is ...*
Wie heißen Sie? *What's your name?* (fml.)
helfen *to help*
Kann ich Ihnen helfen? *Can I help you?*
Hemd (n.) (Hemden) *shirt*
her *here, from*
Wo kommen Sie her? *Where are you from?*
herangehen *to approach*
Herbst (m.) (Herbste) *fall*
Herr (m.) (Herren) *Mr.*
Herrenabteilung (f.) (Herrenabteilungen) *men's department*
herum *around*
hervorragend *outstanding, excellent; very well*
herzlich *warm, sincere*
Herzlichen Glückwunsch! *Congratulations!*
heute *today*
heute Abend *tonight, this evening*
heutzutage *these days*
hier *here*
gleich hier *right here*
Hier Philipp. *Hello, this is Philipp. (on the phone)*
Hilfe (f.) (Hilfen) *help*
hinausgehen *to go out*
hinter *in back of, behind*

hinterlassen *to leave (behind)*
Nachricht (f.) hinterlassen *to leave a message*
Hobby (n.) (Hobbys) *hobby*
einem Hobby nachgehen *to have a hobby*
Hobbyfotograf/-in (m./f.) (Hobbyfotografen/-grafinnen) *amateur photographer*
hoch *high*
am höchsten *highest* (adverb)
hohes Fieber (n.) *high fever*
höchste *highest* (adjective)
höher *higher*
Hochsaison (f.) (Hochsaisons) *peak season*
Hochzeit (f.) (Hochzeiten) *wedding*
hoffen *to hope*
holen *to get, to fetch*
hören *to listen, to hear*
Hör mal. *Listen.*
Hörer (m.) (Hörer) *receiver*
den Hörer auflegen *to hang up the receiver*
Hose (f.) (Hosen) *pair of pants*
Hotel (n.) (Hotels) *hotel*
Hotelzimmer (n.) (Hotelzimmer) *hotel room*
Hühnchen (n.) (Hühnchen) *chicken*
Huhn (n.) (Hühner) *chicken*
Hund (m.) (Hunde) *dog*
hundert *hundred*
einhundert *one hundred*
einhundert(und)eins *one hundred one*
einhundert(und)einundzwanzig *one hundred twenty-one*
hunderttausend *one hundred thousand*
Hunger (m.) (no pl.) *hunger*
Hunger haben *to be hungry*
Husten (m.) (no pl.) *cough*
Husten haben *to have a cough*
Hut (m.) (Hüte) *hat*

I

ich *I*
Ich bin's. *It's me.*
Idee (f.) (Ideen) *idea*
ihm *him/it, to him/it* (dative)
ihn *him* (accusative)
ihnen *them, to them* (dative)
Ihnen *you, to you* (sg. fml./pl. fml.) (dative)
ihr *you* (pl. infml.) (nominative); *her, to her* (dative); *her, their* (possessive)
Ihr *your* (sg. fml./pl. fml.)

im (in + dem) *in/inside/into the*
  im Büro *in an/the office*
  im Januar *in January*
immer *always*
  wie immer *as always*
in *in, inside, into*
inklusive *inclusive*
  Ist das Trinkgeld inklusive? *Is the tip included?*
Innenstadt (f.) (Innenstädte) *city center*
ins (in + das) *in/inside/into the*
  ins Büro *to the office*
intelligent *intelligent*
interessieren *to interest*
inzwischen *in the meantime*

J

Ja. *Yes.*
  Au ja. *Oh yes.*
  Na ja … *Well …*
Jacke (f.) (Jacken) *jacket*
Jahr (n.) (Jahre) *year*
  Ich bin zwanzig Jahre alt. *I am twenty years old.*
  letztes Jahr *last year*
  nächstes Jahr *next year*
  vor vielen Jahren *many years ago*
  Wie alt sind Sie? *How old are you?*
Januar (m.) (Januare) *January*
  im Januar *in January*
Japan (n.) *Japan*
je *ever, each*
  Oh je! *Oh dear!*
Jeans (pl.) *jeans*
jede *each, every*
  jeden Donnerstag *every Thursday*
  jeden Tag *every day*
jemand *someone*
jetzt *now*
joggen *to jog*
Joghurt (m.) (Joghurts) *yogurt*
Journalist/-in (m./f.) (Journalisten/ Journalistinnen) *journalist*
Juli (m.) (Julis) *July*
jung *young*
Junge (m.) (Jungen) *boy*
Juni (m.) (Junis) *June*
Jura (pl.) *the study of law*

K

Kaffee (m.) (Kaffees) *coffee*
  ein Kännchen Kaffee *a portion (lit., a small pot) of coffee*
  eine Tasse Kaffee *a cup of coffee*
Kaffeetasse (f.) (Kafeetassen) *coffee cup*
Kalbfleisch (n.) (no pl.) *veal*
Kalifornien (n.) *California*
kalt *cold*
  Es ist kalt. *It is cold.*
kämmen *to comb*
  sich kämmen *to comb one's hair*
Kanada (n.) *Canada*
Kännchen (n.) (Kännchen) *pot*
  ein Kännchen Kaffee *a portion/a small pot of coffee*
kaputt *broken*
Karate (n.) (no pl.) *karate*
Karatelehrer (m.) (Karatelehrer) *karate teacher*
kariert *checkered*
Karotte (f.) (Karotten) *carrot*
Karriere (f.) (Karrieren) *career*
  Karriere machen *to advance (to make a career)*
Karte (f.) (Karten) *card, map*
  Karten spielen *to play cards*
Kartenspiel (n.) (Kartenspiele) *card game*
Kartoffel (f.) (Kartoffeln) *potato*
Kartoffelsalat (m.) (Kartoffelsalate) *potato salad*
Käse (m.) (no pl.) *cheese*
Kasse (f.) (Kassen) *cashier, checkout*
  an der Kasse *at the cashier, at the checkout*
Katze (f.) (Katzen) *cat*
kaufen *to buy*
Kaufhaus (n.) (Kaufhäuser) *department store*
kein *no, none, not any*
  Keine Sorge. *No worries./Don't worry.*
Keks (m.) (Kekse) *cookie*
Kellner/-in (m./f.) (Kellner/-innen) *waiter/ waitress*
kennen *to know (people, animals, places, and things)*
kennenlernen *to become acquainted with, to meet*
  Leute kennenlernen *to meet people*

Kilogramm (n.) (Kilogramme; no pl. after numbers) *kilogram*

Kilometer (m.) (Kilometer) *kilometer*

Kind (n.) (Kinder) *child*

  ein Kind bekommen *to have a baby*

Kinderzimmer (n.) (Kinderzimmer) *children's room*

Kino (n.) (Kinos) *movie theater*

Klavier (n.) (Klaviere) *piano*

  Klavier spielen *to play the piano*

Kleid (n.) (Kleider) *dress*

  Kleider (pl.) *clothes*

Kleidung (f.) (no pl.) *clothing*

klein *small*

Klient/-in (m./f.) (Klienten/Klientinnen) *client*

klingeln *to ring the doorbell*

klingen *to sound*

  Das klingt aber gut. *That sounds good.*

Kneipe (f.) (Kneipen) *neighborhood bar*

Knie (n.) (Knie) *knee*

Knöchel (m.) (Knöchel) *ankle*

Koch/Köchin (m./f.) (Köche/Köchinnen) *cook*

kochen *to cook*

  gut kochen *to cook well*

Koffer (m.) (Koffer) *suitcase*

Kollege/Kollegin (m./f.) (Kollegen/Kolleginnen) *colleague*

Köln (n.) *Cologne*

kommen *to come*

  Ich komme aus … *I'm from …*

  Das kommt darauf an. *That depends.*

  Wie komme ich … ? *How do I get to … ?*

  Wo kommen Sie her?/Woher kommen Sie? *Where are you from?*

Kommilitone/Kommilitonin (m./f.) (Kommilitonen/Kommilitoninnen) *fellow university student*

Kompliment (n.) (Komplimente) *compliment*

können *can, to be able to*

  Kann ich Ihnen helfen? *Can I help you?*

Kopf (m.) (Köpfe) *head*

Kopfschmerzen (pl.) *headache*

Kopfschmerztablette (f.) (Kopfschmerztabletten) *headache tablet*

Kopfweh (n.) (no pl.) *headache*

  Kopfweh/Kopfschmerzen haben *to have a headache*

kosten *to cost*

krank *sick*

  sich krank fühlen *to feel sick*

Krankenhaus (n.) (Krankenhäuser) *hospital*

Krankenpfleger/Krankenschwester (m./f.) (Krankenpfleger/Krankenschwestern) *nurse*

Krawatte (f.) (Krawatten) *tie*

Kreditkarte (f.) (Kreditkarten) *credit card*

Kreuzung (f.) (Kreuzungen) *intersection*

Kuchen (m.) (Kuchen) *cake*

  ein Stück Kuchen *a piece of cake*

Küche (f.) (Küchen) *kitchen*

kümmern *to concern*

  sich kümmern um … *to take care of …*

küssen *to kiss*

Kunde/Kundin (m./f.) *client, customer*

kurz *short*

L

Laib (m.) (Laibe) *loaf*

  ein Laib Brot *a loaf of bread*

Lamm (n.) (Lämmer) *lamb*

Lampe (f.) (Lampen) *lamp*

Landstraße (f.) (Landstraßen) *country road*

lang *long*

langsam *slow*

lassen *to let, to allow*

lästig *annoying*

Lauf (m.) (Läufe) *course, run*

laufen *to run*

  einen Marathon laufen *to run a marathon*

  Schlittschuh laufen *to go ice-skating*

laut *loud; according to*

lauten *to be*

  meine Nummer lautet … *my (phone) number is …*

  Wie lautet die richtige Antwort? *What's the right answer?*

läuten *to ring the doorbell*

leben *to live*

Leben (n.) (Leben) *life*

  tägliches Leben *everyday life*

Lebenslauf (m.) (Lebensläufe) *résumé*

  den Lebenslauf schreiben *to prepare one's résumé*

Lebensmittel (n.) (Lebensmittel) *food, groceries*

ledig *single*

ledig sein *to be single*
leer *empty*
legen *to put, to place*
  auf die Waage legen *to put on the scale*
Lehrer/-in (m./f.)(Lehrer/-innen) *teacher*
leid *sorry*
  (Es) tut mir leid. *I'm sorry.*
leider *unfortunately*
leihen *to borrow*
leise *quiet*
leisten *to achieve, to manage*
leiten *to lead, to run (a business)*
  ein Geschäft leiten *to run a business*
Leitung (f.)(Leitungen) *line*
  auf der anderen Leitung (sprechen) *(to speak) on the other line*
Lektion (f.)(Lektionen) *lesson*
lernen *to learn*
  viel zu lernen haben *to have a lot to learn*
lesen *to read*
letzte *last*
  letztes Jahr *last year*
  letzten Monat *last month*
  letzte Woche *last week*
Leute (pl.) *people*
  Leute kennenlernen *to meet people*
lieb *nice*
  lieb haben *to like, to love (among family members)*
lieben *to love*
lieber *rather, better*
Liebling (m.)(Lieblinge) *favorite, darling*
  Lieblingsfach (n.) *favorite subject*
liebste *best* (adjective)
  am liebsten *best* (adverb)
liegen *to lie (location)*
lila *violet*
Linie (f.)(Linien) *line*
links *left, to the left*
  links abbiegen *to turn left*
Liter (m.)(Liter) *liter*
  ein Liter Milch *a liter of milk*
loben *to praise*
Löffel (m.)(Löffel) *spoon*
los *loose*
  Was ist denn los? *What's the matter?*
Lust (f.)(Lüste) *pleasure, delight*
  keine Lust haben *to not feel like*

Lust haben *to feel like*
  zu etwas Lust haben *to feel like doing something*
Lyoner (f.) (no pl.) *bologna*

M

machen *to do, to make, to amount to*
  Das macht acht Euro fünfzig. *That's eight euros and fifty cents.*
  Das macht nichts. *It doesn't matter.*
  die Hausaufgaben machen *to do homework*
  eine Pause machen *to take a break*
  ein Picknick machen *to have a picnic*
  eine Verabredung machen *to make an appointment*
  Mach's gut. *Take care.*
  Pläne machen *to make plans*
  Spaß machen *to be fun*
  Urlaub machen *to go on vacation*
  Wie kann ich das wieder gut machen? *How can I make this up to you?*
Mädchen (n.)(Mädchen) *girl*
Magen (m.)(Mägen) *stomach*
Magister (m.)(magister) *master's degree*
  einen Magister machen *to study for a master's degree*
Mai (m.)(Maien) *May*
Mais (m.) (no pl.) *corn*
mal *time* (occasion)
  Bis zum nächsten Mal. *Till next time.*
  Guck mal! *Look!*
  Hör mal. *Listen.*
  jedes Mal *every time*
  zum ersten Mal *for the first time*
malen *to paint*
Mama (f.)(Mamas) *mom*
man *one, they* (indefinite pronoun)
Manager/-in (m./f.)(Manager/-innen) *manager*
manchmal *sometimes*
Mann (m.)(Männer) *man, husband*
  mein Mann *my husband*
  Willst du mein Mann werden? *Will you marry me? (lit., Will you be my husband?)*
Mantel (m.)(Mäntel) *coat*
Marathon (m.)(Marathons) *marathon*
  einen Marathon laufen *to run a marathon*
Marktplatz (m.)(Marktplätze) *market place*
Marmelade (f.)(Marmeladen) *marmalade,*

jam, jelly

Marmorkuchen (m.) (**Marmorkuchen**) *marble cake*

März (m.) (**Märze**) *March*

Maus (f.) (**Mäuse**) *mouse*

Medikament (n.) (**Medikamente**) *medicine, medication*

Medizin (f.) (no pl.) *medicine*

mehr *more*

nicht mehr *any more, no more*

mein *my*

meinen *to mean, to think*

So war das nicht gemeint. *That's not what this was supposed to mean./I didn't mean it that way.*

Meinung (f.) (**Meinungen**) *opinion*

meiste *most* (adjective)

am meisten *most* (adverb)

melden *to report, to notify*

messen *to measure*

Fieber (n.) messen *to take someone's temperature*

Messer (n.) (**Messer**) *knife*

Meter (m.) (**Meter**) *meter*

Metzger/-in (m./f.) (**Metzger/-innen**) *butcher*

mich *me* (accusative); *myself*

mieten *to rent*

Milch (f.) (no pl.) *milk*

ein Liter Milch *a liter of milk*

Milliarde (f.) (**Milliarden**) *billion*

Million (f.) (**Millionen**) *million*

Mineralwasser (n.) (**Mineralwässer/ Mineralwasser**) *mineral water*

eine Flasche Mineralwasser *a bottle of mineral water*

minus *minus*

Minute (f.) (**Minuten**) *minute*

in zehn Minuten *in ten minutes*

mir *me, to me* (dative)

missen *to miss*

mit *with, in*

mit dem Bus *by bus*

Wie wär's mit … *How about …*

Mitarbeiter/-in (m./f.) (**Mitarbeiter/- innen**) *employee, colleague*

Mitbewohner/-in (m./f.) (**Mitbewohner/- innen**) *roommate*

mitbringen *to bring along*

Mitglied (n.) (**Mitglieder**) *member*

mitkommen *to come along*

mitnehmen *to take along*

Mitschüler/-in (m./f.) (**Mitschüler/- innen**) *classmate*

mitspielen *to play along*

Mittag (m.) (**Mittage**) *noon*

zu Mittag essen *to have lunch*

Mittagessen (n.) (**Mittagessen**) *lunch*

Mitte (f.) (**Mitten**) *middle*

Mittwoch (m.) (**Mittwoche**) *Wednesday*

Möbel (pl.) *furniture*

möchten *to like to*

Ich möchte gern … *I'd like …*

mögen *to like (people, things, food, drinks)*

Moment (m.) (**Momente**) *moment*

Einen Moment bitte. *One moment please.*

Monat (m.) (**Monate**) *month*

letzten Monat *last month*

nächsten Monat *next month*

Montag (m.) (**Montage**) *Monday*

am Montag *on Monday*

nächsten Montag *next Monday*

morgen *tomorrow*

Morgen (m.) (**Morgen**) *morning*

am Morgen *in the morning*

Guten Morgen. *Good morning.*

morgens *in the morning*

Motorrad (n.) (**Motorräder**) *motorcycle*

Motorrad fahren *to ride a motorcycle*

müde *tired*

München *Munich*

müssen *to have to*

Mütze (f.) (**Mützen**) *cap, hat*

Mund (m.) (**Münder**) *mouth*

Museum (n.) (**Museen**) *museum*

Musik (f.) (no pl.) *music*

Muster (n.) (**Muster**) *pattern*

Mutter (f.) (**Mütter**) *mother*

N

na *well*

Na also! *See!/There you have it!*

Na dann … *Well, in that case …*

Na endlich! *Finally!/At last!*

Na ja … *Well …*

Na und? *So what?*

nach *to, after, past*

Es ist viertel nach drei. *It is quarter past three.*

Es ist zehn nach zwölf. *It is ten after twelve.*

nach Hause *home*

Nachbar/-in (m./f.) (Nachbarn/ Nachbarinnen) *neighbor*

nachgehen *to pursue, to practice*

einem Hobby nachgehen *to have a hobby*

Nachmittag (m.) (Nachmittage) *afternoon*

am Nachmittag *in the afternoon*

nachmittags *in the afternoon*

Nachprüfung (f.) (Nachprüfungen) *review*

Nachricht (f.) (Nachrichten) *message, (a piece of) news*

Das ist eine gute Nachricht. *That's good news.*

Nachricht hinterlassen *to leave a message*

Nachspeise (f.) (Nachspeisen) *dessert*

als Nachspeise *for dessert*

nächste *next*

Bis zum nächsten Mal. *Till next time.*

nächste Woche *next week*

nächsten Monat *next month*

nächsten Montag *next Monday*

nächstes Jahr *next year*

Nacht (n.) (Nächte) *night*

Nachtisch (m.) (Nachtische) *dessert*

nachts *at night*

nahe *near*

am nächsten *nearest* (adverb)

nächste *nearest* (adjective)

näher *nearer*

Nähe (f.) (Nähen) *closeness*

in der Nähe *nearby*

Name (m.) (Namen) *name*

Auf welchen Namen? *Under which name? (reservation)*

Nase (f.) (Nasen) *nose*

naseweis *meddling, nosy*

nass *wet*

natürlich *naturally, of course*

neben *beside, next to*

Nebenzimmer (n.) (Nebenzimmer) *side room*

Neffe (m.) *nephew*

nehmen *to take*

das Auto nehmen *to take the car*

den Bus nehmen *to take the bus*

die Straßenbahn nehmen *to take the tram*

Nein. *No.*

nett *nice*

neu *new*

ganz neu *brand-new*

neu eröffnen *to reopen*

Was gibt's Neues? *What's new?*

neugierig *curious*

neun *nine*

neunundzwanzig *twenty-nine*

neunzehn *nineteen*

neunzig *ninety*

nicht *not*

gar nicht *not at all*

Nein, noch nicht. *No, not yet.*

nicht mehr *any more, no more*

Nicht wahr? *Isn't that right?*

Nichts passiert. *No harm done.*

Nichte (f.) (Nichten) *niece*

nie *never*

noch *still, yet*

Darf's sonst noch etwas sein? *Anything else? (at a store)*

Nein, noch nicht. *No, not yet.*

noch ein *another*

noch einmal *once more*

noch etwas *some more*

Was brauchen Sie sonst noch? *What else do you need?*

Notaufnahme (f.) (Notaufnahmen) *emergency room*

Note (f.) (Noten) *mark*

Notfall (m.) (Notfälle) *emergency*

nötig *necessary*

November (m.) (November) *November*

Nudeln (pl.) *noodles, pasta*

null *zero*

null Uhr *midnight*

Nummer (f.) (Nummern) *number, size*

meine Nummer lautet … *my (phone) number is …*

nun *now, then*

Nun … *Well …*

nur *only*

O ⸺

ob *if, whether*

Ober (m.) (Ober) *waiter*

Obst (n.) (no pl.) *fruit*

oder *or*
  entweder ... oder ... *either ... or ...*
öffnen *to open*
oft *often*
ohne *without*
Ohrring(m.) **(Ohrringe)** *earring*
Oktober(m.) **(Oktober)** *October*
Oma(f.) **(Omas)** *grandma*
Onkel(m.) **(Onkel)** *uncle*
Opa(m.) **(Opas)** *grandpa*
Orange(f.) **(Orangen)** *orange*
Orangensaft(m.) **(Orangensäfte)** *orange juice*
Ordnung(f.) **(Ordnungen)** *order*
  Ist alles in Ordnung? *Is everything okay?*
Österreich(n.) *Austria*

P

Paar(n.) **(Paare)** *pair, couple*
  ein Paar Schuhe *a pair of shoes*
  ein paar Tage *a couple of days, a few days*
Papa(m.) **(Papas)** *dad(dy)*
Paprika(m.) **(Paprikas)** *pepper (vegetable)*
Park(m.) **(Parks)** *park*
parken *to park*
Parkhaus(n.) **(Parkhäuser)** *parking garage*
  im Parkhaus parken *to park in a parking garage*
Partner/-in(m./f.) **(Partner/-innen)** *partner*
Party(f.) **(Partys)** *party*
  eine Party geben *to have a party*
passen *to fit*
  gut passen *to fit well*
  gut passen zu *to go well with*
passend *matching*
passieren *to happen*
  Nichts passiert. *No harm done.*
Patient/-in(m./f.) **(Patienten/ Patientinnen)** *patient*
Pause(f.) **(Pausen)** *break*
  eine Pause machen *to take a break*
Pausenbrot(n.) **(Pausenbrote)** *something to eat at break*
Pech(n.) (no pl.) *bad luck*
  So ein Pech. *Too bad.*
peinlich *embarrassing*
Penizillin(n.) (no pl.) *penicillin*
Pension(f.) **(Pensionen)** *pension*
  in Pension gehen *to retire*

pensioniert *retired*
perfekt *perfect*
persönlich *personally*
Pfeffer(m.) (no pl.) *pepper (spice)*
Pferd(n.) **(Pferde)** *horse*
pflanzen *to plant*
Pflaster(n.) **(Pflaster)** *adhesive bandage*
Pfund(n.) **(Pfunde)** *pound*
  ein Pfund Tomaten *a pound of tomatoes*
Pianist/-in(m./f.) **(Pianisten/ Pianistinnen)** *pianist*
Picknick(n.) **(Picknicke)** *picnic*
  ein Picknick machen *to have a picnic*
Plan(m.) **(Pläne)** *plan*
  Pläne machen *to make plans*
Polizei(f.) (no pl.) *police*
Post(f.) (no pl.) *post office*
Praktikum(n.) **(Praktika)** *internship*
Praxis(f.) **(Praxen)** *practice, doctor's office*
Preis(m.) **(Preise)** *price*
prima *great, top-quality*
  Prima! *Great!*
pro *per*
probieren *to try*
Problem(n.) **(Probleme)** *problem*
  Kein Problem. *No problem.*
Programm(n.) **(Programme)** *program*
Projekt(n.) **(Projekte)** *project*
Prozent(n.) **(Prozente)** *percent*
Prüfung(f.) **(Prüfungen)** *exam*
Psychologie(f.) **(Psychologien)** *psychology*
pünktlich *punctual*
Pullover(m.) **(Pullover)** *sweater*

R

Rad(n.) **(Räder)** *bike*
  Rad fahren *to bike*
Radio(n.) **(Radios)** *radio*
Radiosprecher/-in(m./f.) **(Radiosprecher/-innen)** *radio announcer*
Radtour(f.) **(Radtouren)** *bike tour*
Rat(m.) **(Räte)** *advice*
Rate(f.) **(Raten)** *rate*
Rathaus(n.) **(Rathäuser)** *town hall*
rauchen *to smoke*
raus *out*
Realschule(f.) **(Realschulen)** *middle school (fifth grade through tenth grade)*

Realschulprüfung (f.)
  (Realschulprüfungen) *middle school exam*
  die Realschulprüfung machen *to take the*
    middle school exam
Rechnung (f.) (Rechnungen) *bill, check, invoice*
Recht (n.) (Rechte) *right*
  Recht haben *to be right*
rechts *right, to the right*
  rechts abbiegen *to turn right*
Rechtsanwalt/Rechtsanwältin (m./f.)
  (Rechtsanwälte/Rechtsanwältinnen) *lawyer*
Redakteur/-in (m./f.) (Redakteure/
  Redakteurinnen) *editor*
reden *to talk*
Regal (n.) (Regale) *shelf*
Regen (m.) (no pl.) *rain*
Regenwetter (n.) (Regenwetter) *rainy weather*
  bei Regenwetter *in rainy weather*
regnen *to rain*
  Es regnet. *It is raining.*
reich *rich*
Reis (m.) (no pl.) *rice*
rennen *to run*
Rente (f.) (Renten) *retirement*
  in Rente gehen *to retire*
reservieren *to reserve*
  einen Tisch reservieren *to reserve a table, to*
    make reservations
Reservierung (f.)
  (Reservierungen) *reservation*
Restaurant (n.) (Restaurants) *restaurant*
Retrospektive (f.)
  (Retrospektiven) *retrospective*
Rezept (n.) (Rezepte) *prescription*
richtig *right, correct; really*
Richtung (f.) (Richtungen) *direction*
  Fahren Sie in Richtung München. *Drive*
    towards/in the direction of Munich.
Rinderbraten (m.) (Rinderbraten) *roast beef*
Rindfleisch (n.) (no pl.) *beef*
Rivale/Rivalin (m./f.) (Rivalen/
  Rivalinnen) *rival*
Rock (m.) (Röcke) *skirt*
Roman (m.) (Romane) *novel*
rosa *pink*
Rose (f.) (Rosen) *rose*
Rostbraten (m.) (Rostbraten) *roast*
rot *red*

Rotwein (m.) (Rotweine) *red wine*
rufen *to call, to yell*
  den Arzt rufen *to call a doctor*

S

Saft (m.) (Säfte) *juice*
sagen *to say*
Salami (f.) (Salamis) *salami*
Salat (m.) (Salate) *salad, lettuce*
Salz (n.) (Salze) *salt*
sammeln *to collect*
Samstag (m.) (Samstage) *Saturday*
Satz (m.) (Sätze) *sentence*
sauer *sour*
Sauerbraten (m.) (Sauerbraten) *braised beef*
Sauerkraut (n.) (no pl.) *sauerkraut*
Schal (m.) (Schale, Schals) *scarf*
Schatz (m.) (Schätze) *treasure, darling,*
  sweetheart
scheinen *to shine*
schenken *to give (as a gift)*
schicken *to send*
Schiff (n.) (Schiffe) *ship*
Schifffahrt (f.) (Schifffahrten) *cruise*
Schild (n.) (Schilder) *sign, signpost*
Schinken (m.) (Schinken) *ham*
Schirm (m.) (Schirme) *umbrella*
schlafen *to sleep*
Schlafzimmer (n.) (Schlafzimmer) *bedroom*
Schläger (m.) (Schläger) *racquet*
schlank *slim*
schlecht *bad*
  Sie sehen schlecht aus. *You look bad/sick.*
schließlich *after all*
Schlittschuh (m.) (Schlittschuhe) *ice skate*
  Schlittschuh laufen *to go ice-skating*
Schlüssel (m.) (Schlüssel) *key*
Schluss (m.) (Schlüsse) *end*
Schlusssatz (m.) (Schlusssätze) *final sentence*
schmecken *to taste, to be to one's taste*
Schmerz (m.) (Schmerzen) *pain*
  Schmerzen haben *to be in pain*
Schnee (m.) (no pl.) *snow*
Schneewetter (n.) (no pl.) *snowy weather*
  bei Schneewetter *in snowy weather*
schneiden *to cut*
schneien *to snow*
  Es schneit. *It is snowing.*

schnell *fast, quick*
schnelllebig *fast-paced*
Schnitzel (n.) (Schnitzel) *cutlet*
Schnupfen (m.) (Schnupfen) *cold*
  Schnupfen haben *to have a runny nose, to have a cold*
Schokolade (f.) (Schokoladen) *chocolate*
schon *already, yet, even, certainly*
  schon, aber … *yes, but …*
  Schon gut. *It's okay.*
schön *beautiful, nice*
  Danke schön. *Thank you.*
schonen *to save, to conserve*
  sich schonen *to take it easy*
Schrank (m.) (Schränke) *closet*
schreiben *to write*
  den Lebenslauf schreiben *to prepare one's résumé*
Schreibtisch (m.) (Schreibtische) *desk*
Schüler/-in (m./f.) (Schüler/-innen) *pupil, schoolboy/girl*
Schuh (m.) (Schuhe) *shoe*
  ein Paar Schuhe *a pair of shoes*
Schuhabteilung (f.) (Schuhabteilungen) *shoe department*
Schuhgeschäft (n.) (Schuhgeschäfte) *shoe store*
schulden *to owe*
Schule (f.) (Schulen) *school*
Schulter (f.) (Schultern) *shoulder*
Schwager (m.) (Schwäger) *brother-in-law*
Schwägerin (f.) (Schwägerinnen) *sister-in-law*
schwanger *pregnant*
  schwanger sein *to be pregnant*
schwarz *black*
Schweinefleisch (n.) (no pl.) *pork*
Schwester (f.) (Schwestern) *sister*
Schwesterchen (n.) (Schwesterchen) *little sister*
Schwiegermutter (f.) (Schwiegermütter) *mother-in-law*
Schwiegervater (m.) (Schwiegerväter) *father-in-law*
schwierig *difficult*
Schwimmbad (n.) (Schwimmbäder) *public pool*
schwimmen *to swim*
sechs *six*
sechsundzwanzig *twenty-six*

sechzehn *sixteen*
sechzig *sixty*
sehen *to see*
sehr *very*
  Bitte sehr. *Here you go.*
  Sehr gut. *Very well.*
sein *to be; his, its*
  Ich bin's. *It's me.*
  tätig sein *to work*
  Wie wär's mit … *How about …*
seit *since, for*
Seite (f.) (Seiten) *page*
Sekt (m.) (Sekte) *champagne, sparkling wine*
selbstständig *self-employed*
selbstverständlich *of course*
September (m.) (September) *September*
Service (n.) (no pl.) *service*
servieren *to serve*
Serviette (f.) (Servietten) *napkin*
Servus. *Hello.*
setzen *to sit, to place, to put*
  sich setzen *to sit down*
Show (f.) (Shows) *show*
sich *yourself* (sg. fml.), *himself, herself, itself, yourselves* (pl. fml.), *themselves*
  sich schonen *to take it easy*
  sich setzen *to sit down*
  sich treffen *to meet*
sicher *sure, certain*
Sie *you* (sg. fml./pl. fml.) (nominative); *you* (sg. fml./ pl. fml.) (accusative)
sie *she, they* (nominative); *her, them* (accusative)
sieben *seven*
siebenundzwanzig *twenty-seven*
siebzehn *seventeen*
siebzig *seventy*
singen *to sing*
sitzen *to sit*
Ski (m.) (Ski, Skier) *ski*
  Ski fahren *to go skiing*
Skifahren (n.) *skiing*
Skigebiet (n.) (Skigebiete) *ski resort*
Snowboard (n.) (Snowboards) *snowboard*
snowboarden *to snowboard*
so *so*
  Ach so. *I see.*
  so … wie *as … as*
  So ein Pech. *Too bad.*

Stimmt so. *That's correct./Keep the change.*
Socken (pl.) *socks*
Sofa (n.) **(Sofas)** *couch*
sofort *at once, right away*
sogar *even*
Sohn (m.) **(Söhne)** *son*
sollen *ought to*
Sommer (m.) **(Sommer)** *summer*
  im Sommer *in the summer*
Sommerurlaub (m.) **(Sommerurlaube)** *summer vacation*
Sonderangebot (n.) **(Sonderangebote)** *special offer*
  im Sonderangebot *on sale*
Sonne (f.) **(Sonnen)** *sun*
Sonntag (m.) **(Sonntage)** *Sunday*
sonst *else*
  Sonst noch etwas? *Anything else?*
  Was brauchen Sie sonst noch? *What else do you need?*
Sorge (f.) *worry*
  Keine Sorge. *No worries./Don't worry.*
Spaß (m.) **(Späße)** *fun*
  Spaß machen *to be fun*
  Viel Spaß! *Enjoy!/Have fun!*
spät *late*
  Wie spät ist es? *What is the time?*
  spät aufstehen *to get up late*
später *later*
spazieren *to stroll*
  spazieren gehen *to go for a walk*
Speisekarte (f.) **(Speisekarten)** *menu*
Spezialität (f.) **(Spezialitäten)** *specialty*
Spiegel (m.) **(Spiegel)** *mirror*
Spiel (n.) **(Spiele)** *game*
spielen *to play*
  Fußball spielen *to play soccer*
  Gitarre spielen *to play the guitar*
  Karten spielen *to play cards*
Spielzeug (n.) **(Spielzeuge)** *toy*
Spinat (m.) (no pl.) *spinach*
Sport (m.) (no pl.) *sport*
  Sport treiben *to play sports*
Sportart (f.) **(Sportarten)** *sport*
Sportler/-in (m./f.) **(Sportler/-innen)** *athlete*
Sportstudio (n.) **(Sportstudios)** *sports center*
sprechen *to speak*
Spritze (f.) **(Spritzen)** *shot (medical), syringe*

Squash (n.) (no pl.) *squash*
  Squash spielen *to play squash*
Stadion (n.) **(Stadien)** *stadium*
Stadt (f.) **(Städte)** *city, town*
  in der Stadt *around town*
Stadtplan (m.) **(Stadtpläne)** *(city) map*
Stadtrundfahrt (f.) **(Stadtrundfahrten)** *city tour*
  eine Stadtrundfahrt machen *to take a city tour*
ständig *constantly*
stark *strong*
Statistik (f.) **(Statistiken)** *statistics*
statt *instead of*
Stau (m.) **(Staus)** *traffic jam, stopped traffic*
  im Stau stecken *to be stuck in traffic*
  im Stau stehen *to be stopped in traffic*
Steak (n.) **(Steaks)** *steak*
stecken *to be stuck*
  im Stau stecken *to be stuck in traffic*
stehen *to stand, to suit*
  gut stehen *to look good on (somebody)*
  im Stau stehen *to be stopped in traffic*
steigen *to climb, to rise, to increase*
  Berg steigen *to go mountain climbing*
Stelle (f.) **(Stellen)** *place, position, job*
  sich auf eine Stelle bewerben *to apply for a job, to apply for a position*
stellen *to place, to put*
Stellenanzeige (f.) **(Stellenanzeigen)** *job announcement, help-wanted ad*
Stellenmarkt (m.) **(Stellenmärkte)** *job announcements, help-wanted ads; job market*
Stiefel (m.) **(Stiefel)** *boots*
still *quiet*
Stimme (f.) **(Stimmen)** *voice*
stimmen *to be right*
  Das stimmt! *That's true!*
  Stimmt so. *That's correct./Keep the change.*
stolz *proud*
Straße (f.) **(Straßen)** *street*
  zwei Straßen weiter *two blocks farther*
Straßenbahn (f.) **(Straßenbahnen)** *street car*
  die Straßenbahn nehmen *to take the tram*
  mit der Straßenbahn *by tram*
stricken *to knit*
Student/-in (m./f.) **(Studenten/-innen)** *student*
studieren *to study (at a university)*

Studium (n.) (Studien) *study, studies*
Stück (n.) (Stücke) *piece*
  am Stück *in one piece*
  ein Stück Kuchen *a piece of cake*
Stuhl (m.) (Stühle) *chair*
Stunde (f.) (Stunden) *hour*
  in einer Stunde *in an hour*
  vor einer Stunde *an hour ago*
suchen *to search, to look for*
Südafrika (n.) *South Africa*
süß *sweet*
süßsauer *sweet-and-sour*
Süßspeise (f.) (Süßspeisen) *sweets, dessert*
super *super, great*
Supermarkt (m.) (Supermärkte) *grocery store*
Suppe (f.) (Suppen) *soup*
  ein Teller Suppe *a bowl of soup*

T

Tablette (f.) (Tabletten) *pill*
Tag (m.) (Tage) *day*
  den ganzen Tag *all day*
  ein paar Tage *a couple of days, a few days*
  Guten Tag. *Hello./Good day.*
  jeden Tag *every day*
Tageszeitung (f.) (Tageszeitungen) *daily
  newspaper*
täglich *daily*
  tägliches Leben *everyday life*
Tango (m.) (Tangos) *tango*
tanken *to get gas*
Tankstelle (f.) (Tankstellen) *gas station*
Tankwart/-in (m./f.) (Tankwarte/-innen) *gas
  station attendant*
Tante (f.) (Tanten) *aunt*
tanzen *to dance*
Tasche (f.) (Taschen) *bag*
Taschengeld (n.) (Taschengelder) *allowance*
Tasse (f.) (Tassen) *cup*
  eine Tasse Kaffee *a cup of coffee*
tätig *active*
  freiberuflich tätig sein *to freelance*
  tätig sein *to work*
tauchen *to (scuba) dive*
tausend *thousand*
  eintausend *one thousand*
  eintausendeinhundert *one thousand one
  hundred*

hunderttausend *one hundred thousand*
zehntausend *ten thousand*
zweitausend *two thousand*
Taxi (n.) (Taxis; Taxen) *taxi*
  ein Taxi rufen *to call a cab*
  mit dem Taxi fahren *to go by cab*
Taxifahrer (m.) (Taxifahrer) *taxi driver*
Teilzeit (f.) (no pl.) *part-time*
Teilzeitbeschäftigung (f.)
  (Teilzeitbeschäftigungen) *part-time
  employment*
Telefon (n.) (Telefone) *telephone*
telefonieren *to call*
Telefonnummer (f.) (Telefonnummern) *phone
  number*
Teller (m.) (Teller) *plate, bowl*
  ein Teller Suppe *a bowl of soup*
Temperatur (f.) (Temperaturen) *temperature*
  erhöhte Temperatur *elevated temperature*
Tennis (n.) (no pl.) *tennis*
  Tennis spielen *to play tennis*
Tennisschläger (m.) (Tennisschläger) *tennis
  racquet*
Tennisschuhe (pl.) *tennis shoes*
Termin (m.) (Termine) *appointment*
Terrasse (f.) (Terrassen) *terrace*
teuer *expensive*
Tisch (m.) (Tische) *table*
  einen Tisch bestellen *to reserve a table, to
    make reservations*
  einen Tisch reservieren *to reserve a table, to
    make reservations*
Tischler/-in (m./f.) (Tischler/-innen) *carpenter*
Tochter (f.) (Töchter) *daughter*
Toilette (f.) (Toiletten) *bathroom, toilet*
Tomate (f.) (Tomaten) *tomato*
  ein Pfund Tomaten *a pound of tomatoes*
Ton (m.) (no pl.) *clay*
töpfern *to make pottery*
Tourist/-in (m./f.) (Touristen/
  Touristinnen) *tourist*
tragen *to wear*
Traube (f.) (Trauben) *bunch of grapes*
Traum (m.) (Träume) *dream*
traurig *sad*
treffen *to hit*
  sich treffen *to meet*
treiben *to drive, to do*

Sport treiben *to play sports*

trinken *to drink*

Trinkgeld (n.) **(Trinkgelder)** *tip*

  ein Trinkgeld geben *to leave a tip, to tip*

  Ist das Trinkgeld inklusive? *Is the tip included?*

Tropfen (m.) **(Tropfen)** *drop*

trotz *despite*

trotzdem *nevertheless*

Tschüss. *Bye.*

Tür (f.) **(Türen)** *door*

tun *to do*

  (Es) tut mir leid. *I'm sorry.*

  viel zu tun haben *to have a lot to do*

U

über *over, above, across, about*

übermorgen *the day after tomorrow*

Überstunde (f.) **(Überstunden)** *overtime*

  Überstunden machen *to work overtime*

Uhr (f.) **(Uhren)** *clock, watch, o'clock*

  Es ist sechs Uhr fünfzehn. *It is six fifteen.*

  Es ist vier Uhr dreißig. *It is four thirty.*

  Es ist zehn Uhr. *It's ten o'clock.*

  null Uhr *midnight*

  um ein Uhr *at one o'clock*

  um fünf Uhr *at five o' clock*

  Wieviel Uhr ist es? *What time is it?*

Uhrzeit (f.) **(Uhrzeiten)** *time, time of day*

  Um welche Uhrzeit? *For what time? (reservation)*

um *at, around, about*

  um ein Uhr *at one o'clock*

  um fünf Uhr *at five o' clock*

umdrehen *to make a U-turn, to turn around*

umgehen *to circulate, to be going around*

  Die Grippe geht um. *The flu is going around.*

Umkleidekabine (f.) **(Umkleidekabinen)** *fitting room*

umsteigen *to change trains/buses*

umtauschen *to (ex)change*

und *and*

  Na und? *So what?*

Universität (f.) **(Universitäten)** *university*

uns *us* (accusative); *us, to us* (dative); *ourselves*

unser *our*

unter *under, beneath, among*

unterbrechen *to interrupt*

Unterhaltung (f.) **(Unterhaltungen)** *entertainment*

Unterricht (m.) (no pl.) *lessons*

unterrichten *to teach*

untersuchen *to examine*

unterwegs *on the way*

  unterwegs sein *to be on the way (baby)*

Urlaub (m.) **(Urlaube)** *vacation*

  (sich) Urlaub nehmen *to take a vacation, take leave*

  Urlaub machen *to go on vacation*

Urlaubsplan (m.) **(Urlaubspläne)** *vacation plans*

Ursache (f.) **(Ursachen)** *cause, reason, motive*

  Keine Ursache! *Don't mention it!*

V

Vase (f.) **(Vasen)** *vase*

Vater (m.) **(Väter)** *father*

verabreden *to arrange*

Verabredung (f.) **(Verabredungen)** *appointment, date*

  eine Verabredung machen (Verabredungen machen) *to make an appointment*

Verband (m.) **(Verbände)** *bandage*

  einen Verband anlegen *to put on a bandage*

verbessern *to improve*

verbinden *to connect*

Verbindung (f.) **(Verbindungen)** *connection*

Verein (m.) **(Vereine)** *club*

  einem Verein beitreten *to join a club*

vereinbaren *to arrange*

vergessen *to forget*

verheiratet *married*

  verheiratet sein *to be married*

verkaufen *to sell*

Verkäufer/-in (m./f.) **(Verkäufer/-innen)** *salesperson*

Verkehr (m.) (no pl.) *traffic*

Verkehrsdurchsage (f.) **(Verkehrsdurchsagen)** *traffic announcement*

verleihen *to lend*

verletzen *to hurt, to injure*

  sich verletzen *to hurt oneself*

verlobt *engaged*

  verlobt sein *to be engaged*

verpassen *to miss*

verschieben *to move, to postpone*

verschreiben *to prescribe*

verstehen *to understand*
Verzeihung (f.) (Verzeihungen) *forgiveness*
  Verzeihung. *Forgive me.*
viel *much, a lot*
  Viel Glück! *Good luck!*
  Viel Spaß! *Enjoy!/Have fun!*
  viel zu lernen haben *to have a lot to learn*
  viel zu tun haben *to have a lot to do*
viele *many*
  Vielen Dank. *Many thanks.*
  Vielen Dank für die Blumen! *Thanks for*
    the compliment! (lit., Thanks for the flowers.
    [often used ironically])
vielleicht *maybe*
vier *four*
viertel *quarter*
  Es ist viertel nach drei. *It is quarter past*
    three.
  Es ist viertel vor drei. *It is quarter to three.*
Viertel (n.) (Viertel) *quarter*
  akademische Viertel *academic quarter*
Viertelstunde (f.) (Viertelstunden) *quarter of*
  an hour
  nur noch ein Viertelstündchen *just another*
    fifteen minutes
vierundzwanzig *twenty-four*
vierzehn *fourteen*
vierzig *forty*
violet *purple*
voll *full*
Volleyball (m.) (no pl.) *volleyball (game)*
  Volleyball spielen *to play volleyball*
Vollzeitbeschäftigug (f.)
  (Vollzeitbeschäftigungen) *full-time*
  employment
Volontariat (n.) (Valontariate) *internship*
  (newspaper)
  ein Volontariat machen *to intern at a*
    newspaper
vom (von + dem) *from/by the*
von *from, by*
  von ... bis *from ... to*
vor *in front of, before, ago*
  Es ist viertel vor drei. *It is quarter to three.*
  Es ist zehn vor zwölf. *It is ten to twelve.*
  vor einer Stunde *an hour ago*
vorbei *over, finished*
vorbereiten *to prepare*

Vorgesetzte (m./f.) (Vorgesetzten) *superior*
vorgestern *the day before yesterday*
vorhin *a little while ago*
vorlesen *to read to, to read out loud*
vorletzte *the ... before last*
Vorsicht (f.) (no pl.) *caution, attention*
  Vorsicht! *Careful!*
Vorspeise (f.) (Vorspeisen) *appetizer*
  als Vorspeise *as an appetizer*

W

Waage (f.) (Waagen) *scale*
  auf die Waage legen *to put on the scale*
Wahl (f.) (Wahlen) *choice*
wahr *true, real*
  Nicht wahr? *Isn't that right?*
während *during*
wandern *to hike*
wann *when*
warm *warm*
  Es ist warm. *It is warm.*
warten *to wait*
  warten auf *to wait for*
warum *why*
was *what*
waschen *to wash*
  sich waschen *to wash oneself*
Wasser (n.) (Wasser; Wässer) *water*
wechseln *to (ex)change*
Weg (m.) (Wege) *way, path*
wegen *because*
weh tun *to hurt*
Weihnachten (n.) (Weihnachten) *Christmas*
weil *because*
Wein (m.) (Weine) *wine*
  eine Flasche Wein *a bottle of wine*
  ein Glas Wein *a glass of wine*
weinen *to cry (tears)*
Weinkarte (f.) (Weinkarten) *wine list*
weiß *white*
Weißwein (m.) (Weißweine) *white wine*
weit *far*
  Wie weit ... ? *How far ... ?*
weiter *farther*
  zwei Straßen weiter *two blocks farther*
welcher *which*
  welche Größe (f.) *what size*
Welt (f.) (Welten) *world*

wenig *little*
wenige *few*
weniger *less*
wenn *if, when*
wer *who*
werden *to become, to happen*
  geschieden werden *to get divorced*
  Willst du mein Mann werden? *Will you marry me? (lit., Will you be my husband?)*
  Willst du meine Frau werden? *Will you marry me? (lit., Will you be my wife?)*
wessen *whose*
Wetter (n.) (Wetter) *weather*
  bei gutem Wetter *in good weather*
  bei schlechtem Wetter *in bad weather*
WG (f.) (WGs) *shared flat*
wichtig *important*
wie *how, as*
  Wie alt sind Sie? *How old are you?*
  Wie bitte? *Excuse me/I'm sorry?*
  Wie geht es Ihnen? *How are you?* (fml.)
  Wie geht's? *How are you?* (infml.)
  Wie heißen Sie? *What's your name?* (fml.)
  Wie wär's mit … *How about …*
  wie immer *as always*
  Wie wär's mit … *How about …*
wieder *again*
  Wie kann ich das wieder gut machen? *How can I make this up to you?*
wiederholen *to repeat*
wiedersehen *to see again*
  Auf Wiedersehen. *Goodbye.*
  Auf Wiedersehen bis dann. *Good-bye until then.*
wiegen *to weigh*
wie viel *how much*
  Wie viel Uhr ist es? *What time is it?*
wie viele *how many*
Willkommen. *Welcome.*
  Willkommen zurück. *Welcome back.*
Winter (m.) (Winter) *winter*
  im Winter *in the winter*
Winterurlaub (m.) (Winterurlaube) *winter vacation*
wir *we*
wirklich *really*
  Wirklich? *Really?*
wissen *to know (facts)*

  Nicht dass ich wüsste. *Not that I know of.*
  Woher wusstest du das? *How did you know that?*
Wissenschaftler/-in (m./f.) (Wissenschaftler/-innen) *scientist, academic*
wo *where*
  Wo kommen Sie her? *Where are you from?*
Woche (f.) (Wochen) *week*
  letzte Woche *last week*
  nächste Woche *next week*
  pro Woche *per week*
Wochenende (n.) (Wochenenden) *weekend*
  am Wochenende *on the weekend*
woher *where from*
  Woher kommen Sie? *Where are you from?*
  Woher wusstest du das? *How did you know that?*
wohl *well*
  Auf dein Wohl! *To your health!*
  sich wohl fühlen *to feel well*
  Zum Wohl! *Cheers! (lit., To wellness!)*
wohlhabend *wealthy, prosperous*
wohnen *to reside, to live*
  Ich wohne in Berlin. *I live in Berlin.*
  Wo wohnen Sie? *Where do you live?*
Wohngemeinschaft (f.) (Wohngemeinschaften) *shared flat*
Wohnung (f.) (Wohnungen) *apartment*
Wohnzimmer (n.) (Wohnzimmer) *living room*
wollen *to want to*
wünschen *to wish*
Wunde (f.) (Wunden) *wound*
  Wunde auswaschen *to clean the wound*
Wurstaufschnitt (m.) (no pl.) *cold cuts*

Y

Yoga (m./n.) (no pl.) *yoga*
Yogastudio (n.) (Yogastudios) *Yoga studio*

Z

Zahn (m.) (Zähne) *tooth*
Zahnarzt/Zahnärztin (m./f.) (Zahnärzte/Zahnärztinnen) *dentist*
Zahnschmerzen (pl.) *toothache*
Zahnweh (n.) (no pl.) *toothache*
  Zahnweh haben *to have a toothache*
Zehe (f.) (Zehen) *toe*
zehn *ten*

zeichnen *to draw*
zeigen *to show*
Zeit (f.) (Zeiten) *time*
Zeitung (f.) (Zeitungen) *newspaper*
Zeitungsartikel (m.)
   (Zeitungsartikel) *newspaper article*
Zeugnis (n.) (Zeugnisse) *report card*
ziehen *to pull*
Zimmer (n.) (Zimmer) *room*
zu *to, towards* (preposition); *too* (adverb)
   um ... zu *in order to*
   zu etwas Lust haben *to feel like doing
      something*
   zu Mittag essen *to have lunch*
Zucker (m.) (no pl.) *sugar*
zuckersüß *sugar sweet*
zuerst *first*
Zufall (m.) (Zufälle) *coincidence*
Zug (m.) (Züge) *train*
Zuhause (n.) (no pl.) *home*
zuhören *to listen*
zum (zu + dem) *to/toward the*
   Zum Wohl! *Cheers! (lit., To wellness!)*
zumachen *to close*
zur (zu + der) *to/toward the*
zurück *back*
   Willkommen zurück. *Welcome back.*
zurückrufen *to call back*
zusammen *together*
   Alles zusammen? *One check? (at a restaurant)*
Zuschauer/-in (m./f.) (Zuschauer/-
   innen) *viewer*
zwanzig *twenty*
zwei *two*
zweiundzwanzig *twenty-two*
Zwiebel (f.) (Zwiebeln) *onion*
zwischen *between*
zwölf *twelve*

English-German

A

a/an *ein*
able to (to be) *können*
about *etwa, um, über*
above *über*
academic *akademisch*
   academic quarter *akademische Viertel* (n.)
according to *laut*
accountant *Buchhalter/-in* (m./f.) (Buchhalter/-
   innen)
achieve (to) *leisten*
acquainted with (to become) *kennenlernen*
across *über*
   across from *gegenüber*
active *tätig*
addition (in addition) *außerdem*
address *Adresse* (f.) (Adressen)
admire (to) *bewundern*
advice *Rat* (m.) (Räte)
Africa *Afrika* (n.)
after *nach*
   after all *schließlich*
   It is ten after twelve. *Es ist zehn nach zwölf.*
afternoon *Nachmittag* (m.) (Nachmittage)
   in the afternoon *am Nachmittag, nachmittags*
afterwards *danach*
again *wieder*
   see again (to) *wiedersehen*
against *gegen*
age *Alter* (n.) (Alter)
   at the age of *im Alter von*
ago *vor*
   a little while ago *vorhin*
   an hour ago *vor einer Stunde*
   many years ago *vor vielen Jahren*
airport *Flughafen* (m.) (Flughäfen)
all *alle*
   all day *den ganzen Tag*
allergic *allergisch*
   allergic to cats (to be) *gegen Katzen allergisch
      sein*
allow (to) *lassen*
   allowed to (to be) *dürfen*
allowance *Taschengeld* (n.) (Taschengelder)
almost *fast*

already *schon*

also *auch*

alter (to) *ändern*

always *immer*
  as always *wie immer*

amateur filmmaker *Amateur-Filmemacher/-in*
  (m./f.) *(Amateur-Filmemacher/-innen)*

amateur photographer *Hobbyfotograf/-in*
  (m./f.) *(Hobbyfotografen/Hobbyfotografinnen)*

amazing *erstaunlich*

America *Amerika* (n.)

American *Amerikaner/-in* (m./f.) *(Amerikaner/-innen)*

among *unter*

amount to (to) *machen*

and *und*

angry *böse*

ankle *Knöchel* (m.) *(Knöchel)*

announce (to) *ansagen*

annoy (to) *ärgern*
  annoyed (to be) *sich ärgern*

annoying *lästig*

another *andere, noch ein*

answer *Antwort* (f.) *(Antworten)*
  What's the right answer? *Wie lautet die
  richtige Antwort?*

answer (to) *antworten*

answering machine *Anrufbeantworter* (m.)
  (Anrufbeantworter)

apartment *Wohnung* (f.) *(Wohnungen)*

apologize (to) *entschuldigen*

apparatus *Apparat* (m.) *(Apparate)*

appear (to) *aussehen*

appetite *Appetit* (m.) (no pl.)

appetizer *Vorspeise* (f.) *(Vorspeisen)*
  as an appetizer *als Vorspeise*

apple *Apfel* (m.) *(Äpfel)*

apple juice *Apfelsaft* (m.) *(Apfelsäfte)*

apply (to) *bewerben*
  apply for a job/position (to) *sich auf eine
  Stelle bewerben*

appointment *Termin* (m.) *(Termine),
Verabredung* (f.) *(Verabredungen)*
  make an appointment (to) *eine Verabredung
  machen (Verabredungen machen)*

apprentice *Auszubildende* (m./f.)
(Auszubildenden), Azubi (m./f.) *(Azubis)*

apprentice (to) *eine Ausbildung machen*

apprenticeship *Ausbildungsstelle* (f.)
  (Ausbildungsstellen), Ausbildung (f.)
  (Ausbildungen)

approach (to) *herangehen*

approve (to) *genehmigen*

approximately *etwa*

April *April* (m.) *(Aprile)*

architect *Architekt/-in* (m./f.) *(Architekten/
Architektinnen)*

arm *Arm* (m.) *(Arme)*

around *um, herum*
  around the corner *um die Ecke*
  around town *in der Stadt*
  going around (to be) *umgehen*
  know one's way around (to) *sich auskennen*
  turn around (to) (U-turn) *umdrehen*

arrange (to) *verabreden, vereinbaren*

arrive (to) *ankommen*

article *Artikel* (m.) *(Artikel)*

as *wie, als*
  as … as *so … wie*
  as always *wie immer*

ask (to) *fragen*

aspirin *Aspirin* (n.) (no pl.)

assistant *Assistent/-in* (m./f.) *(Assistenten/
Assistentinnen)*

at *um, bei, an*
  at five o' clock *um fünf Uhr*
  at once *sofort*
  at one o'clock *um ein Uhr*
  at the corner *an der Ecke*

athlete *Sportler/-in* (m./f.) *(Sportler/-innen)*

attention *Vorsicht* (f.) (no pl.)
  Pay attention! *Pass auf!*

August *August* (m.) *(Auguste)*

aunt *Tante* (f.) *(Tanten)*

Austria *Österreich* (n.)

B

baby *Kind* (n.) *(Kinder)*
  have a baby (to) *ein Kind bekommen*

back *zurück*
  in back of *hinter*
  Welcome back. *Willkommen zurück.*

bad *schlecht, böse*
  bad luck *Pech* (n.) (no pl.)
  Too bad. *So ein Pech.*
  You look bad/sick. *Sie sehen schlecht aus.*

bag *Tasche* (f.) *(Taschen)*
bake (to) *backen*
baker *Bäcker/-in* (m.) *(Bäcker/Bäckerinnen)*
bakery *Bäckerei* (f.) *(Bäckereien)*
balcony *Balkon* (m.) *(Balkone)*
ball *Ball* (m.) *(Bälle)*
ballet classes *Ballettunterricht* (m.) (no pl.)
banana *Banane* (f.) *(Bananen)*
bandage *Verband* (m.) *(Verbände)*
  bandage (adhesive bandage) *Pflaster* (n.) *(Pflaster)*
  put on a bandage (to) *Verband anlegen*
bank (financial institution) *Bank* (f.) *(Banken)*
bar (neighborhood bar) *Kneipe* (f.) *(Kneipen)*
basketball (game) *Basketball* (m.) (no pl.)
  play basketball (to) *Basketball spielen*
bathroom *Bad* (n.) *(Bäder)*, *Badezimmer* (n.) *(Badezimmer)*, *Toilette* (f.) *(Toiletten)*
be (to) *sein, lauten*
beautiful *schön*
because *wegen, weil, denn*
become (to) *werden*
bed *Bett* (n.) *(Betten)*
  go to bed (to) *ins Bett gehen*
bedroom *Schlafzimmer* (n.) *(Schlafzimmer)*
beef *Rindfleisch* (n.) (no pl.)
  braised beef *Sauerbraten* (m.) *(Sauerbraten)*
beer *Bier* (n.) *(Biere)*
before *vor*
begin (to) *anfangen, beginnen*
behind *hinter*
believe (to) *glauben*
belly *Bauch* (m.) *(Bäuche)*
belong to (to) *gehören*
belt *Gürtel* (m.) *(Gürtel)*
bench *Bank* (f.) *(Bänke)*
beneath *unter*
beside *neben*
best (adjective) *liebste, beste*
  best (adverb) *am liebsten, am besten*
better *lieber, besser*
between *zwischen*
  in between *dazwischen*
beverage *Getränk* (n.) *(Getränke)*
bicycle *Fahrrad* (n.) *(Fahrräder)*
  ride a bicycle (to) *Fahrrad fahren*
big *groß*
  bigger *größer*

biggest (adjective) *größte*
  biggest (adverb) *am größten*
bike *Rad* (n.) *(Räder)*
  bike (to) *Rad fahren*
bike tour *Radtour* (f.) *(Radtouren)*
bill *Rechnung* (f.) *(Rechnungen)*
billion *Milliarde* (f.) *(Milliarden)*
biology *Biologie* (f.) (no pl.)
birthday *Geburtstag* (m.) *(Geburtstage)*
  Happy birthday! *Alles Gute zum Geburtstag!*
black *schwarz*
blouse *Bluse* (f.) *(Blusen)*
blue *blau*
bologna *Lyoner* (f.) (no pl.)
book *Buch* (n.) *(Bücher)*
book page *Buchseite* (f.) *(Buchseiten)*
booked out *ausgebucht*
boots *Stiefel* (m.) *(Stiefel)*
borrow (to) *leihen*
boss *Boss* (m.) *(Bosse)*, *Chef/-in* (m./f.) *(Chefs/Chefinnen)*
both *beide*
bottle *Flasche* (f.) *(Flaschen)*
  a bottle of mineral water *eine Flasche Mineralwasser*
  a bottle of wine *eine Flasche Wein*
boutique *Boutique* (f.) *(Boutiquen)*
bowl *Teller* (m.) *(Teller)*
  a bowl of soup *ein Teller Suppe*
boy *Junge* (m.) *(Jungen)*
boyfriend *Freund* (m.) *(Freunde)*
braised beef *Sauerbraten* (m.) *(Sauerbraten)*
brand-new *ganz neu*
bread *Brot* (n.) *(Brote)*
  a loaf of bread *ein Laib Brot*
break *Pause* (f.) *(Pausen)*
  take a break (to) *eine Pause machen*
break (to) *brechen*
breakfast *Frühstück* (n.) *(Frühstücke)*
breakfast roll *Brötchen* (n.) *(Brötchen)*
bring (to) *bringen*
  bring along (to) *mitbringen*
broken *kaputt*
brother *Bruder* (m.) *(Brüder)*
brother-in-law *Schwager* (m.) *(Schwäger)*
brown *braun*
brunch *Brunch* (m.) *(Brunches/Brunche)*
bus *Bus* (m.) *(Busse)*

by bus *mit dem Bus*
take the bus (to) *den Bus nehmen*
bus stop *Bushaltestelle* (f.) *(Bushaltestellen)*
business *Geschäft* (n.) *(Geschäfte)*
  run a business (to) *ein Geschäft leiten*
business trip *Geschäftsreise* (f.)
  (Geschäftsreisen)
businessman *Geschäftsmann* (m.)
  (Geschäftsmänner)
busy (phone line) *besetzt*
but *aber*
  yes, but ... *schon, aber ...*
butcher *Metzger/-in* (m./f.) *(Metzger/-innen)*
butter *Butter* (f.) (no pl.)
buy (to) *kaufen*
by *von, bei, durch*
  by bus *mit dem Bus*
  by car *mit dem Auto*
  by chance *etwa*
  by profession *von Beruf*
  by tram *mit der Straßenbahn*
  go by cab/taxi (to) *mit dem Taxi fahren*
  go by foot (to) *zu Fuß gehen*
  go by means of ... (to) *fahren mit ...*
Bye. *Tschüss.*

C

cab *Taxi* (n.) *(Taxis; Taxen)*
  call a cab (to) *ein Taxi rufen*
  go by cab (to) *mit dem Taxi fahren*
cab driver *Taxifahrer* (m.) *(Taxifahrer)*
cake *Kuchen* (m.) *(Kuchen)*
  a piece of cake *ein Stück Kuchen*
California *Kalifornien* (n.)
call (to) *rufen, anrufen, telefonieren*
  called (to be) *heißen*
  call a doctor (to) *den Arzt rufen*
call back (to) *zurückrufen*
can *können*
  Can I help you? *Kann ich Ihnen helfen?*
Canada *Kanada* (n.)
cancel (to) *absagen*
cap (hat) *Mütze* (f.) *(Mützen)*
car *Auto* (n.) *(Autos)*
  by car *mit dem Auto*
  take the car (to) *das Auto nehmen*
card *Karte* (f.) *(Karten)*
  play cards (to) *Karten spielen*

card game *Kartenspiel* (n.) *(Kartenspiele)*
career *Karriere* (f.) *(Karrieren)*
  advance (to make a career) (to) *Karriere*
  machen
Careful! *Vorsicht!*
  Be careful! *Pass gut auf dich auf!*
carpenter *Tischler/-in* (m./f.) *(Tischler/-innen)*
carrot *Karotte* (f.) *(Karotten)*
cashier *Kasse* (f.) *(Kassen)*
  at the cashier *an der Kasse*
cat *Katze* (f.) *(Katzen)*
catch a cold (to) *sich erkälten, eine Erkältung*
  bekommen
catch something (somebody else's illness)
  (to) *sich anstecken*
cause *Ursache* (f.) *(Ursachen)*
caution *Vorsicht* (f.) (no pl.)
celebrate (to) *feiern*
cell phone *Handy* (n.) *(Handys)*
cell phone number *Handynummer* (f.)
  (Handynummern)
certain *bestimmt, sicher*
certainly *bestimmt, schon*
chair *Stuhl* (m.) *(Stühle)*
champagne *Champagner* (m.) (no pl.)
chance *Chance* (f.) *(Chancen)*
  by chance *etwa*
change (to) *umtauschen, wechseln, ändern*
change (trains/buses) (to) *umsteigen*
cheap *billig*
check *Rechnung* (f.) *(Rechnungen)*
  One check? (at a restaurant) *Alles*
  zusammen?
checkered *kariert*
Cheers! (lit., To wellness!) *Zum Wohl!*
cheese *Käse* (m.) (no pl.)
chicken *Hühnchen* (n.) *(Hühnchen), Huhn* (n.)
  (Hühner)
child *Kind* (n.) *(Kinder)*
children's room *Kinderzimmer* (n.)
  (Kinderzimmer)
chocolate *Schokolade* (f.) *(Schokoladen)*
choice *Wahl* (f.) *(Wahlen)*
Christmas *Weihnachten* (n.) *(Weihnachten)*
circulate (to) *umgehen*
city *Stadt* (f.) *(Städte)*
city center *Innenstadt* (f.) *(Innenstädte)*
city tour *Stadtrundfahrt* (f.) *(Stadtrundfahrten)*

take a city tour (to) *eine Stadtrundfahrt machen*
classified ad *Annonce* (f.) (*Annoncen*)
classmate *Mitschüler/-in* (m./f.) (*Mitschüler/-innen*)
clay *Ton* (m.) (no pl.)
clean (to) *reinigen, auswaschen*
  clean the wound (to) *Wunde auswaschen*
client *Klient/-in* (m./f.) (*Klienten/Klientinnen*), *Kunde/Kundin* (m./f.)
climb (to) *steigen*
clock *Uhr* (f.) (*Uhren*)
close (to) *zumachen*
closeness *Nähe* (f.) (*Nähen*)
closet *Schrank* (m.) (*Schränke*)
clothes *Kleider* (pl.)
clothing *Kleidung* (f.) (*Kleidungen*)
club *Verein* (m.) (*Vereine*)
  join a club (to) *einem Verein beitreten*
coat *Mantel* (m.) (*Mäntel*)
coffee *Kaffee* (m.) (*Kaffees*)
  a cup of coffee *eine Tasse Kaffee*
  a portion (lit., a small pot) of coffee *ein Kännchen Kaffee*
coffee cup *Kaffeetasse* (f.) (*Kafeetassen*)
coincidence *Zufall* (m.) (*Zufälle*)
cold *kalt; Erkältung* (f.) (*Erkältungen*), *Schnupfen* (m.) (*Schnupfen*)
  catch a cold (to) *eine Erkältung bekommen*
  have a cold (to) *Schnupfen haben*
  It is cold. *Es ist kalt.*
cold cuts *Wurstaufschnitt* (m.) (no pl.)
colleague *Arbeitskollege/Arbeitskollegin* (m./f.) (*Arbeitskollegen/Arbeitskolleginnen*), *Kollege/Kollegin* (m./f.) (*Kollegen/Kolleginnen*), *Mitarbeiter/-in* (m./f.) (*Mitarbeiter/-innen*)
collect (to) *sammeln*
Cologne *Köln* (n.)
color *Farbe* (f.) (*Farben*)
comb (to) *kämmen*
  comb one's hair (to) *sich kämmen*
come (to) *kommen*
  come along (to) *mitkommen*
company *Firma* (f.) (*Firmen*)
complete *ganz*
completely *ganz*
compliment *Kompliment* (n.) (*Komplimente*)
computer *Computer* (m.) (*Computer*)

concern (to) *kümmern, betreffen*
congratulation *Glückwunsch* (m.) (*Glückwünsche*)
  Congratulations! *Herzlichen Glückwunsch!*
connect (to) *verbinden*
connection *Verbindung* (f.) (*Verbindungen*)
conserve (to) *schonen*
constantly *ständig*
contagious *ansteckend*
continue straight ahead (to) *geradeaus gehen*
cook *Koch/Köchin* (m./f.) (*Köche/Köchinnen*)
cook (to) *kochen*
  cook well (to) *gut kochen*
cookie *Keks* (m.) (*Kekse*)
corn *Mais* (m.) (no pl.)
corner *Ecke* (f.) (*Ecken*)
  around the corner *um die Ecke*
  at the corner *an der Ecke*
correct *richtig*
cost (to) *kosten*
couch *Couch* (f.) (*Couches*), *Sofa* (n.) (*Sofas*)
cough *Husten* (m.) (no pl.)
  have a cough (to) *Husten haben*
couple *Paar* (n.) (*Paare*)
  a couple of days *ein paar Tage*
course *Lauf* (m.) (*Läufe*)
cousin *Cousin/Cousine* (m./f.) (*Cousins/Cousinen*)
cover (to) *belegen*
credit card *Kreditkarte* (f.) (*Kreditkarten*)
crochet (to) *häkeln*
crosswalk *Fußgängerüberweg* (m.) (*Fußgängerüberwege*)
  Take the crosswalk. *Gehen Sie über den Fußgängerüberweg.*
cruise *Schifffahrt* (f.) (*Schifffahrten*)
cry (tears) (to) *weinen*
cucumber *Gurke* (f.) (*Gurken*)
cup *Tasse* (f.) (*Tassen*)
  a cup of coffee *eine Tasse Kaffee*
curious *neugierig*
customer *Kunde/Kundin* (m./f.)
cut (to) *schneiden*
cutlet *Schnitzel* (n.) (*Schnitzel*)

D

dad(dy) *Papa* (m.) (*Papas*)
daily *täglich*

dance (to) *tanzen*
dangerous *gefährlich*
darling *Schatz* (m.) *(Schätze), Liebling* (m.)
  (Lieblinge)
date *Verabredung* (f.) *(Verabredungen)*
daughter *Tochter* (f.) *(Töchter)*
day *Tag* (m.) *(Tage)*
  a couple of days, a few days *ein paar Tage*
  all day *den ganzen Tag*
  every day *jeden Tag*
  Good day. *Guten Tag.*
  the day after tomorrow *übermorgen*
  the day before yesterday *vorgestern*
  these days *heutzutage*
December *Dezember* (m.) *(Dezember)*
decide (to) *bestimmen, entscheiden*
decrease (to) *abnehmen*
definite *bestimmt*
definitely *bestimmt*
degree *Grad* (m.) *(Grade)*
delight *Lust* (f.) *(Lüste)*
dentist *Zahnarzt/Zahnärztin* (m./f.)
  (Zahnärzte/Zahnärztinnen)
department store *Kaufhaus* (n.) *(Kaufhäuser)*
  men's department *Herrenabteilung* (f.)
    (Herrenabteilungen)
  shoe department *Schuhabteilung* (f.)
    (Schuhabteilungen)
departure *Abfahrt* (f.) *(Abfahrten), Abreise* (f.)
  (Abreisen)
describe (to) *beschreiben*
desk *Schreibtisch* (m.) *(Schreibtische)*
despite *trotz*
dessert *Nachspeise* (f.) *(Nachspeisen), Nachtisch*
  (m.) *(Nachtische), Süßspeise* (f.) *(Süßspeisen)*
  for dessert *als Nachspeise*
determine (to) *bestimmen*
differently *anders*
difficult *schwierig*
dining room *Esszimmer* (n.) *(Esszimmer)*
dining table *Esstisch* (m.) *(Esstische)*
dinner *Abendessen* (n.) *(Abendessen)*
direction *Richtung* (f.) *(Richtungen)*
  Drive towards/in the direction of
    Munich. *Fahren Sie in Richtung München.*
directly *direkt*
dive (scuba dive) (to) *tauchen*
divorced *geschieden*

get divorced (to) *geschieden werden*
do (to) *machen, tun, treiben*
  have a lot to do (to) *viel zu tun haben*
doctor *Arzt/Ärztin* (m./f.) *(Ärzte/Ärztinnen)*
doctor's office *Praxis* (f.) *(Praxen)*
dog *Hund* (m.) *(Hunde)*
door *Tür* (f.) *(Türen)*
draw (to) *zeichnen*
dream *Traum* (m.) *(Träume)*
dress *Kleid* (n.) *(Kleider)*
dress (to) *anziehen*
drink *Getränk* (n.) *(Getränke)*
drink (to) *trinken*
drive (to) *fahren, treiben*
  Drive safely! *Gute Fahrt!*
drop *Tropfen* (m.) *(Tropfen)*
drugstore *Drogerie* (f.) *(Drogerien)*
during *während*

E

each *jede, je*
earlier *früher*
early *früh*
earring *Ohrring* (m.) *(Ohrringe)*
eat (to) *essen*
editor *Redakteur/-in* (m./f.) *(Redakteure/*
  Redakteurinnen)
education *Ausbildung* (f.) *(Ausbildungen)*
eight *acht*
eighteen *achtzehn*
eighty *achtzig*
either *entweder*
  either … or … *entweder … oder …*
elbow *Ellbogen* (m.) *(Ellbogen)*
electrician *Elektriker/-in* (m./f.) *(Elektriker/-*
  innen)
elementary school (first grade through fourth
  grade) *Grundschule* (f.) *(Grundschulen)*
eleven *elf*
else *sonst*
  Anything else? *Sonst noch etwas?/Darf's*
    sonst noch etwas sein?
  What else do you need? *Was brauchen Sie*
    sonst noch?
e-mail *E-Mail* (f.) *(E-Mails)*
embarrassing *peinlich*
emergency *Notfall* (m.) *(Notfälle)*
emergency room *Notaufnahme* (f.)

(Notaufnahmen)
employee *Arbeitnehmer/-in* (m./f.)
  (Arbeitnehmer/-innen), Angestellte (m./f.)
  (Angestellten), Mitarbeiter/-in (m./f.)
  (Mitarbeiter/-innen)
employment *Beschäftigung* (f.)
  (Beschäftigungen)
  full-time employment *Vollzeitbeschäftigug*
    (f.) *(Vollzeitbeschäftigungen)*
  part-time employment *Teilzeitbeschäftigung*
    (f.) *(Teilzeitbeschäftigungen)*
  self-employed *selbstständig*
empty *leer*
end *Ende* (n.) *(Enden), Schluss* (m.) *(Schlüsse)*
end (to) *beenden*
engaged *verlobt*
  engaged (to be) *verlobt sein*
Enjoy! *Viel Spaß!*
  Enjoy your meal! *Guten Appetit!*
enough *genug*
entertainment *Unterhaltung* (f.)
  (Unterhaltungen)
entire *ganz*
entrance *Einfahrt* (f.) *(Einfahrten)*
euro *Euro* (m.) *(Euros)*
evaluation *Beurteilung* (f.) *(Beurteilungen)*
even *schon, sogar, auch*
evening *Abend* (m.) *(Abende)*
  Good evening. *Guten Abend.*
  in the evening *am Abend, abends*
  this evening *heute Abend*
ever *je*
every *jede*
  every day *jeden Tag*
  every Thursday *jeden Donnerstag*
  every time *jedes Mal*
everyday life *tägliches Leben*
everything *alles*
  Is everything okay? *Ist alles in Ordnung?*
  That's everything. *Das ist alles.*
exam *Prüfung* (f.) *(Prüfungen)*
  high school exam *Abitur* (n.) *(Abiture)*
  middle school exam *Realschulprüfung* (f.)
    (Realschulprüfungen)
  school-leaving exam (lower
    level) *Hauptschulabschluß* (m.)
    (Hauptschulabschlüsse)
  take the high school exam (to) *das Abitur*

machen
  take the middle school exam (to) *die*
    Realschulprüfung machen
examine (to) *untersuchen*
excellent *ausgezeichnet, hervorragend*
except for *außer*
exchange (to) *umtauschen, wechseln*
excited *aufgeregt*
excitedly *aufgeregt*
excuse *Entschuldigung* (f.) *(Entschuldigungen)*
  Excuse me. *Entschuldigung.*
excuse (to) *entschuldigen*
  Excuse me. *Entschuldige.*
  Excuse me?/I'm sorry? *Wie bitte?*
exit *Ausfahrt* (f.) *(Ausfahrten)*
expensive *teuer*
experience *Erfahrung* (f.) *(Erfahrungen)*
explain (to) *erklären*
expression *Ausdruck* (m.) *(Ausdrücke)*
eye *Auge* (n.) *(Augen)*
  keep an eye on (to) *aufpassen*

F

fall *Herbst* (m.) *(Herbste)*
  fall (to) *fallen*
  fall asleep (to) *einschlafen*
family *Familie* (f.) *(Familien)*
  family life *Familienleben* (n.) (no pl.)
  family photographs *Familienfotos* (pl.)
  start a family (to) *eine Familie gründen*
fantastic *fantastisch*
far *weit*
  How far … ? *Wie weit … ?*
fare *Fahrgeld* (n.) (no pl.)
farther *weiter*
  two blocks farther *zwei Straßen weiter*
fast *schnell*
fast-paced *schnelllebig*
fat *dick*
  fattening (to be) *dick machen*
father *Vater* (m.) *(Väter)*
father-in-law *Schwiegervater* (m.)
  (Schwiegerväter)
favorite *Liebling* (m.) *(Lieblinge)*
  favorite subject *Lieblingsfach* (n.)
February *Februar* (m.) *(Februare)*
feel (to) *fühlen, sich fühlen*
  feel healthy (to) *sich gesund fühlen*

feel like (to) *Lust haben*
feel like doing something (to) *zu etwas Lust haben*
feel sick (to) *sich krank fühlen*
feel well (to) *sich wohl fühlen*
not feel like (to) *keine Lust haben*
fetch (to) *holen*
fever *Fieber* (n.) *(Fieber)*
  high fever *hohes Fieber*
  take someone's temperature (to) *Fieber messen*
few *wenige*
fifteen *fünfzehn*
  It is six fifteen. (time) *Es ist sechs Uhr fünfzehn.*
fifty *fünfzig*
  from the fifties ('50s) *aus den Fünfzigern*
final sentence *Schlusssatz* (m.) *(Schlusssätze)*
finally *endlich*
  Finally! *Na endlich!*
find (to) *finden*
finger *Finger* (m.) *(Finger)*
finished *fertig, vorbei*
fire (to) *entlassen*
first *zuerst, erst mal*
  at first *erst*
  for the first time *zum ersten Mal*
fish *Fisch* (m.) *(Fische)*
fit *fit*
fit (to) *passen*
  fit well (to) *gut passen*
fitness club *Fitnessclub* (m.) *(Fitnessclubs)*
fitting room *Umkleidekabine* (f.) *(Umkleidekabinen)*
five *fünf*
flexible working hours *gleitende Arbeitszeit* (f.)
flower *Blume* (f.) *(Blumen)*
flu *Grippe* (f.) *(Grippen)*
  have the flu (to) *Grippe haben*
  The flu is going around. *Die Grippe geht um.*
follow (to) *folgen*
food *Lebensmittel* (n.) *(Lebensmittel)*
foot *Fuß* (m.) *(Füße)*
  go by foot (to) *zu Fuß gehen*
for *für, seit*
foreign *fremd*
forget (to) *vergessen*
Forgive me. *Entschuldigung./Verzeihung.*

forgiveness *Verzeihung* (f.) *(Verzeihungen)*
fork *Gabel* (f.) *(Gabeln)*
forty *vierzig*
found (to) *gründen*
four *vier*
fourteen *vierzehn*
foyer *Diele* (f.) *(Dielen)*
France *Frankreich* (n.) (no pl.)
freelance (adjective/adverb) *freiberuflich*
freelance (to) *freiberuflich arbeiten, freiberuflich tätig sein*
Frenchman *Franzose* (m.) *(Franzosen)*
fresh *frisch*
Friday *Freitag* (m.) *(Freitage)*
friend *Freund/Freundin* (m./f.) *(Freunde/ Freundinnen)*
friendly *freundlich*
from *von, aus, her*
  from … to *von … bis*
  I'm from … *Ich komme aus …*
  Where are you from? *Wo kommen Sie her?/ Woher kommen Sie?*
front (in front of) *vor*
fruit *Obst* (n.) (no pl.)
full *voll*
full-time employment *Vollzeitbeschäftigug* (f.) *(Vollzeitbeschäftigungen)*
fully *ganz*
fun *Spaß* (m.) *(Späße)*
  fun (to be) *Spaß machen*
  Have fun! *Viel Spaß!*
furniture *Möbel* (pl.)

G

game *Spiel* (n.) *(Spiele)*
garden *Garten* (m.) *(Gärten)*
  work in the garden (to) *im Garten arbeiten*
garden work *Gartenarbeit* (f.) *(Gartenarbeiten)*
gas (to get) *tanken*
gas station *Tankstelle* (f.) *(Tankstellen)*
gas station attendant *Tankwart/-in* (m./f.) *(Tankwarte/-innen)*
German (language) *Deutsch* (n.) (no pl.)
  in German *auf Deutsch*
German (person) *Deutscher/Deutsche* (m./f.) *(Deutschen)*
Germany *Deutschland* (n.) (no pl.)
get (to) *holen, bekommen*

How do I get to … ? *Wie komme ich … ?*
get up (to) *aufstehen*
  get up early (to) *früh aufstehen*
  get up late (to) *spät aufstehen*
gift *Geschenk* (n.) *(Geschenke)*
  as a gift for … *als Geschenk für …*
girl *Mädchen* (n.) *(Mädchen)*
girlfriend *Freundin* (f.) *(Freundinnen)*
give (as a gift) (to) *schenken*
give (to) *geben*
glad (to be) *freuen*
glass *Glas* (n.) *(Gläser)*
  a glass of wine *ein Glas Wein*
gliding *gleitend*
gloves *Handschuhe* (pl.)
go (to) *gehen, fahren*
  go by means of … (to) *fahren mit …*
  go by cab (to) *mit dem Taxi fahren*
  go by foot (to) *zu Fuß gehen*
  go for a walk (to) *spazieren gehen*
  go ice-skating (to) *Schlittschuh laufen*
  go on vacation (to) *Urlaub machen*
  go to bed (to) *ins Bett gehen*
  go skiing (to) *Ski fahren*
  go swimming (to) *schwimmen gehen*
  go well with (to) *gut passen zu*
go out (to) *ausgehen, hinausgehen*
going around (to be) *umgehen*
  The flu is going around. *Die Grippe geht um.*
golf *Golf* (n.)
  play golf (to) *Golf spielen*
golf course *Golfplatz* (m.) *(Golfplätze)*
good *gut*
  Good day. *Guten Tag.*
  Good evening. *Guten Abend.*
  good-looking *gutaussehend*
  Good luck! *Viel Glück!*
  Good morning. *Guten Morgen.*
Goodbye. *Auf Wiedersehen.*
  Good-bye until then. *Auf Wiedersehen bis dann.*
gram *Gramm* (n.) *(Gramme; but no pl. after numbers)*
grandchild *Enkelkind* (n.) *(Enkelkinder)*
granddaughter *Enkelin* (f.) *(Enkelinnen)*
grandfather *Großvater* (m.) *(Großväter)*
grandma *Oma* (f.) *(Omas)*
grandmother *Großmutter* (f.) *(Großmütter)*

grandpa *Opa* (m.) *(Opas)*
grandparents *Großeltern* (pl.)
grandson *Enkel* (m.) *(Enkel)*
grapes (bunch of) *Traube* (f.) *(Trauben)*
grass *Gras* (n.) *(Gräser)*
gray *grau*
great *prima, super*
  Great! *Prima!*
green *grün*
groceries *Lebensmittel* (f.) *(Lebensmittel)*
grocery store *Gemüseladen* (m.) *(Gemüseläden), Supermarkt* (m.) *(Supermärkte)*
guest *Gast* (m.) *(Gäste)*
guitar *Gitarre* (f.) *(Gitarren)*
  play the guitar (to) *Gitarre spielen*

H

hair *Haar* (n.) *(Haare)*
half *halb*
  It is half past seven. *Es ist halb acht.*
ham *Schinken* (m.) *(Schinken)*
hand *Hand* (f.) *(Hände)*
  on the other hand *dagegen*
handball (game) *Handball* (m.) (no pl.)
  play handball (to) *Handball spielen*
handsome *gutaussehend*
hang (to) *hängen*
hang up (to) *auflegen*
  hang up the receiver (to) *den Hörer auflegen*
happen (to) *werden, geschehen, passieren*
Happy birthday! *Alles Gute zum Geburtstag!*
hard *hart*
hasten (to) *beeilen*
hat *Hut* (m.) *(Hüte), Mütze* (f.) *(Mützen)*
have (to) *haben*
  have a baby (to) *ein Kind bekommen*
  have a hobby (to) *einem Hobby nachgehen*
  have a picnic (to) *ein Picknick machen*
  I would like to have … *Ich hätte gern …*
  There you have it! *Na also!*
have to (to) *müssen*
he *er*
head *Kopf* (m.) *(Köpfe)*
headache *Kopfweh* (n.) (no pl.), *Kopfschmerzen* (pl.)
  have a headache (to) *Kopfweh/ Kopfschmerzen haben*
headache tablet *Kopfschmerztablette* (f.)

(Kopfschmerztabletten)

healthy *gesund*
 feel healthy (to) *sich gesund fühlen*
 To your health! *Auf dein Wohl!*
hear (to) *hören*
Hello. *Guten Tag./Grüß Gott./Servus.*
 Hello, this is Philipp. (on the phone) *Hier Philipp.*
help *Hilfe* (f.) *(Hilfen)*
help (to) *helfen*
 Can I help you? *Kann ich Ihnen helfen?*
help-wanted ad *Stellenanzeige* (f.) *(Stellenanzeigen)*, *Stellenmarkt* (m.) *(Stellenmärkte)*
her (accusative) *sie*
 her, to her (dative) *ihr*
 her (possessive) *ihr*
here *hier, her*
 Here you go. *Bitte sehr.*
 right here *gleich hier*
herself *sich*
Hi. *Hallo.*
high *hoch*
 high fever *hohes Fieber* (n.)
 higher *höher*
 highest (adjective) *höchste*
 highest (adverb) *am höchsten*
highway (interstate) *Autobahn* (f.) *(Autobahnen)*
 state highway *Landstraße* (f.) *(Landstraßen)*
hike (to) *wandern*
him (accusative) *ihn*
 him, to him (dative) *ihm*
himself *sich*
hire (to) *einstellen*
his *sein*
hit (to) *treffen*
hobby *Hobby* (n.) *(Hobbys)*
 have a hobby (to) *einem Hobby nachgehen*
hold (to) *halten*
home *Zuhause* (n.) (no pl.), *zu Hause, nach Hause*
homework *Hausaufgaben* (pl.)
 do homework (to) *die Hausaufgaben machen*
honest *ehrlich*
hope (to) *hoffen*
horse *Pferd* (n.) *(Pferde)*
hospital *Krankenhaus* (n.) *(Krankenhäuser)*
hot *heiß*

It is hot. *Es ist heiß.*
hotel *Hotel* (n.) *(Hotels)*
hotel room *Hotelzimmer* (n.) *(Hotelzimmer)*
hour *Stunde* (f.) *(Stunden)*
 an hour ago *vor einer Stunde*
 in an hour *in einer Stunde*
 quarter of an hour *Viertelstunde* (f.) *(Viertelstunden)*
house *Haus* (n.) *(Häuser)*
how *wie*
 How about … *Wie wär's mit …*
 How are you? (fml.) *Wie geht es Ihnen?*
 How are you? (infml.) *Wie geht's?*
 how many *wie viele*
 how much *wie viel*
hundred *hundert*
 one hundred *einhundert*
 one hundred one *einhundert(und)eins*
 one hundred thousand *hunderttausend*
 one hundred twenty-one *einhundert(und) einundzwanzig*
hunger *Hunger* (m.) (no pl.)
hungry (to be) *Hunger haben*
hurry (to) *beeilen, sich beeilen*
hurt (to) *verletzen, weh tun*
 hurt oneself (to) *sich verletzen*
husband *Ehemann* (m.) *(Ehemänner)*, *Gatte* (m.) *(Gatten)*, *Mann* (m.) *(Männer)*
 my husband *mein Mann*

I

I *ich*
 I'm sorry. *(Es) tut mir leid.*
ice cream *Eis* (n.) (no pl.)
ice skate *Schlittschuh* (m.) *(Schlittschuhe)*
 go ice-skating (to) *Schlittschuh laufen*
idea *Idee* (f.) *(Ideen)*
if *wenn, ob*
immediately *gleich*
important *wichtig*
impressive *beeindruckend*
improve (to) *verbessern*
in *in, mit*
in order to *um … zu*
inclusive *inklusive*
increase (to) *steigen, erhöhen*
infect (to) *anstecken*
injure (to) *verletzen*

inside *in*
instead *dafür*
instead of *statt, anstatt*
intelligent *intelligent*
intention *Absicht* (f.) *(Absichten)*
interest (to) *interessieren*
internship *Volontariat* (n.) *(Valontariate)*
 internship (newspaper) *Praktikum* (n.)
  (Praktika)
 intern at a newspaper (to) *ein Volontariat
  machen*
interrupt (to) *unterbrechen*
intersection *Kreuzung* (f.) *(Kreuzungen)*
into *in*
invitation *Einladung* (f.) *(Einladungen)*
invite (to) *einladen*
invoice *Rechnung* (f.) *(Rechnungen)*
issue *Frage* (f.) *(Fragen)*
it (nominative) *es*
 it (accusative) *es*
 it, to it (dative) *ihm*
its *sein*
itself *sich*

J

jacket *Jacke* (f.) *(Jacken)*
jam *Marmelade* (f.) *(Marmeladen)*
January *Januar* (m.) *(Januare)*
 in January *im Januar*
Japan *Japan* (n.)
jeans *Jeans* (pl.)
jelly *Gelee* (m.) *(Gelees)*
job *Aufgabe* (f.) *(Aufgaben), Beruf* (m.)
 (Berufe), Stelle (f.) *(Stellen), Arbeitsstelle* (f.)
 (Arbeitsstellen)
job announcement *Stellenanzeige* (f.)
 (Stellenanzeigen), Stellenmarkt (m.)
 (Stellenmärkte)
job opportunity *Berufsaussicht* (f.)
 (Berufsaussichten); Berufschance (f.)
 (Berufsschancen)
job-oriented *beruflich*
jog (to) *joggen*
join (to) *beitreten*
 join a club (to) *einem Verein beitreten*
journalist *Journalist/-in* (m./f.) *(Journalisten/
 Journalistinnen)*
juice *Saft* (m.) *(Säfte)*

July *Juli* (m.) *(Julis)*
June *Juni* (m.) *(Junis)*
junior high school (fifth grade through ninth
 grade) *Hauptschule* (f.) *(Hauptschulen)*
just *gerade, eben, gleich, einfach*

K

karate *Karate* (n.) *(no pl.)*
karate teacher *Karatelehrer* (m.) *(Karatelehrer)*
keep an eye on (to) *aufpassen*
Keep the change. *Stimmt so.*
key *Schlüssel* (m.) *(Schlüssel)*
kilogram *Kilogramm* (n.) *(Kilogramme; but no
 pl. after numbers)*
kilometer *Kilometer* (m.) *(Kilometer)*
kind *freundlich*
kiss (to) *küssen*
kitchen *Küche* (f.) *(Küchen)*
knee *Knie* (n.) *(Knie)*
knife *Messer* (n.) *(Messer)*
knit (to) *stricken*
know (facts) (to) *wissen*
 know (people, animals, places, and things)
  (to) *kennen*
 How did you know that? *Woher wußtest du
  das?*
 know one's way around (to) *sich auskennen*
 Not that I know of. *Nicht dass ich wüsste.*

L

lacking (to be) *fehlen*
lady *Dame* (f.) *(Damen)*
lamb *Lamm* (n.) *(Lämmer)*
lamp *Lampe* (f.) *(Lampen)*
last *letzte*
 At last! *Na endlich!*
 last month *letzten Monat*
 last night *gestern Abend*
 last week *letzte Woche*
 last year *letztes Jahr*
 the ... before last *vorletzte*
late *spät*
later *später*
law (the study of law) *Jura* (pl.)
lawyer *Anwalt/Anwältin* (m./f.) *(Anwälte/
 Anwältinnen), Rechtsanwalt/Rechtsanwältin*
 (m./f.) *(Rechtsanwälte/Rechtsanwältinnen)*
lay on (to) *anlegen*

layoff *Entlassung* (f.) (*Entlassungen*)
lead (to) *leiten*
learn (to) *lernen*
  have a lot to learn (to) *viel zu lernen haben*
leave (to) *fahren, abfahren, hinterlassen*
  leave a message (to) *Nachricht* (f.)
   hinterlassen
left, to the left *links*
  turn left (to) *links abbiegen*
leg *Bein* (n.) (*Beine*)
leisure time *Freizeit* (f.) (no pl.)
leisure time activity *Freizeitbeschäftigung* (f.)
  (*Freizeitbeschäftigungen*)
lend (to) *verleihen*
less *weniger*
lesson *Lektion* (f.) (*Lektionen*)
  lessons *Unterricht* (m.) (no pl.)
let (to) *lassen*
  let go (to) *gehen lassen, entlassen*
letter *Brief* (m.) (*Briefe*)
lettuce *Salat* (m.) (*Salate*)
lie (to) (location) *liegen*
life *Leben* (n.) (*Leben*)
  everyday life *tägliches Leben*
lightning *Blitz* (m.) (*Blitze*)
like (to) *gern haben*
  like (to) (among family members) *lieb haben*
  like (to) (people, things, food, drinks) *mögen*
  like to (would) *möchten*
  I don't like it. *Das gefällt mir nicht.*
  I like it. *Das gefällt mir.*
  I'd like ... *Ich möchte gern ...*
  I'd like to have ... *Ich hätte gern ...*
line *Linie* (f.) (*Linien*), *Leitung* (f.) (*Leitungen*)
  (to speak) on the other line *auf der anderen*
   Leitung (sprechen)
listen (to) *hören, zuhören*
  Listen. *Hör mal.*
liter *Liter* (m.) (*Liter*)
  a liter of milk *ein Liter Milch*
little *wenig*
  a little bit *ein bisschen*
  little brother *Brüderchen* (n.) (*Brüderchen*)
  little sister *Schwesterchen* (n.)
   (*Schwesterchen*)
live (to) *leben, wohnen*
  I live in Berlin. *Ich wohne in Berlin.*
  Where do you live? *Wo wohnen Sie?*

living room *Wohnzimmer* (n.) (*Wohnzimmer*)
loaf *Laib* (m.) (*Laibe*)
  a loaf of bread *ein Laib Brot*
long *lang*
look (to) *gucken, aussehen*
  Look! *Guck mal!*
  look good on (somebody) (to) *gut stehen*
  You look bad/sick. *Sie sehen schlecht aus.*
look for (to) *suchen*
look forward to ... (to) *sich auf ... freuen*
loose *los*
lose weight (to) *abnehmen*
lot (a lot) *viel*
  have a lot to learn (to) *viel zu lernen haben*
  have a lot to do (to) *viel zu tun haben*
loud *laut*
love (to) *lieben*
luck *Glück* (n.) (no pl.)
  bad luck *Pech* (n.) (no pl.)
  Good luck! *Viel Glück!*
lunch *Mittagessen* (n.) (*Mittagessen*)
  have lunch (to) *zu Mittag essen*

M

mail (to) *abschicken*
main course *Hauptgericht* (n.) (*Hauptgerichte*),
 Hauptspeise (f.) (*Hauptspeisen*)
  as a main course *als Hauptspeise*
maintain (to) *erhalten*
make (to) *machen*
  How can I make this up to you? *Wie kann ich*
   das wieder gut machen?
  make plans (to) *Pläne machen*
man *Mann* (m.) (*Männer*)
  men's department *Herrenabteilung* (f.)
   (*Herrenabteilungen*)
manage (to) *leisten*
manager *Manager/-in* (m./f.) (*Manager/-innen*)
many *viele*
  how many *wieviele*
  many years ago *vor vielen Jahren*
map *Karte* (f.) (*Karten*)
  map (city map) *Stadtplan* (m.) (*Stadtpläne*)
marathon *Marathon* (m.) (*Marathons*)
  run a marathon (to) *einen Marathon laufen*
marble cake *Marmorkuchen* (m.)
  (*Marmorkuchen*)
March *März* (m.) (*Märze*)

mark Note (f.) *(Noten)*
market place *Marktplatz* (m.) *(Marktplätze)*
marmalade *Marmelade* (f.) *(Marmeladen)*
married *verheiratet*
  married (to be) *verheiratet sein*
  get married (to) *heiraten*
Marry me! *Heirate mich!*
  Will you marry me? (lit., Will you be my husband?) *Willst du mein Mann werden?*
  Will you marry me? (lit., Will you be my wife?) *Willst du meine Frau werden?*
master's degree *Magister* (m.) *(Magister)*
  study for a master's degree (to) *einen Magister machen*
matching *passend*
May *Mai* (m.) *(Maie)*
maybe *vielleicht*
me (accusative) *mich*
  me, to me (dative) *mir*
  It's me. *Ich bin's.*
meal *Essen* (n.) *(Essen)*
mean (to) *meinen, beabsichtigen*
  That's not what this was supposed to mean./I didn't mean it that way. *So war das nicht gemeint.*
meantime (in the meantime) *inzwischen*
measure (to) *messen*
meat *Fleisch* (n.) (no pl.)
meddling *naseweis*
medication *Medikament* (n.) *(Medikamente)*
medicine *Medizin* (f.) (no pl.), *Medikament* (n.) *(Medikamente)*
meet (to) *kennenlernen, sich treffen*
  meet people (to) *Leute kennenlernen*
meeting *Besprechung* (f.) *(Besprechungen)*
member *Mitglied* (n.) *(Mitglieder)*
menu *Speisekarte* (f.) *(Speisekarten)*
message *Nachricht* (f.) *(Nachrichten)*
  leave a message (to) *Nachricht hinterlassen*
meter *Meter* (m.) *(Meter)*
middle *Mitte* (f.) *(Mitten)*
midnight *null Uhr*
milk *Milch* (f.) (no pl.)
  a liter of milk *ein Liter Milch*
million *Million* (f.) *(Millionen)*
mineral water *Mineralwasser* (n.) *(Mineralwässer/Mineralwasser)*
  a bottle of mineral water *eine Flasche Mineralwasser*
minus *minus*
minute *Minute* (f.) *(Minuten)*
  in ten minutes *in zehn Minuten*
mirror *Spiegel* (m.) *(Spiegel)*
Miss *Fräulein* (n.) *(Fräulein)*
miss (to) *missen, verpassen*
missing (to be) *fehlen*
mom *Mama* (f.) *(Mamas)*
moment *Moment* (m.) *(Momente)*
  at the moment *gerade*
  One moment please. *Einen Moment bitte.*
Monday *Montag* (m.) *(Montage)*
  next Monday *nächsten Montag*
  on Monday *am Montag*
money *Geld* (n.) *(Gelder)*
month *Monat* (m.) *(Monate)*
  last month *letzten Monat*
  next month *nächsten Monat*
more *mehr*
  not any more, no more *nicht mehr*
  once more *noch einmal*
  some more *noch etwas*
morning *Morgen* (m.) *(Morgen)*
  Good morning. *Guten Morgen.*
  in the morning *am Morgen, morgens*
most (adjective) *meiste*
  most (adverb) *am meisten*
mother *Mutter* (f.) *(Mütter)*
mother-in-law *Schwiegermutter* (f.) *(Schwiegermütter)*
motive *Beweggrund* (m.) *(Beweggründe)*
motorcycle *Motorrad* (n.) *(Motorräder)*
  ride a motorcycle (to) *Motorrad fahren*
mountain *Berg* (m.) *(Berge)*
  go mountain climbing (to) *Berg steigen*
mouse *Maus* (f.) *(Mäuse)*
  computer mouse *Computermaus* (f.) *(Computermäuse)*
mouth *Mund* (m.) *(Münder)*
move (to) *verschieben*
movie *Film* (m.) *(Filme)*
movie theater *Kino* (n.) *(Kinos)*
Mr. *Herr* (m.) *(Herren)*
Mrs./Ms. *Frau* (f.) *(Frauen)*
much *viel*
  how much *wie viel*
Munich *München*

museum *Museum* (n.) (*Museen*)
music *Musik* (f.) (no pl.)
my *mein*
  My name is … *Ich heiße …*
  My pleasure! *Gern geschehen!*
myself *mich*

N

name *Name* (m.) (*Namen*)
  My name is … *Ich heiße …*
  Under which name? (reservation) *Auf welchen Namen?*
  What's your name? (fml.) *Wie heißen Sie?*
named (to be) *heißen*
napkin *Serviette* (f.) (*Servietten*)
naturally *natürlich*
near *nahe, dabei*
  nearby *in der Nähe*
  nearer *näher*
  nearest (adjective) *nächste*
  nearest (adverb) *am nächsten*
necessary *nötig*
need (to) *brauchen*
neighbor *Nachbar/-in* (m./f.) (*Nachbarn/ Nachbarinnen*)
nephew *Neffe* (m.)
never *nie*
nevertheless *trotzdem*
new *neu*
  brand-new *ganz neu*
  What's new? *Was gibt's Neues?*
news (a piece of news) *Nachricht* (f.) (*Nachrichten*)
  That's good news. *Das ist eine gute Nachricht.*
newspaper *Zeitung* (f.) (*Zeitungen*)
  daily newspaper *Tageszeitung* (f.) (*Tageszeitungen*)
  newspaper article *Zeitungsartikel* (m.) (*Zeitungsartikel*)
next *nächste*
  next Monday *nächsten Montag*
  next month *nächsten Monat*
  next week *nächste Woche*
  next year *nächstes Jahr*
  Till next time. *Bis zum nächsten Mal.*
  Until next time. (on the phone) *Auf Wiederhören.*
next to *neben*

nice *nett, schön*
nicely *lieb*
niece *Nichte* (f.) (*Nichten*)
night *Nacht* (n.) (*Nächte*)
  at night *nachts*
  last night *gestern Abend*
nine *neun*
nineteen *neunzehn*
ninety *neunzig*
no *kein*
  No. *Nein.*
none *kein*
noodles *Nudeln* (pl.)
noon *Mittag* (m.) (*Mittage*)
nose *Nase* (f.) (*Nasen*)
nosy *naseweis*
not *nicht*
  not any *kein*
  not at all *gar nicht*
  not feel like (to) *keine Lust haben*
  No, not yet. *Nein, noch nicht.*
notify (to) *melden*
novel *Roman* (m.) (*Romane*)
November *November* (m.) (*November*)
now *jetzt, nun*
number *Nummer* (f.) (*Nummern*)
  my (phone) number is … *meine Nummer lautet …*
nurse *Krankenpfleger/Krankenschwester* (m./f.) (*Krankenpfleger/Krankenschwestern*)

O

o'clock *Uhr* (f.) (*in time expressions*)
  at five o' clock *um fünf Uhr*
  at one o'clock *um ein Uhr*
  It's ten o'clock. *Es ist zehn Uhr.*
occupation *Beruf* (m.) (*Berufe*)
October *Oktober* (m.) (*Oktober*)
of course *natürlich, selbstverständlich*
offer *Angebot* (n.) (*Angebote*)
  special offer *Sonderangebot* (n.) (*Sonderangebote*)
office *Büro* (n.) (*Büros*), *Arbeitszimmer* (n.) (*Arbeitszimmer*)
  in an office *im Büro*
  to the office *ins Büro*
often *oft*
oh *ach*

okay (It's okay.) *Schon gut.*
  Is everything okay? *Ist alles in Ordnung?*
old *alt*
  How old are you? *Wie alt sind Sie?*
  I am twenty years old. *Ich bin zwanzig Jahre alt.*
on *an, auf*
  on top of *auf*
once *einmal*
  once more *noch einmal*
one *eins*
  one (indefinite pronoun) *man*
one-way street *Einbahnstraße* (f.) *(Einbahnstraßen)*
onion *Zwiebel* (f.) *(Zwiebeln)*
only *nur, erst*
onto *auf*
open (to) *aufmachen, öffnen, eröffnen*
opinion *Meinung* (f.) *(Meinungen)*
or *oder*
orange *Orange* (f.) *(Orangen)*
orange juice *Orangensaft* (m.) *(Orangensäfte)*
order *Ordnung* (f.) *(Ordnungen)*
order (to) *bestellen*
other *andere*
  the others *die anderen*
ought to *sollen*
our *unser*
ourselves *uns*
out *raus*
  out of *aus*
outside *draußen*
outstanding *hervorragend*
over *über, vorbei*
overtime *Überstunde* (f.) *(Überstunden)*
  work overtime (to) *Überstunden machen*
owe (to) *schulden*

P

page *Seite* (f.) *(Seiten)*
  book page *Buchseite* (f.) *(Buchseiten)*
pain *Schmerz* (m.) *(Schmerzen)*
  in pain (to be) *Schmerzen haben*
paint (to) *malen*
pair *Paar* (n.) *(Paare)*
  a pair of shoes *ein Paar Schuhe*
pants (pair of pants) *Hose* (f.) *(Hosen)*
parents *Eltern* (pl.)

park *Park* (m.) *(Parks)*
park (to) *parken*
  park in a parking garage (to) *im Parkhaus parken*
parking garage *Parkhaus* (n.) *(Parkhäuser)*
partner *Partner/-in* (m./f.) *(Partner/-innen)*
part-time *Teilzeit* (f.) (no pl.)
  part-time employment *Teilzeitbeschäftigung* (f.) *(Teilzeitbeschäftigungen)*
party *Party* (f.) *(Partys)*
  have a party (to) *eine Party geben*
passenger *Fahrgast* (n.) *(Fahrgäste)*
past *nach*
  It is quarter past three. *Es ist viertel nach drei.*
pasta *Nudeln* (pl.)
path *Weg* (m.) *(Wege)*
patient *Patient/-in* (m./f.) *(Patienten/ Patientinnen)*
pattern *Muster* (n.) *(Muster)*
pay (to) *bezahlen*
  Pay attention! *Pass auf!*
pea soup *Erbsensuppe* (f.) *(Erbsensuppen)*
peak season *Hochsaison* (f.) *(Hochsaisons)*
pedestrian *Fußgänger* (m.) *(Fußgänger)*
  pedestrian zone *Fußgängerzone* (f.) *(Fußgängerzonen)*
penicillin *Penizillin* (n.) (no pl.)
pension *Pension* (f.) *(Pensionen)*
people *Leute* (pl.)
  meet people (to) *Leute kennenlernen*
pepper (spice) *Pfeffer* (m.) (no pl.)
pepper (vegetable) *Paprika* (m.) *(Paprikas)*
per *pro*
percent *Prozent* (n.) *(Prozente)*
perfect *perfekt*
personally *persönlich*
Ph.D. *Doktor* (m.) *(Doktoren)*
  study for a Ph.D. (to) *einen Doktor machen*
pharmacy *Apotheke* (f.) *(Apotheken)*
photo *Bild* (n.) *(Bilder)*
photograph *Foto* (n.) *(Fotos)*
  family photographs *Familienfotos* (pl.)
photograph (to) *fotografieren*
pianist *Pianist/-in* (m./f.) *(Pianisten/ Pianistinnen)*
piano *Klavier* (n.) *(Klaviere)*
  play the piano (to) *Klavier spielen*

picnic Picknick (n.) (Picknicke)
  have a picnic (to) ein Picknick machen
picture Bild (n.) (Bilder)
piece Stück (n.) (Stücke)
  a piece of cake ein Stück Kuchen
  in one piece am Stück
pill Tablette (f.) (Tabletten)
pink rosa
place Stelle (f.) (Stellen)
place (to) stellen, legen, setzen
plan Plan (m.) (Pläne)
  make plans (to) Pläne machen
plant (to) pflanzen
plate Teller (m.) (Teller)
play (to) spielen
  play along (to) mitspielen
  play basketball (to) Basketball spielen
  play cards (to) Karten spielen
  play soccer (to) Fußball spielen
  play sports (to) Sport treiben
  play the guitar (to) Gitarre spielen
  play the piano (to) Klavier spielen
please bitte
  Yes, please. Ja, gern.
please (to) gefallen
pleasure Lust (f.) (Lüste)
  My pleasure! Gern geschehen!
  With pleasure! Aber gern!
police Polizei (f.) (no pl.)
pool (public pool) Schwimmbad (n.)
  (Schwimmbäder)
poor arm
popular beliebt
pork Schweinefleisch (n.) (no pl.)
position Stelle (f.) (Stellen)
post office Post (f.) (no pl.)
postpone (to) verschieben
pot Kännchen (n.) (Kännchen); Topf (m.) (Töpfe)
  a portion (lit., a small pot) of coffee ein
    Kännchen Kaffee
potato Kartoffel (f.) (Kartoffeln)
potato salad Kartoffelsalat (m.) (Kartoffelsalate)
pottery (to make) töpfern
pound Pfund (n.) (Pfunde)
  a pound of tomatoes ein Pfund Tomaten
practice (doctor's office) Praxis (f.) (Praxen)
practice (to) nachgehen
praise (to) loben

pregnant schwanger
  pregnant (to be) schwanger sein
prepare (to) vorbereiten
prescribe (to) verschreiben
prescription Rezept (n.) (Rezepte)
price Preis (m.) (Preise)
problem Problem (n.) (Probleme)
  No problem. Kein Problem.
profession Beruf (m.) (Berufe)
  by profession von Beruf
  professional experience Berufserfahrung (f.)
    (Berufserfahrungen)
  professional outlook Berufsaussicht (f.)
    (Berufsaussichten)
  professional training Ausbildung (f.)
    (Ausbildungen)
professionally beruflich
program Programm (n.) (Programme)
project Projekt (n.) (Projekte)
promote (to) befördern
promotion Beförderung (f.) (Beförderungen)
prosperous wohlhabend
proud stolz
prove (to) beweisen
psychology Psychologie (f.) (Psychologien)
punctual pünktlich
pupil Schüler/-in (m./f.) (Schüler/-innen)
purple violet
pursue (to) nachgehen
put (to) stellen, anlegen, legen, setzen
  put on the scale (to) auf die Waage legen
put on (to) anlegen, anziehen
  put on a bandage (to) Verband anlegen

Q

quarter (adjective) viertel
  It is quarter past three. Es ist viertel nach
    drei.
  It is quarter to three. Es ist viertel vor drei.
quarter (noun) Viertel (n.) (Viertel)
  academic quarter akademische Viertel
  quarter of an hour Viertelstunde (f.)
    (Viertelstunden)
question Frage (n.) (Fragen)
  question time Fragestunde (f.) (Fragestunden)
quick schnell
quiet leise, still
quite ganz

R

racquet *Schläger* (m.) *(Schläger)*
radio *Radio* (n.) *(Radios)*
  radio announcer *Radiosprecher/-in* (m./f.) *(Radiosprecher/-innen)*
rain *Regen* (m.) (no pl.)
rain (to) *regnen*
  It is raining. *Es regnet.*
rainy weather *Regenwetter* (n.) *(Regenwetter)*
  in rainy weather *bei Regenwetter*
raise *Erhöhung* (f.) *(Erhöhungen)*
  raise (in salary) *Gehaltserhöhung* (f.) *(Gehaltserhöhungen)*
raise (to) *erhöhen*
rate *Rate* (f.) *(Raten)*
rather *lieber*
reach (to) *erreichen*
read (to) *lesen*
  read out loud (to) *vorlesen*
real *wahr*
really *wirklich, richtig*
  Really? *Wirklich?*
reason *Ursache* (f.) *(Ursachen)*
receive (to) *bekommen, erhalten*
receiver *Hörer* (m.) *(Hörer)*
  hang up the receiver (to) *den Hörer auflegen*
recommend (to) *empfehlen*
red *rot*
red wine *Rotwein* (m.) *(Rotweine)*
remain (to) *bleiben*
remove (to) *abnehmen*
rent (to) *mieten*
reopen (to) *neu eröffnen*
repeat (to) *wiederholen*
reply to (to) *beantworten*
report (to) *melden*
report card *Zeugnis* (n.) *(Zeugnisse)*
reservation *Reservierung* (f.) *(Reservierungen)*
reserve (to) *reservieren*
  reserve a table (to) *einen Tisch bestellen, einen Tisch reservieren*
reside (to) *wohnen*
restaurant *Restaurant* (n.) *(Restaurants)*
résumé *Lebenslauf* (m.) *(Lebensläufe)*
  prepare one's résumé (to) *den Lebenslauf schreiben*
retire (to) *in Rente gehen, in Pension gehen*

retired *pensioniert*
retirement *Rente* (f.) *(Renten)*
retrospective *Retrospektive* (f.) *(Retrospektiven)*
review *Nachprüfung* (f.) *(Nachprüfungen)*
rice *Reis* (m.) (no pl.)
rich *reich*
ride a bicycle (to) *Fahrrad fahren*
right *richtig, gleich; Recht* (n.) *(Rechte)*
  right (to be) *Recht haben, stimmen*
  Isn't that right? *Nicht wahr?*
  right away *sofort*
  right here *gleich hier*
  to the right *rechts*
  turn right (to) *rechts abbiegen*
ring the doorbell (to) *läuten, klingeln*
rise (to) *steigen*
rival *Rivale/Rivalin* (m./f.) *(Rivalen/Rivalinnen)*
road (country road) *Landstraße* (f.) *(Landstraßen)*
roast *Braten* (m.) *(Braten)*
roast beef *Rinderbraten* (m.) *(Rinderbraten)*
room *Zimmer* (n.) *(Zimmer)*
  children's room *Kinderzimmer* (n.) *(Kinderzimmer)*
  dining room *Esszimmer* (n.) *(Esszimmer)*
roommate *Mitbewohner/-in* (m./f.) *(Mitbewohner/-innen)*
rose *Rose* (f.) *(Rosen)*
round up (the amount) (to) *aufrunden*
run (to) *rennen, laufen, leiten*
  run a business (to) *ein Geschäft leiten*
  run a marathon (to) *einen Marathon laufen*
runny nose (to have a runny nose) *Schnupfen haben*

S

sad *traurig*
salad *Salat* (m.) *(Salate)*
salami *Salami* (f.) *(Salamis)*
salary *Gehalt* (n.) *(Gehälter)*
sale (on sale) *im Angebot, im Sonderangebot*
salesperson *Verkäufer/-in* (m./f.) *(Verkäufer/-innen)*
salt *Salz* (n.) *(Salze)*
same *gleich, egal*
  at the same time *dabei*
Saturday *Samstag* (m.) *(Samstage)*

sauerkraut *Sauerkraut* (n.) (no pl.)
save (to) *schonen*
say (to) *sagen*
scale *Waage* (f.) *(Waagen)*
  put on the scale (to) *auf die Waage legen*
scarf *Schal* (m.) *(Schale, Schals)*
school *Schule* (f.) *(Schulen)*
  comprehensive school *Gesamtschule* (f.)
    (Gesamtschulen)
  elementary school (first grade through
    fourth grade) *Grundschule* (f.)
    (Grundschulen)
  high school (fifth grade through twelfth
    grade) *Gymnasium* (n.) *(Gymnasien)*
  junior high school (fifth grade
    through ninth grade) *Hauptschule* (f.)
    (Hauptschulen)
  middle school (fifth grade through tenth
    grade) *Realschule* (f.) *(Realschulen)*
  vocational school *Berufsschule* (f.)
    (Berufsschulen)
  schoolboy/girl *Schüler/-in* (m./f.) *(Schüler/-
    innen)*
scientist *Wissenschaftler/-in* (m./f.)
  (Wissenschaftler/-innen)
search (to) *suchen*
see (to) *sehen*
  I see. *Ach so./Aha!*
  See! *Na also!*
  see again (to) *wiedersehen*
  See you soon. *Bis bald.*
self-employed *selbstständig*
sell (to) *verkaufen*
send (to) *schicken*
send off (to) *abschicken*
sentence *Satz* (m.) *(Sätze)*
  final sentence *Schlusssatz* (m.) *(Schlusssätze)*
September *September* (m.) *(September)*
serve (to) *servieren*
service *Service* (m.) (no pl.)
seven *sieben*
seventeen *siebzehn*
seventy *siebzig*
shared flat *Wohngemeinschaft* (f.)
  (Wohngemeinschaften), WG (f.) *(WGs)*
she (nominative) *sie*
shelf *Regal* (n.) *(Regale)*
shine (to) *scheinen*

ship *Schiff* (n.) *(Schiffe)*
shirt *Hemd* (n.) *(Hemden)*
shoe *Schuh* (m.) *(Schuhe)*
  a pair of shoes *ein Paar Schuhe*
  shoe department *Schuhabteilung* (f.)
    (Schuhabteilungen)
  shoe store *Schuhgeschäft* (n.) *(Schuhgeschäfte)*
shop (to) *einkaufen*
  go (grocery) shopping (to) *einkaufen gehen*
  go (window-)shopping (to) *bummeln gehen*
  shopping list *Einkaufsliste* (f.) *(Einkaufslisten)*
short *kurz*
shot (medical) *Spritze* (f.) *(Spritzen)*
shoulder *Schulter* (f.) *(Schultern)*
show *Show* (f.) *(Shows)*
show (to) *zeigen*
siblings *Geschwister* (pl.)
sick *krank*
  feel sick (to) *sich krank fühlen*
  You look bad/sick. *Sie sehen schlecht aus.*
side room *Nebenzimmer* (n.) *(Nebenzimmer)*
sidewalk *Gehweg* (m.) *(Gehwege)*
signpost *Schild* (n.) *(Schilder)*
silverware *Besteck* (n.) *(Bestecke)*
simple *einfach*
simply *eben, einfach*
since *denn, seit*
sincere *herzlich*
sing (to) *singen*
single *ledig*
  single (to be) *ledig sein*
sister *Schwester* (f.) *(Schwestern)*
sister-in-law *Schwägerin* (f.) *(Schwägerinnen)*
sit (to) *sitzen, sich setzen*
  sit down (to) *sich setzen*
six *sechs*
sixteen *sechzehn*
sixty *sechzig*
size *Größe* (f.) *(Größen), Nummer* (f.) *(Nummern)*
  what size *welche Größe*
ski *Ski* (m.) *(Ski; Skier)*
  go skiing (to) *Ski fahren*
  ski resort *Skigebiet* (n.) *(Skigebiete)*
skiing *skifahren* (n.)
skirt *Rock* (m.) *(Röcke)*
sleep (to) *schlafen*
slim *schlank*
slow *langsam*

small *klein*
smoke (to) *rauchen*
snow *Schnee* (m.) (no pl.)
snow (to) *schneien*
   It is snowing. *Es schneit.*
snowboard *Snowboard* (n.) (*Snowboards*)
snowboard (to) *snowboarden*
snowy weather *Schneewetter* (n.) (no pl.)
   in snowy weather *bei Schneewetter*
so *so, also*
   So what? *Na und?*
soccer *Fußball* (m.) (no pl.)
   play soccer (to) *Fußball spielen*
socks *Socken* (pl.)
some *etwas*
   some more *noch etwas*
someone *jemand*
something *etwas*
   something like that *so etwas*
sometimes *manchmal*
somewhat *etwas*
son *Sohn* (m.) (*Söhne*)
soon *bald*
   See you soon. *Bis bald.*
sore throat *Halsschmerzen* (pl.)
sorry *leid*
   Sorry. *Entschuldigung.*
   I'm sorry. *(Es) tut mir leid.*
sound (to) *klingen*
   That sounds good. *Das klingt aber gut.*
soup *Suppe* (f.) (*Suppen*)
   a bowl of soup *ein Teller Suppe*
   pea soup *Erbsensuppe* (f.) (*Erbsensuppen*)
sour *sauer*
South Africa *Südafrika* (n.)
sparkling wine *Sekt* (m.) (*Sekte*)
speak (to) *sprechen*
speaking *am Apparat*
   Honberg speaking. *Honberg am Apparat.*
   Who is speaking? *Wer ist am Apparat?*
special offer *Sonderangebot* (n.)
   (*Sonderangebote*)
specialty *Spezialität* (f.) (*Spezialitäten*)
spice *Gewürz* (n.) (*Gewürze*)
spinach *Spinat* (m.) (no pl.)
spoon *Löffel* (m.) (*Löffel*)
sport *Sport* (m.) (no pl.), *Sportart* (f.) (*Sportarten*)
   play sports (to) *Sport treiben*

sports center *Sportstudio* (n.) (*Sportstudios*)
spring *Frühling* (m.) (*Frühlinge*)
squash *Squash* (n.) (no pl.)
   play squash (to) *Squash spielen*
stadium *Stadion* (n.) (*Stadien*)
stamp *Briefmarke* (f.) (*Briefmarken*)
stand (to) *stehen*
start a family (to) *eine Familie gründen*
statistics *Statistik* (f.) (*Statistiken*)
stay (to) *bleiben*
   stay in shape (to) *fit bleiben*
steak *Steak* (n.) (*Steaks*)
still *noch*
stomach *Bauch* (m.) (*Bäuche*), *Magen* (m.)
   (*Mägen*)
stomachache *Bauchschmerzen* (pl.), *Bauchweh*
   (n.) (no pl.)
stop *Haltestelle* (f.) (*Haltestellen*)
store *Geschäft* (n.) (*Geschäfte*)
straight *direkt*
   straight (ahead) *geradeaus*
   continue straight ahead (to) *geradeaus gehen*
strange *fremd*
street *Straße* (f.) (*Straßen*)
   one-way street *Einbahnstraße* (f.)
   (*Einbahnstraßen*)
street car *Straßenbahn* (f.) (*Straßenbahnen*)
striped *gestreift*
stroll (to) *bummeln, spazieren*
strong *stark*
stuck (to be) *stecken*
   stuck in traffic (to be) *im Stau stecken*
student *Student/-in* (m./f.) (*Studenten/-innen*)
   fellow university student *Kommilitone/*
   Kommilitonin (m./f.) (*Kommilitonen/*
   Kommilitoninnen)
studies *Studium* (n.) (*Studien*)
study *Studium* (n.) (*Studien*)
study (to) (at a university) *studieren*
   study for a Ph.D. (to) *einen Doktor machen*
subject *Fach* (n.) (*Fächer*)
   favorite subject *Lieblingsfach* (n.)
successful *erfolgreich*
sugar *Zucker* (m.) (no pl.)
sugar sweet *zuckersüß*
suit *Anzug* (m.) (*Anzüge*)
suit (to) *stehen, passen*
suitcase *Koffer* (m.) (*Koffer*)

summer *Sommer* (m.) *(Sommer)*
  in the summer *im Sommer*
summer vacation *Sommerurlaub* (m.)
  (Sommerurlaube)
sun *Sonne* (f.) *(Sonnen)*
Sunday *Sonntag* (m.) *(Sonntage)*
super *super*
superior *Vorgesetzte* (m./f.) *(Vorgesetzten)*
sure *sicher*
  Sure! *Bestimmt!*
sweater *Pullover* (m.) *(Pullover)*
  woman's sweater *Damenpullover* (m.)
  (Damenpullover)
sweet *süß*
sweet-and-sour *süßsauer*
sweetheart *Schatz* (m.) *(Schätze)*
sweets *Süßspeise* (f.) *(Süßspeisen)*
swim (to) *schwimmen*
  go swimming (to) *schwimmen gehen*
syringe *Spritze* (f.) *(Spritzen)*

T

table *Tisch* (m.) *(Tische)*
  dining table *Esstisch* (m.) *(Esstische)*
  reserve a table (to) *einen Tisch bestellen,*
  einen Tisch reservieren
take (to) *fahren, nehmen*
  take a city tour (to) *eine Stadtrundfahrt*
  machen
  take along (to) *mitnehmen*
  Take care. *Mach's gut.*
  take care of … (to) *sich kümmern um …*
  Take good care of yourself! *Pass gut auf dich*
  auf!
  take it easy (to) *sich schonen*
  take the bus (to) *den Bus nehmen*
  take the car (to) *das Auto nehmen*
  take the daughter to school (to) *die Tochter*
  in die Schule fahren
  take the high school exam (to) *das Abitur*
  machen
  take the tram (to) *die Straßenbahn nehmen*
talk (to) *reden*
tango *Tango* (m.) *(Tangos)*
task *Aufgabe* (f.) *(Aufgaben)*
taste (to)/one's taste (to be) *schmecken*
taxi *Taxi* (n.) *(Taxis; Taxen)*
  call a taxi (to) *ein Taxi rufen*

go by taxi (to) *mit dem Taxi fahren*
taxi driver *Taxifahrer/-in* (m./f.) *(Taxifahrer/-*
  innen)
teach (to) *unterrichten*
teacher *Lehrer/-in* (m./f.) *(Lehrer/-innen)*
telephone *Telefon* (n.) *(Telefone)*
  on the phone *am Apparat*
  phone number *Telefonnummer* (f.)
  (Telefonnummern)
television *Fernsehen* (n.) (no pl.)
  television (set) *Fernseher* (m.) *(Fernseher)*
  on TV *im Fernsehen*
temperature *Temperatur* (f.) *(Temperaturen)*
  elevated temperature *erhöhte Temperatur*
ten *zehn*
tennis *Tennis* (n.) (no pl.)
  play tennis (to) *Tennis spielen*
tennis racquet *Tennisschläger* (m.)
  (Tennisschläger)
tennis shoes *Tennisschuhe* (pl.)
terrace *Terrasse* (f.) *(Terrassen)*
than *als*
thank (to) *danken*
  Thank you. *Danke./Danke schön.*
thanks *Dank* (m.) (no pl.)
  Many thanks. *Vielen Dank.*
  Thanks for the compliment! *Vielen Dank*
  für die Blumen! (lit., Thanks for the flowers.
  [often used ironically])
that (conjunction) *dass*
  that (demonstrative pronoun) *das*
  That sounds good. *Das klingt aber gut.*
the (nominative) *der* (m.), *das* (n.), *die* (f./pl.)
  the (accusative) *den* (m.), *das* (n.), *die* (f./pl.)
  the (dative) *dem* (m./n.), *der* (f.), *den* (pl.)
  of the (genitive) *des* (m./n.), *der* (f./pl.)
their *ihr*
them (accusative) *sie*
  them, to them (dative) *ihnen*
themselves *sich*
then *denn, nun, dann, da*
there *dort, da*
there is/are *es gibt*
therefore *also, deshalb*
these days *heutzutage*
they (nominative) *sie* (pl.)
  they (indefinite pronoun) *man*
thing *Gegenstand* (m.) *(Gegenstände)*

think (to) *glauben, meinen, denken*
  I don't think so. *Ich glaube nicht.*
  I think so, too. *Das finde ich auch.*
thirteen *dreizehn*
thirty *dreißig*
  It is four thirty. *Es ist vier Uhr dreißig.*
thirty-one *einunddreißig*
this *dieser*
  This is … *Das ist …*
those *jene, die* (pl.)
  Those are … *Das sind …*
thousand *tausend*
  one hundred thousand *hunderttausend*
  one thousand *eintausend*
  one thousand one
    hundred *eintausendeinhundert*
  ten thousand *zehntausend*
  two thousand *zweitausend*
three *drei*
  three times *dreimal*
through *durch*
thunder *Donner* (m.) (no pl.)
Thursday *Donnerstag* (m.) (*Donnerstage*)
  every Thursday *jeden Donnerstag*
ticket *Fahrkarte* (f.) (*Fahrkarten*)
tie *Krawatte* (f.) (*Krawatten*)
tight *eng*
time *Zeit* (f.) (*Zeiten*), *Uhrzeit* (f.) (*Uhrzeiten*)
  time (occasion) *mal*
  every time *jedes Mal*
  for the first time *zum ersten Mal*
  For what time? (reservation) *Um welche Uhrzeit?*
  question time *Fragestunde* (f.) (*Fragestunden*)
  Till next time. *Bis zum nächsten Mal.*
  What is the time? *Wie spät ist es?*
  What time is it? *Wieviel Uhr ist es?*
tip *Trinkgeld* (n.) (*Trinkgelder*)
  Is the tip included? *Ist das Trinkgeld inklusive?*
tip (to) *ein Trinkgeld geben*
tired *müde*
to *an, zu, nach*
  It is quarter to three. *Es ist viertel vor drei.*
  It is ten to twelve. *Es ist zehn vor zwölf.*
  To your health! *Auf dein Wohl!*
today (to) *heute*
toe (to) *Zehe* (f.) (*Zehen*)

together (to) *zusammen*
toilet *Toilette* (f.) (*Toiletten*)
tomato *Tomate* (f.) (*Tomaten*)
  a pound of tomatoes *ein Pfund Tomaten*
tomorrow *morgen*
  the day after tomorrow *übermorgen*
tonight *heute Abend*
too *auch, zu*
  Too bad. *So ein Pech.*
tooth *Zahn* (m.) (*Zähne*)
toothache *Zahnweh* (n.) (no pl.), *Zahnschmerzen* (pl.)
  have a toothache (to) *Zahnweh haben*
tourist *Tourist/-in* (m./f.) (*Touristen/ Touristinnen*)
toward *zu, gegen*
town *Stadt* (f.) (*Städte*)
  around town *in der Stadt*
town hall *Rathaus* (n.) (*Rathäuser*)
toy *Spielzeug* (n.) (*Spielzeuge*)
trade *Handwerk* (n.) (*Handwerke*)
traffic *Verkehr* (m.) (no pl.)
traffic announcement *Verkehrsdurchsage* (f.) (*Verkehrsdurchsagen*)
traffic jam *Stau* (m.) (*Staus*)
  stopped in traffic (to be) *im Stau stehen*
  stuck in traffic (to be) *im Stau stecken*
traffic light *Ampel* (f.) (*Ampeln*)
  at the traffic light *an der Ampel*
train *Zug* (m.) (*Züge*)
train station *Bahnhof* (m.) (*Bahnhöfe*)
tram *Straßenbahn* (f.) (*Straßenbahnen*)
  by tram *mit der Straßenbahn*
  take the tram (to) *die Straßenbahn nehmen*
treat (to) *behandeln*
trip *Fahrt* (f.) (*Fahrten*)
true *wahr*
  That's true! *Das stimmt!*
try (to) *probieren*
try on (to) *anprobieren*
Tuesday *Dienstag* (m.) (*Dienstage*)
turn (to) *abbiegen*
  turn left (to) *links abbiegen*
  turn right (to) *rechts abbiegen*
  turn around (to) (U-turn) *umdrehen*
twelve *zwölf*
twenty *zwanzig*
twenty-eight *achtundzwanzig*

twenty-five *fünfundzwanzig*
twenty-four *vierundzwanzig*
twenty-nine *neunundzwanzig*
twenty-one *einundzwanzig*
twenty-seven *siebenundzwanzig*
twenty-six *sechsundzwanzig*
twenty-three *dreiundzwanzig*
twenty-two *zweiundzwanzig*
two *zwei*

U

Uh … *Äh …*
umbrella *Schirm* (m.) *(Schirme)*
uncle *Onkel* (m.) *(Onkel)*
under *unter*
  Under which name? (reservation) *Auf welchen Namen?*
understand (to) *verstehen*
unemployed *arbeitslos*
  unemployed (people) *Arbeitslose* (m./f.) *(Arbeitslosen)*
unemployment rate *Arbeitslosenquote* (f.) *(Arbeitslosenquoten)*
unfortunately *leider*
university *Universität* (f.) *(Universitäten)*
  fellow university student *Kommilitone/ Kommilitonin* (m./f.) *(Kommilitonen/ Kommilitoninnen)*
until *bis*
  not until *erst*
  Till next time. *Bis zum nächsten Mal.*
  Until next time. (on the phone) *Auf Wiederhören.*
upright *aufrecht*
urgent *eilig, dringend*
urgently *dringend*
us (accusative); us, to us (dative) *uns*
use (to) *benutzen*
  being used *besetzt*

V

vacant *frei*
vacation *Urlaub* (m.) *(Urlaube), Ferien* (pl.)
  go on vacation (to) *Urlaub machen*
  take a vacation (to) *(sich) Urlaub nehmen*
vacation apartment *Ferienwohnung* (f.) *(Ferienwohnungen)*
vacation plans *Urlaubsplan* (m.) *(Urlaubspläne)*

vase *Vase* (f.) *(Vasen)*
veal *Kalbfleisch* (n.) (no pl.)
vegetables *Gemüse* (n.) (no pl.)
very *sehr*
  Very well. *Sehr gut.*
viewer *Zuschauer/-in* (m./f.) *(Zuschauer/-innen)*
village *Dorf* (n.) *(Dörfer)*
violet *lila*
visit *Besuch* (m.) *(Besuche)*
  on a visit (to be) *zu Besuch sein*
visit (to) *besuchen*
voice *Stimme* (f.) *(Stimmen)*
volleyball (game) *Volleyball* (m.) (no pl.)
  play volleyball (to) *Volleyball spielen*

W

wait (to) *warten*
  wait for (to) *warten auf*
waiter *Ober* (m.) *(Ober), Kellner* (m.) *(Kellner)*
waitress *Bedienung* (f.) (no pl.), *Kellnerin* (f.) *(Kellnerinnen)*
walk (to) *zu Fuß gehen*
  go for a walk (to) *spazieren gehen*
wallet *Geldbeutel* (m.) *(Geldbeutel)*
want to (to) *wollen*
warm *warm, herzlich*
  It is warm. *Es ist warm.*
wash (to) *waschen*
  wash oneself (to) *sich waschen*
wash out (to) *auswaschen*
watch *Uhr* (f.) *(Uhren)*
watch (to) *aufpassen*
water *Wasser* (n.) *(Wasser; Wässer)*
way *Weg* (m.) *(Wege)*
  on the way *unterwegs*
  on the way (to be) (baby) *unterwegs sein*
we *wir*
wealthy *wohlhabend*
wear (to) *anziehen, tragen*
weather *Wetter* (n.) *(Wetter)*
  in bad weather *bei schlechtem Wetter*
  in good weather *bei gutem Wetter*
  in rainy weather *bei Regenwetter*
  in snowy weather *bei Schneewetter*
wedding *Hochzeit* (f.) *(Hochzeiten)*
Wednesday *Mittwoch* (m.) *(Mittwoche)*
week *Woche* (f.) *(Wochen)*
  last week *letzte Woche*

next week *nächste Woche*
per week *pro Woche*
weekend *Wochenende* (n.) *(Wochenenden)*
  on the weekend *am Wochenende*
weigh (to) *wiegen*
Welcome. *Willkommen.*
  Welcome back. *Willkommen zurück.*
  You're welcome! *Bitte./Gern geschehen!*
well *na, wohl*
  feel well (to) *sich wohl fühlen*
  very well *hervorragend*
  Very well. *Sehr gut.*
  Well... *Na ja... /Nun...*
  Well done! *Bravo!*
wet *nass*
what *was*
  So what? *Na und?*
  What's new? *Was gibt's Neues?*
  What's the matter? *Was ist denn los?*
  What's your name? (fml.) *Wie heißen Sie?*
when (question) *wann*
  when (conjunction) *wenn, als*
where *wo*
  where from *woher*
  Where are you from? *Woher kommen Sie?/*
    Wo kommen Sie her?
whether *ob*
which *welch-* (all genders, numbers, cases)
white *weiß*
white wine *Weißwein* (m.) *(Weißweine)*
who (question) *wer*
  who (relative pronoun, nominative) *der* (m.), *das*
    (n.), *die* (f./pl.)
  Who is speaking? *Wer ist am Apparat?*
whole *ganz*
whom (relative pronoun, accusative) *den* (m.), *das*
  (n.), *die* (f./pl.)
  to whom (relative pronoun, dative) *dem* (m./n.),
    der (f.), *denen* (pl.)
whose (question) *wessen*
  whose (relative pronoun) *dessen* (m./n.), *deren*
    (f./pl.)
why *warum*
wife *Ehefrau* (f.) *(Ehefrauen), Frau* (f.) *(Frauen)*
  my wife *meine Frau*
win (to) *gewinnen*
window *Fenster* (n.) *(Fenster)*
wine *Wein* (m.) *(Weine)*

a bottle of wine *eine Flasche Wein*
a glass of wine *ein Glas Wein*
red wine *Rotwein* (m.) *(Rotweine)*
sparkling wine *Sekt* (m.) *(Sekte)*
white wine *Weißwein* (m.) *(Weißweine)*
wine list *Weinkarte* (f.) *(Weinkarten)*
winter *Winter* (m.) *(Winter)*
  in the winter *im Winter*
winter vacation *Winterurlaub* (m.)
  (Winterurlaube)
wish *Glückwunsch* (m.) *(Glückwünsche)*
wish (to) *wünschen*
with *mit, bei*
  With pleasure! *Aber gern!*
without *ohne*
woman *Frau* (f.) *(Frauen)*
wonder (to) *fragen*
work *Arbeit* (m.) *(Arbeiten)*
  flexible working hours *gleitende Arbeitszeit*
    (f.)
work (to) *arbeiten, tätig sein*
  work overtime (to) *Überstunden machen*
work hours *Arbeitszeit* (f.) *(Arbeitszeiten)*
  flexible working hours *gleitende Arbeitszeit*
worker *Arbeiter/-in* (m./f.) *(Arbeiter/-innen)*
workplace *Arbeitsplatz* (m.) *(Arbeitsplätze),*
  Arbeitsstelle (f.) *(Arbeitsstellen)*
world *Welt* (f.) *(Welten)*
worry *Sorge* (f.) *(Sorgen)*
  No worries./Don't worry. *Keine Sorge.*
wound *Wunde* (f.) *(Wunden)*
  clean the wound (to) *Wunde auswaschen*
write (to) *schreiben*
wrong *falsch*

Y

year *Jahr* (n.) *(Jahre)*
  I am twenty years old. *Ich bin zwanzig Jahre*
    alt.
  last year *letztes Jahr*
  many years ago *vor vielen Jahren*
  next year *nächstes Jahr*
yell (to) *rufen*
yellow *gelb*
Yes. *Ja.*
  Oh yes. *Au ja.*
  yes, but... *schon, aber...*
yesterday *gestern*

the day before yesterday *vorgestern*

yet *noch, schon*

  No, not yet. *Nein, noch nicht.*

yoga *Yoga* (m./n.) (no pl.)

yoga studio *Yogastudio* (n.) *(Yogastudios)*

yogurt *Joghurt* (m.) *(Joghurts)*

you (nominative) *du* (sg. infml.), *Sie* (sg. fml./pl. fml.), *ihr* (pl. infml.)

  you (accusative) *dich* (sg. infml.), *Sie* (sg. fml./pl. fml.), *euch* (pl. infml.)

  you, to you (dative) *dir* (sg. infml.), *euch* (pl. infml.), *Ihnen* (sg. fml./pl. fml.)

you, to you (dative) *euch* (pl. infml.)

young *jung*

your *Ihr* (sg. fml./pl. fml.), *dein* (sg. infml.), *euer* (pl. infml.)

yourself *sich* (sg. fml.), *dich* (sg. infml.)

yourselves *sich* (pl. fml.), *euch* (pl. infml.)

Z

zero *null*